Fresh from the Garden

If you can cook a really delicious meal using vegetables you have bought in the shops, just think how much more delicious it could be if you were to cook it with vegetables fresh from your own garden. Roger Grounds and Robin Howe have collaborated to provide a complete book for the home vegetable grower.

Roger Grounds gives advice on the best possible way to grow your vegetables and fruit. An enthusiastic natural gardener, he suggests ways of getting the best flavour from your home-grown food rather than concerning himself with size and colour.

Robin Howe has spent most of her life travelling the world and brings together her extensive knowledge of cookery to give new and imaginative ways of cooking fresh vegetables and fruits.

Finally, Brenda Sanctuary's chapter on freezing is a complete guide to what you can and can't freeze, how to achieve the best results and the length of time the frozen food will keep.

Fresh from the Garden

ROGER GROUNDS
ROBIN HOWE
and Brenda Sanctuary

MAGNUM BOOKS
Methuen Paperbacks Ltd

A Magnum Book

FRESH FROM THE GARDEN
ISBN 0 417 03670 1

First published 1979 by Magnum Books

Copyright (c) 1979 by Roger Grounds, Robin Howe
and Brenda Sanctuary

Magnum Books are published
by Methuen Paperbacks Ltd
11 New Fetter Lane, London EC4P 4EE

Made and printed in Great Britain by
Hazell, Watson & Viney Ltd
Aylesbury, Bucks

❧ Contents

🌿 Introduction

If you can cook a really delicious meal using vegetables you have bought in the shops, just think how much more delicious it could be if you were to cook it with vegetables fresh from your own garden.

It is not just wish fulfilment on the part of those enthusiasts who grow their own vegetables that makes them claim that what they grow for themselves tastes better than what they buy. It is a fact. And for some very simple reasons.

The commercial vegetable grower, producing vast crops for supermarket outlets, has to concentrate on growing a relatively limited range of varieties, because what he grows has to measure up to some very rigid criteria. He has to select a variety that he can be sure will give him a very heavy crop, otherwise he won't be able to make ends meet. He tends to go for bulk, not flavour, because he is paid by the volume he produces, rather than refinements of taste. His produce has got to travel well, it has got to have a good shelf life, and worst of all, it has got to be the right colour, not by daylight, but by the artificial irradiance of fluorescent tubes. Really, once he has considered all those factors, he does not have much time to spare to think about flavour.

In your own garden you can throw out all the commercial grower's criteria and go all out for flavour. It really is the main thing with which you should concern yourself when you are growing your own vegetables. It simply does not matter what colour your asparagus is under fluorescent tubes; you'll probably eat it by candlelight anyway.

You have one or two other advantages over the shops. You can ring the changes on the varieties you grow, not merely from year to year, but within the same season. You

can grow five or six different sorts of radish, carrot and lettuce, at the same time or one after the other; it keeps your
taste buds on their toes. And you can harvest any vegetable
at the very moment you think it should be picked, regardless
of what size, shape or colour the shops choose to sell it. If you
like your marrows bitter you can pick them when they are
only six inches long; and if you prefer them so large that the
skin is hard as horn, you can wait till they are three feet
long. The options are yours.

Of course, one of the reasons why many people have never
quite got around to growing their own vegetables, is that
they think they are boring. The British have been moaning
about their boring vegetables for eighty years and more; the
ones they grow and the way they cook them.

It has all changed. And it is going on changing fast. Perhaps the increased ease and comfort of modern travel has
widened our horizons and increased our expectations.

Be that as it may, if you don't want to get left behind
somewhere in the first half of the twentieth century, you
really do need to start growing your own vegetables as soon
as you can. Because only then can you get the real benefit of
the new and exciting thinking about new ways of cooking
vegetables.

In the last few years there has been a revolution in the
vegetables we can grow in Britain. It is a revolution that
makes it possible for both grower and cook to co-operate in
ways that were simply not possible before.

It is now possible to grow in the cool, inclement climate of
Britain a whole host of vegetables that once were thought, by
most of us, as the joys of the sun-baked Mediterranean
countries. They were too tender to grow out of doors in this
country: to grow them one needed a vast area of heated
glass, so most of us did not bother. We purchased them,
rarely, at enormous price, from the few purveyors of green-
groceries who had such delicacies. But modern advances in
plant breeding have produced hardier strains of many of
these vegetables: aubergines, sweet corn, courgettes and
many others. And because we can grow them ourselves, we

can eat them more often and be more adventurous in the way we cook them. Which in turn tunes us in to being more adventurous with the more everyday vegetables.

Even our everyday vegetables have been improved almost beyond recognition by the plant breeders. The common cabbage, for example, has improved in flavour so much that it seems to have little relation to its forefathers of twenty years ago. There is even a cabbage now that doesn't smell like cabbage while it is cooking. Not so very long ago the swede was a thing with coarse flesh and a rank flavour, usually considered fit only for cattle. Of course, there were always good cooks who knew how to make a delicacy of such an indelicacy. The swedes of today almost melt in your mouth, and have a curiously subtle flavour. And there are many other improvements: string beans aren't stringy any more, and a new 'superspud' is on its way.

With these modern advances it really is possible, provided there is a competent gardener in the family, and a competent cook, to eat a great deal better at home than you would if you went out. And eating well does not cost the earth. Practically nothing need be wasted: what you can't eat today, you can freeze for tomorrow. And if you compare the price of a packet of seeds with the cost of the vegetables in the shops, you can quickly work out the sort of savings you'll be making.

It is worth remembering though, however much you come to enjoy vegetables fresh from your own garden, and however much you become convinced that they do you good – and they really are very good for your skin and your general well-being – they contain relatively little in the way of protein. What you save by growing your own vegetables, is all extra money to spend on meat, fish, cheese and the other protein-packed foods with gold-plated prices.

Not only is vegetable growing more exciting today than ever before, but so too is vegetable cookery. So be adventurous. Try two or three new vegetables each year, and a new vegetable recipe at least once a week.

THE GARDEN
by Roger Grounds

❧ First Thoughts

Most people's first thoughts about growing their own vegetables is that, really, they just don't have the time.

But how much time does it really take?

About two hours a week, averaged out across the year.
That's all it takes to till and cultivate enough ground to keep
a family of four supplied with all the vegetables they need,
year in, year out.

You haven't got two hours a week? Then find it or make
it, because the rewards you will reap from growing your
own vegetables will be far greater than whatever sacrifice
you have to make.

The chances are that you, like most of modern mankind,
spend the greater part of your life indoors, caged in by walls
and windows, utterly unaware of the world beyond. Probably you take your relaxation indoors – modern man tends
to.

It would do you a power of good to get out and make
friends with the sun and the soil once in a while, to get to
know and to relate your own life to the changing rhythms of
the seasons. The air and exercise you gain in cultivating
your crops do just as much to make you healthier and hap-
pier as do your home-grown vegetables. The two hours a
week you may not think you can spare at the moment could,
if you take the longer view, add ten years to your life. Two
hours, once a week, isn't that much. It's about as long as it
takes to watch a game of football from your armchair. And
a great deal better for you.

Two hours a week is an average figure, taking the year as
a whole. You need to spend more time on the land in the
summer, when it is a joy to be out of doors, and less during

the winter, when it may not be quite such a pleasure. Indeed, if you manage things well, you may not need to get out on your land at all some weeks when the weather is really foul. By a happy chance, you do the heaviest work in the winter, when you are probably reluctant to take much other exercise; and least in summer, when it can get too hot for heavy digging.

What with the wind to blow the cobwebs out of your brains, the exercise to put a healthier complexion on your face, and the summer's suntan you'll gain while you harvest your crops, growing vegetables could make a new person of you, while the good they'll do you when you eat them is indisputable, especially if they are cooked in some of the delicious ways suggested in this book.

🌺 Basics

If you are not already a confirmed gardener, you probably think of soil as something that is called mud when it gets wet, and that bakes hard when it is dry. You may also have noticed that plants tend to stick out of the top of it. You need to know a little more than that if you are to grow worthwhile vegetable crops.

It is very easy to dismiss the soil as an inert mineral substance, but actually it is a little more complicated than that.

The soil itself is made up of three things: mineral particles, humus and a complex population of soil-living organisms. In the perfect soil, these three things occur in roughly equal quantities. The soil as you find it in the garden contains two other things, often overlooked, but actually extremely important: air and water, preferably in about equal parts.

The mineral particles in your soil are the result of the erosion of the rocks which form the earth's crust. Usually the mineral particles will have been eroded from local rock: if you live on sandstone you'll probably have a sandy soil, and so on. There are exceptions. If you live on a clay or gravel soil the mineral particles may have come to you from halfway across a land mass, carried on the backs of the glaciers during an ice age. These particles determine your basic soil type. That is a function of the size of the particles. They also determine the flavour of your soil, that is, whether it is acid or alkaline.

If you live in Britain, the chances are that you will be gardening on one of the three basic types of soil; clay, sand or loam. A clay soil is defined as one in which 30% of the mineral particles measure 0·002 mm diameter or less. A sand soil is one in which 35% of the particles are between

0·10 mm and 0·50 mm diameter. A loam is a soil in which one-third of the particles are typical clay size, one-third typical sand soil size, and one-third silt size, which is between 0·002 mm and 0·05 mm diameter. All of which sounds, and probably is, rather academic, since it is not necessary to rush out and accurately measure the size of the mineral particles in your soil to grow good crops. There are easier ways of finding out which type of soil you have.

Each of the three basic soil types has its own peculiar characteristics. Clay soils are usually very rich in plant foods, but they are heavy and difficult to work. In wet weather they are very sticky, and the soil particles tend to cling together with quite surprising tenacity. In hot weather clay soils bake hard. Overall, clay soils are badly drained: the particle size is so small that the gaps between them are necessarily similarly small with the result that water can only drain through very slowly. Sandy soils, on the other hand, are almost too easy to work at any time of year. They have a light, open structure, and because of this are usually free-draining. One consequence of this is that plant foods tend to get washed through sandy soils very quickly, leaving them poor in plant nutrients. A loam soil is, in essence, a happy balance between these two.

The simplest way of finding out what sort of soil you have is, quite literally, to feel the quality. Take a small quantity of soil from your future vegetable patch, and put it in the palm of your hand, then gradually dampen it, at the same time rolling it between finger and thumb. Add water little by little, and keep on moulding the soil until it forms a small ball, with enough adhesion to hold itself together, but with no free water. Now you can make some elementary deductions about your soil. The first thing is to decide how gritty it feels. If it feels very gritty, the chances are you have a sandy soil; a good loam feels only slightly gritty; a clay soil hardly feels gritty at all. You can cross-check your first finding by deciding how much polish there is to your ball of soil. A smooth, shiny, polished ball contains a relatively large number of fine mineral particles, indicating clay; loam soils produce less-polished balls, while sandy soils produce balls with practically no polish on them at all. A final cross-check is to test the ball for stickiness. A clay ball will be extremely sticky: you may have problems getting the clay off your hands. A ball made from a sandy soil will be so lacking in stickiness that it will probably fall apart in your hands.

If you are still in any doubt about what sort of soil you have, roll a lump into a ball between the palms of your hands, and having got it into a ball, then try to roll it out into a worm. If you've got a sandy soil, you won't get very far, because you won't even be able to get the ball to stick together. If you have a good loam soil, you'll be able to make the ball all right, but when you try to make a worm you'll find that it will fall apart. If you have a clay soil you will have no difficulty at all not only in making a ball but in making the worm as well.

Having played around with your soil in this way, you should have a pretty fair idea of the type of soil you have so far as the mineral particles are concerned. The next thing you need to check for is humus. You do this simply by drop-ping the ball of soil you already have in your hand into a tumbler of water, stirring it round with a teaspoon until the water is really cloudy, and then allowing it to settle. Most soils will settle to the bottom of the tumbler in three, more or less distinct, layers. At the very bottom will be the mineral particles: in a sandy soil these are clearly visible as sand. Above this will be a layer of smaller particles. The upper-most layer, which will be the one that takes longest to settle, will be the humus; this is usually dark brown in colour. If you have a good, thick layer of humus, keep smiling; if the layer is very thin, your soil lacks humus, and you are going to have to do something to put that right.

Humus has a totally different origin from the mineral particles: it is organic. It is what remains of animal and vegetable matter which has been broken down in and on the soil by the actions of wind, rain and soil micro-organisms. It is a highly complex material, black and brown in colour, colloidal (jelly-like) in texture, and is rich in fats, carbo-hydrates and protein.

The importance of humus in your soil cannot be suffici-ently stressed. It does four things which nothing else can do. First, it acts as a store for plant foods which tend to adhere very tightly to its particle surfaces, making them less likely to be washed away, and it is, in itself, the only store in the soil for nitrogen, which is essential to all plant growth. Secondly, it binds the mineral particles together, making them less likely to be washed away by wind or rain. Thirdly, it plays a vital role in the texture of the soil, increasing the speed at which surplus water can drain away, while acting as a sponge to prevent all the moisture drying out. Lastly, and in some ways just as importantly, it provides food for the micro-organisms in the soil. Because if your soil does not have a rich and thriving population of micro-organisms, it will never produce healthy, thriving plants.

A healthy soil contains, in its own way, a population as diverse and varied as the air above it. What you probably don't realise, as you turn the soil, is that there are, in any averagely fertile soil, some 100,000 micro-organisms to each cubic centimetre. That's an awful lot of life to find in a substance that most people consider inert. If the soil popula-tion is as rich and varied as it should be, it will contain plants and creatures ranging in size from microscopic, single-celled organisms such as bacteria, to highly visible things like earthworms.

A rich and diverse soil population does a number of things which are highly beneficial to plant growth. In the first place they convert dead animal and vegetable matter into humus, thereby converting it into a type of food that the plants can actually use. In the second place they work the soil, and keep air and drainage channels open.

What is interesting about soil micro-organisms is that they do best under exactly the same conditions as the roots of plants. They work together to try to create those conditions in the soil. Like the roots of plants, they need both air and water to live, and like the roots of plants, they inhale oxygen and exhale carbon dioxide; they also compete directly with the roots of plants for the same nutrients. Curiously enough, such competition is highly desirable. It prevents specialised plant disease organisms from becoming dominant.

You can encourage a healthy and diverse soil population by adding all the rotting vegetable matter you can to the soil. The micro-organisms will turn this into humus. The more you feed them, the more they will thrive, and the more humus there will be for your plants to feed on.

However, your plants won't be able to live at all unless there is both air and water in the soil. The actual bulk of most plants is made up mainly of water: a courgette, for example, is over 90% water. So water is pretty crucial to plant growth. But it is important in another way too. Plants can only absorb the nutrients they need in the form of weak solutions, so they need water in order to be able to feed. However, they need water in the right quantities: too little water, and they wilt and die of desiccation; too much and the roots literally suffocate and die. The only way you can really make sure that your plants are not getting too much nor too little water is to ensure a good soil structure with plenty of humus and a thriving micro-organic population.

The water that is of use to plants is held in the spaces between the particles in the soil. The smaller the particles, the more tightly it is held, and the poorer the drainage; the larger the particles the more loosely the water is held, and the more rapid drainage. Plainly, from the plant's point of view, a soil containing both large and small particles is most desirable.

One implication of this is obvious, but easily overlooked. Air is held in those spaces between the soil particles that are not already occupied by water. Thus a soil that contains an excess of water is, of necessity, short of air, and one in which there is too little water, has far too much air. Again, the only way to be sure that your soil suffers from neither extreme is to keep it liberally supplied with humus.

Both plant roots and soil micro-organisms need air in order to live. Both inhale oxygen and exhale carbon dioxide.

Provided that there are adequate pore spaces in the soil, there is a continual interchange of oxygen and carbon dioxide. However, if the pores become blocked by a surplus of water, carbon dioxide builds up in the soil, and carbon dioxide in high concentrations is just as poisonous to plants and micro-organisms as it is to people.

If the free exchange of oxygen and carbon dioxide is interrupted, as it easily can be in flood conditions, the carbon dioxide build-up damages the roots directly by poisoning them, but it also does something worse. It produces an acute imbalance in the soil population. Only those micro-organisms which can use high levels of carbon dioxide survive. These normally feed off dead or decaying matter in the soil, but once the carbon dioxide balance shifts, they attack the weakened roots, which further weakens the plants, making them susceptible to a whole host of other diseases. Normally population explosions of these undesirable organisms are kept in check by natural competition with other soil micro-organisms. You can only avoid the sort of problems that accompany carbon dioxide imbalance by ensuring a healthy soil with a healthy and competitive micro-organic community. Which again comes back to adding all the decaying vegetable matter you can to the soil.

Far from the soil being an inert mineral substance, it vibrates with life and activity. The important thing is to keep it that way.

❧ The Living Plant

It may have surprised you to find out just how alive the seemingly dead earth actually is. And that may have made you wonder just how alive a plant really is. It is all too easy to take it for granted that you stick a seedling in the soil and it grows, and, in time, you pull it up from the soil and eat it. The plant packs an awful lot of living into the time in between, and even a brief understanding of how a plant lives, and what it expects from the world it lives in, will help you to grow better crops.

Anyway, what is a plant?

Well, all living things are alive because they are consuming energy. Ultimately all living things on earth derive their energy from the sun. However, there are two totally different ways of deriving that energy. There is their way; and there is our way. Theirs is to use the energy directly from the sun; ours is to derive it from substances in which it has been stored. Living things which derive energy directly from the sun are plants; the rest of us are animals.

What a plant actually does is to take the energy from sunlight and use it to weld together six molecules of carbon dioxide and six molecules of water, thereby producing one molecule of glucose, and in the process discarding six molecules of oxgyen. Most of the energy contained in the glucose is then, almost immediately, converted by a chain of complex chemical reactions into thirty-eight molecules of ATP (adenosine triphosphate) which is, as it were, the universal currency of plant energy. It is in this form that energy travels round the plant to be used for cell-division which is the basis of growth, and for other functions which are necessary to keep a plant alive and healthy. Energy not used at once can be stored in the form of carbohydrates, fats and proteins. It is usually in one of those forms that we, as humans, consume the energy needed to keep our batteries charged.

The process of using the energy from sunlight to convert the carbon dioxide and water into glucose is called photosynthesis. That is what a plant is programmed to do. However, in order to accomplish it, it has to perform a number of, what are called in computer jargon, sub-routines. Photosynthesis and all its sub-routines are all gated to start with the coming of sunlight at dawn.

Two of these sub-routines are of supreme importance, because they are the ones that provide the plant with the carbon dioxide and water they need for photosynthesis to take place at all. Plants obtain carbon dioxide by a process known as respiration, and they obtain the water they need by transpiration.

Respiration is, in effect, breathing. What the plants do is absorb air through the pores in their leaves, and filter this to extract the carbon dioxide they need, after which they exhale the oxygen balance. When you realise that the concentration of carbon dioxide in the air is as little as three parts in every ten thousand, you begin to see just how much air the leaves have to filter to obtain sufficient carbon dioxide to run the photosynthesis factory.

The amount of water plants get through is even more amazing. Not only do they have to match every six molecules of carbon dioxide with six molecules of water, but they use water to cool the power house too. The sub-routine by which this is achieved is called transpiration. Water absorbed by the root and root hairs is passed through fine capillary tubes in the stem to the leaves and then is given off as water vapour through the stomata, or pores, in the leaves. Evaporation of water at the surface of the leaves creates suction: that suction causes a constant compensatory suction back through the twigs, stems and down to the roots. The sheer force of the suction created by evaporation is staggering. It is a pull of 1,000 atmospheres. That corresponds to the pull on a rope 3 mm in diameter by a man of eleven stone suspended from it. Each of the tiny capillary vessels that carry the water from the roots to the leaves may individually be subjected to pressures as great as thirty-five atmospheres. Suction of that magnitude causes the capillaries to shrink. Since the sap ducts run side by side, the stem of a plant actually shrinks under the pull of this suction. The rate of evaporation is greatest, the stem consequently thinnest, at about 2 pm. It is fattest around 4 am when evaporation is minimal.

There is a critical interplay between transpiration and another sub-routine, the one known as osmosis, which is the means by which plants absorb water and mineral salts in solution from the soil. What osmosis amounts to is this. When a solution with a high concentration of dissolved salts (such as that contained in the roots of a plant) is separated by a semi-permeable membrane (such as that of plant tissue) from a weaker solution (such as that contained in the soil round a plant's roots), water will pass from the weaker solution to the stronger solution in an attempt to neutralise the difference. And that is exactly how plants absorb water from the ground around them. Normally the amount of water absorbed through the roots balances the amount of water being evaporated by the leaves. All of which assumes sufficient water in the soil for this to happen.

The moment the amount of water being given off through the leaves by evaporation exceeds the amount of water the roots can absorb from the soil, a crisis occurs. The power-house no longer has water with which to cool its system, nor water to combine with carbon dioxide to make sugars. The power-house has to close down. Unless water becomes available to the roots through the soil, either from rainfall or watering, a situation is soon reached in which the concentration of dissolved salts in the soil is higher than that in the plants: then reverse osmosis occurs, the water moving from the plant into the surrounding soil. As a result of this water loss to the soil, the plant wilts.

All these sub-routines are handled automatically by the

plant in its day-to-day living, in very much the same way
that our parasympathetic nervous system handles our heart-
beat and breathing sub-routines, without our having to
think about it.

There is relatively little you can do about any of these
systems in plants, except to recognise that they need water,
air and sunlight to live, just as much as do you or I, and to
make sure that they do not have to go without any of these
unnecessarily.

Even in good light, the proportion of radiant energy from
sunlight which plants convert into bonded or chemical
energy, is rather less than 1%. That assumes clear skies;
heavy cloud cover can reduce the light intensity to as little
as 5%, with a corresponding decrease in the amount of
energy fixed by the plants. If you plant sun-loving vegetables
in shade, they will not be able to convert sunlight into the
energy they need to build their own tissues efficiently, and
growth will be poor. If you allow them to lack water, they
have to close down the power-house, and this again causes a
loss of growth. The only element you can tamper with to
good effect is the concentration of carbon dioxide in the
atmosphere: at higher concentrations, the rate of plant
growth is slightly increased. Even then, carbon dioxide
enrichment can only be done under glass, and is really still
very much in its experimental stages.

So it is probably better not to waste more time on things
you can do very little about, and pass on to aspects of plant
growth about which you can do something really useful.
Like feeding your plants, and making sure that their roots
are happily at home in your soil.

❧ What Plants Eat

Plants eat mineral salts. These they absorb from the soil in a weak solution. Their diet is mixed and very, very varied, containing some very surprising delicacies, including rare and precious metals such as gold, platinum, caesium and even boron. Fortunately they only need these in minute amounts. Luckily there is no need to feed gold to your tomatoes.

The minerals essential to plant growth are divided into those which are important – the macro-elements – and those which are not nearly so important – the micro-elements.

The macro-elements include all the major minerals needed by plants to make healthy growth. By far the most important of these is one that is very often passed over in silence. Perhaps its presence in the soil is taken for granted. It is calcium. Plants need calcium to build their skeletal structure just as we need calcium to build strong bones. It is calcium that forms the great skeletons left standing in the deserts of America when a giant saguaro cactus dies. It is calcium that makes lettuce leaves crisp, and it is calcium that makes the spines of a thistle stiff enough to stick into you. What calcium is actually used for is to build the cell walls of the plants, all the cell walls, not only in the leaves, but in the stems and roots too.

In most soils calcium is present in sufficient quantities without your having to worry about adding it. But some people do try to add it. That is one of the reasons why people put lime on the soil where they are going to grow vegetables. Lime is rich in calcium. There are many other reasons why people put lime on the soil, so we'll take a closer look at lime in a minute.

Apart from calcium, there are three other macro-elements which are needed by all plants if they are to make healthy growth. These are nitrogen, phosphorus and potassium: N, P and K.

Nitrogen is possibly the most important of these. Its prime use to plants is for growth. Apply liquid nitrogen round the roots of any fast-growing plant, a lettuce for example, and you will be able to see the rate of growth accelerate literally within a couple of days. Of course, such rapid growth is of little use to the plant unless other macro-elements are present in abundance: a plant growing in a soil rich in nitrogen but poor in potassium will grow fast but lack the skeletal strength to hold itself upright.

Phosphorus is used by plants to help them come out the right colour. A lettuce without phosphorus will grow a most extraordinary sort of almost bright yellow colour. It needs phosphorus to help it grow green. If it lacks that green colouring, it will not be able to photosynthesise properly and then, no matter how well you cultivate it, its growth will be impaired; you will get a poor crop.

Potassium is used by plants chiefly for forming their flowers and setting their fruit. Its presence in the soil is most important for those plants whose flowers you are going to eat (like cauliflowers and broccoli) or whose fruits you are going to eat (like tomatoes and marrows).

Those are the macro- or major elements plants need in their diet. They are all elements you can work into the soil to help ensure healthy growth in your crops.

The micro-elements, also known as trace elements because only traces of them are necessary, are used by plants in relatively small quantities. There are literally dozens of these trace elements, including the precious metals mentioned above, but they are usually present in any good fertile soil in sufficient quantity for the plants' requirements.

There are just two micro-elements of which plants do occasionally run short. These are magnesium and boron. Indeed, modern findings suggest that these two elements are somewhat more important to plant growth than used to be thought the case. While not as important as the macro-elements, they seem to be considerably more important than the rest of the micro-elements. You are most likely to have plants suffering from magnesium or boron deficiencies if you grow your plants on an exceptionally fast-draining soil. The problem is that these two elements are very readily leached out of the soil by weathering. However, if you keep your soil in good condition by the techniques recommended in this book you really should not run into magnesium or boron deficiencies, even on the fastest-draining soils.

Plants, like people, need the right diet if they are to be healthy and happy. You can make sure that they have plenty of carbon dioxide and water available to them by keeping your soil in good heart; you can make sure that they get all the macro-elements they need by feeding them correctly, which will also ensure that they have all the trace elements they need. The one area where you might run into problems is ensuring that they get sufficient calcium in their diet. There is usually plenty of calcium in the soil; the problem is that some plants are inhibited from using it because the soil is too acid or too alkaline. That is a matter of the 'flavour' of your soil, and the flavour of your soil is measured on what is called the pH scale.

❧ Soil Tasting

The 'flavour' of your soil is determined by its hydrogen ion content. Depending upon how much or how little it has it will be either acid or alkaline. A soil with an excess of hydrolyx (OH-) is alkaline. Where there is an excess of hydrogen ions it is acid. Where the hydrolyx ions and the hydrogen ions are present in equal quantities, the soil is neither acid nor alkaline, it is neutral.

Whether your soil is acid, alkaline or neutral is something that can be measured on what is known as the pH scale (pH = potential of hydrogen). The scale runs from 0 to 14. Both extremes burn. 0 is as acid as hydrochloric acid. 14 is as caustic as caustic soda. Very little indeed will grow at these extremes of the scale. In garden terms it is very unlikely that your soil will be more acid than pH 4·5, or more alkaline than pH 8·5. pH 4·5 is fine for rhododendrons; pH 8·5 is fine for lilacs. However, if you want to grow first-rate vegetables you need to aim for a soil that is virtually neutral, somewhere between 6·5 and 7. Which may be interesting intellectually, but how do you actually find out, in plain practical terms, whether your soil is acid, alkaline or neutral?

The simplest and oldest way is to look around your garden and see what is growing there. All plants have a preference for a soil with a particular flavour. Rhododendrons have a taste for an acid soil, so does bracken, and so do most of the heathers. So if any of these are growing in your garden the soil must be on the acid side. Lilacs and groundsel thrive in alkaline soils, though both will tolerate neutral soils: they should only be taken as a sure guide to an alkaline soil if there are no rhododendrons to be seen anywhere round your garden or your neighbours' gardens.

However valid the conclusions you may draw from your observations of the plants growing in your garden, those observations will be valid only at the time you observe them. The fact is that once you start to cultivate your soil you start to change its pH. In general, cultivation tends to shift the pH towards the acid end of the scale. One simple way of checking this is to grow a hydrangea right in the middle of your vegetable patch. Hydrangeas start producing blue flowers at pH 5, which is far too acid for most vegetables. They produce muddled sort of pinky-mauvy-bluey flowers at about pH 5·5, which gives you an early warning of a pH shift.

There is, quite frankly, only one accurate way to find out whether your soil is acid or alkaline, and that is to test it. Go along to your local garden centre and buy yourself a lime-testing kit. Be sure to ask for a lime-testing kit. If you ask for a soil-testing kit it will cost you an enormous amount more, and give you information you may not need. All a lime-testing kit does is tell you whether your soil is acid or alkaline, and usually that is all you need to know.

What you do is you take a sample of damp but not wet soil from the part of the garden in which you intend to grow your vegetables. You tip this into a small test-tube supplied with the kit, and then add a liquid catalyst which also comes with the kit. You shake the catalyst and soil around in the tube, and then leave them to settle. The catalyst will change colour according to the degree of acidity in your soil. All you then have to do is compare the colour of the liquid with the colours on the pH scale that comes with the kit, and just read off the pH of your soil.

What you will have established is the flavour of your soil. Why this is important is because it is one of the limiting factors plants have: did they not have such limiting factors it would, at least theoretically, be possible for one genus or species to take over the whole globe.

Suppose, after testing it, you find that your soil has the wrong flavour to grow vegetables well: what do you do?

Give up? Or rush out and cover the vegetable patch with lime? Which is what lots of people do, very often for the wrong reasons.

❧ Lime and Liming

At some time or other lime has been considered a cure for practically every imaginable ill in the vegetable garden. But this is partly because the term 'lime' is used very loosely, and partly because the different types of lime applied under different names achieve different ends.

The term 'lime' is properly used of the compound CaO, which is the oxide of the metal calcium, which is obtained by heating chalk or limestone in a kiln with coal until it is red-hot. The end product is properly called quicklime.

From the vegetable grower's point of view, quicklime has some interesting and useful qualities. Firstly, when it is wetted (as for example by rain), or simply dampened by lying on moist soil, it swells up and crumbles into a fine, white powder. This fine white powder is known as slaked lime.

It is slaked lime that is generally of most use in the vegetable garden. Slaked lime is only very slightly soluble in water, and when mixed with it produces an alkaline solution. This solution readily absorbs the gas carbon dioxide, which makes it even less soluble.

Carbon dioxide is a very weak acid, so that it is easily displaced from the slaked lime by other acids, especially those commonly found in the soil. When these soil acids combine with the carbon in the slaked lime, they are neutralised. In effect, slaked lime absorbs the acids in acid soils and neutralises them, leaving the soil sweet. This effect can be measured as a shift on the pH scale from acid to neutral.

Therefore one of the uses of lime is to render an acid soil less acid. But lime performs other functions too.

One of the most useful of these is to ameliorate the texture of clay soils. It does this by a process known as flocculation. What actually happens is that particles of lime cause the minute particles of clay to cling together in groups. This increases the particle size, and thereby improves both the drainage and aeration of clay soils.

Another useful thing lime does is to encourage the activities of the soil micro-organisms responsible for the decomposition of organic matter, turning it into humus. However, it can only do this where there is adequate decomposable matter in the soil. Light dressings of lime on soils that have been adequately supplied with decomposable vegetable matter can help to produce thriving crops. The problem is that continued dressings of lime on soils that lack readily decomposable vegetable matter will actually make the soil increasingly less and less fertile, so that crops will get poorer and poorer season by season.

From this it would seem that all is well so long as you add plenty of compost or manure, and a little slaked lime. And all is well – so long as you do not add them both together. The moment lime comes into contact with materials containing salts of ammonia, as most compost does, it causes ammonia gases to be liberated into the air.

If you want to use both lime and organic matter on your soil, the golden rule is to apply the lime first – at least a month before you apply the organic matter.

There's another golden rule about lime, and that is that you add slaked lime to the surface of the soil, and leave it there. The action of the weather will work the lime into the ground. There is no need for you to dig it in.

There is just one exception to this rule, and that is when you use lime to try to rid the soil of the organisms that cause club root in vegetables of the cabbage family – the Brassicas. If this is your purpose in applying lime, you should use quicklime, not slaked lime, and the quicker the better. When quicklime gets damp it gets hot, and the quicker the lime the hotter it gets. So you need to dig quicklime well into the soil where you want to grow Brassicas, so that it will burn the organisms that cause club root. The problem with using lime in this way is that it also burns many of the highly desirable organisms in the soil too.

The heat in quicklime does not last so very long, and once the quicklime has been thoroughly wetted, it cools, and what remains in the ground is slaked lime. Because you now have slaked lime in the soil, you need to apply a liberal dressing of organic matter, but not until at least a month after you applied the quicklime.

So while lime has its uses, it is certainly not something that should be scattered on the soil every time you have a bare patch of land in your vegetable plot, as used to be the fashion until relatively recently, and is still sometimes recommended. It should be used for specific purposes: for changing the pH of the soil, for increasing the rate of decomposition of organic matter, or for ridding the soil of club root, but never just added haphazardly. And never ever without a complementary dose of organic matter.

Probably the most frequent use of lime today is for changing the flavour of the soil, for making an acid soil neutral or alkaline. The problem here is that there is no standard rate of application. Different soils need different amounts of lime to achieve the same change in the pH. It takes only 1·8 kg of lime to raise a light sandy soil from pH 4·5 to pH 5; but it takes 4·5 kg to raise the pH in a heavy clay soil by the same amount. To make life easier for you, consult the Liming Table on the next page. If in doubt about the rate at which to apply lime, always go for the lesser amount, rather than the greater amount.

It has become so much a part of the lore or folklore of gardening that if you want to grow vegetables you add lime to the soil, that few people have stopped to consider what you do to the soil if it is already too alkaline to grow vegetables. It is sometimes recommended that you add flowers of sulphur or aluminium sulphate, at various rates. In fact, both are to be avoided like the plague. Both leave in the soil deposits of aluminium and aluminium is poisonous to most plants. It is also poisonous to most people, so it is rather foolish to add it to any soil where you are going to grow plants you intend to eat.

In fact there is little need to do anything drastic in order to make an alkaline soil more acid. The mere fact that you cultivate it, that you feed it with manure and/or compost, will gradually make it more and more acid.

Liming is not a ritual to be performed at regular intervals: it is something to be done for a specific reason, to achieve a specific end. If you intend to use lime on your vegetable garden, be sure why you are using it, that you are using the right type of lime, and that you are applying it at the right rate.

LIMING TABLE

pH	Soil acidity	Light sandy soils	Sandy loam or silt soils	Medium loam soils	Clay loam soils	Heavy clay soils
6·0	Moderate	·9 kg (2 lb)	1·4 kg (3 lb)	1·8 kg (4 lb)	2·2 kg (5 lb)	2·5–2·7 kg (5½–6 lb)
5·5	Strong	1·4 kg (3 lb)	1·8 kg (4 lb)	2·6 kg (5¾ lb)	3·1 kg (7 lb)	3·5 kg (7¾ lb)
5·0	Very strong	1·7 kg (3¾ lb)	2·6 kg (5¾ lb)	3·2 kg (7¼ lb)	3·6 kg (8 lb)	4·1 kg (9¼ lb)
4·5	Extreme	1·8 kg (4 lb)	2·9 kg (6½ lb)	3·6 kg (8 lb)	4 kg (8¾ lb)	4·5 kg (10 lb)

Amount of hydrated lime required to raise pH 6·5, the optimum level. Rate per 9 sq m (100 sq ft).

❧ Improving Your Soil

There was a time, and not so very long ago at that, when the only materials known to man for improving his soil were muck and sand. Muck is still very popular. Sand, somehow, seems to have been forgotten. Which is a shame, because it has an important part to play in soil improvement.

The thinking behind the muck and sand recipe was very sound, if somewhat anthropomorphic: the idea was that plants, like us, need roughage in their diet, as well as goodness. So the old gardeners gave their plants sand, where today we eat bran buds.

Muck is a valuable commodity. It contains nearly all the essential foods that plants need, together with most of the trace elements as well. Seemingly, you can go on applying it to the soil forever, and there is a widespread assumption that you can go on applying it forever without doing the soil any harm.

The thinking behind the muck, muck and more muck argument is this: soil organisms need organic matter upon which to thrive. So the more organic matter you add to the soil the greater the population of micro-organisms will be. So far, so good. The micro-organisms mix the organic matter in with the mineral matter in the soil, thereby producing the perfect growing mix. And up to a point this is true. But it is a matter of balance and proportion. If you add six inches of manure to the land every year, after a hundred years you are going to have a huge pile of manure on top of your soil, and the soil will be so far down below the surface that the micro-organisms, most of whom live only in the top layer of soil (about the depth of a spade) simply cannot mix the soil and organic matter. Ultimately the endless adding of organic matter becomes self-defeating. A few feet below the surface of your hundred-year thick layer of manure, you would finish up with a layer somewhat resembling a vast cowpat. You avoid this by adding sand: it gives the organic matter some bulk to build itself around.

Very few of us are likely to go on adding muck to our vegetable plots for a hundred years. For one thing, muck is not that easy to come by any more. But the point is one worth bearing in mind, if only because so long as muck is in fashion, you'll find people advocating adding nothing but organic materials to your soil to improve it. But you need to add sand too. The problem is that sand is often even harder to come by than muck.

There is sand and sand. The sort of sand you need for the garden is very coarse sand, that is, sand with large individual particles: large individual particles have large spaces between them as they rest against each other, and that means good drainage. Sand with small particles, and consequently small spaces between the particles, drains very badly. If you look at a pile of the yellow sand builders use for mixing cement, you will notice that puddles form on it after a heavy rainstorm. Sand like that is useless in the garden. You might just as well add clay.

The sort of sand you want is what builder's merchants usually sell under the name of washed river sand. It is usually used as a foundation upon which to lay paving. A quarter yard every couple of years, spread over your vegetable area, will do much to improve the texture of your soil, no matter what sort of soil you start with, provided that you also follow a regular regime of adding organic matter to the soil.

If you doubt the beneficial effects of sand in the garden, there is an experiment that it would be well worth your trying. Take a couple of cuttings of something that roots easily, weeping willow, goat willow, forsythia, something like that, and try one cutting in one of the modern soilless growing mixes that contains no sand and is virtually pure peat, and the other in pure washed river sand or silver sand.

Both will root, but the one in the soilless growing mix will produce only a small number of thick, white, rather straight roots, while the one in the sand will produce a larger number of much finer roots, which will branch and twist and spread in all directions. In terms of quantity, the one in the sand will produce more root matter than the one in the soilless growing mix. In terms of quality the ones in the sand will be better than those in the soilless growing mix. Pot them on into any good soil, and it is the plant that formed its roots in sand that will romp away.

Which is not to deny the benefit of muck on the ground. It is simply to stress that the more organic matter you add to the land, the more important it becomes that you also add grit in some form, coarse sand being ideal.

In the days when muck and sand were the only means available for improving the land, there was plenty of muck around. But then everyone had a horse or more. Today everyone has a car or more, and the problem with cars, so far as the good gardener is concerned, is that they do not produce droppings which can be used to improve the land.

If you can get organic manure, from a farm, a riding school, or even just someone who happens to keep a horse, use it. Manure is manure, whether it comes from a cow or a horse or is a mixture of both. Pig manure has its uses too, though you may find neighbours complaining of the smell.

If you cannot obtain organic manure, use whatever organic materials you can obtain to improve your ground. The choice is wide. You can probably obtain at least one and probably more likely several of the following: bone, blood, fish meal, sewage sludge, town waste, spent hops, shoddy, peat or seaweed. All these contain the essential nutrients needed by plants, but in differing proportions. For that reason it is wise if you possibly can, to use one type of organic manure one year, and something different next year. Ring the changes.

Of course, one of the finest sources of all the organic manures available to you is already right there, literally on your doorstep. That is waste vegetable matter, either from the garden or from the kitchen. Instead of throwing it away, all you have to do is compost it, and you will have turned it into one of the finest organic soil improvers around.

🎕 Blending Your Own Compost

In the old days a compost heap was a necessary evil. The garden produced weeds, and you had to put them somewhere. That somewhere gradually grew into an untidy heap called the compost heap. When it got too large you put the more thoroughly rotted parts of it back on the garden, mainly because you did not know what else to do with it.

Today a compost bin is a neat and tidy affair, designed to consume as much vegetable matter as you can supply it with, and to convert that as rapidly as possible into a nutrient-rich material somewhat resembling peat, which you can put on your land to improve the soil.

If you haven't already got a compost bin, you can either buy or build one. Whichever you do it really is important to understand exactly how a compost bin works. In fact, it works very much like a bonfire. In a bonfire, it is a flame that consumes the waste matter; in a compost bin it is bacteria that consume the waste material. A bonfire needs a good draught and plenty of air if the flame is to do a thorough job of consuming what is there. The bacteria in a compost bin need just as much air and just about as much of a draught if they are to consume thoroughly everything you put in the bin.

If you are thinking of building your own bin, the first thing to think about is where to put it. It needs plenty of air circulating freely around it on all sides, and it needs to be in sun. Apart from that, the choice is yours. There is a wide range of materials from which you can build your compost bin. You can make it of wood – things like timber planks, pine poles, split pine poles, chestnut palings; or you can make it of more durable things like brick, concrete, breeze blocks. What is important is that whatever you make it from, it must have a space beneath it so that air can circulate underneath it, and there must be plenty of holes in the sides, otherwise the bacteria will not be able to consume matter resting against the sides of the bin. Probably the best plan is to make the holes fairly large, and to line the bin with a plastic coated fine-mesh wire netting. This provides plenty of air without allowing even relatively small pieces of the compost material, like lawn clippings, to fall out.

The bin should be either square or round in plan. And it should be of a convenient size, neither too big nor too small. If it is too small it won't hold enough, and if it is too big you'll have problems in getting the matured compost out, or else in using it. The ideal is usually to build two or three bins, all the same size, and to use them in rotation. A fairly reasonable size for a bin is about a metre each way – wide, long and tall. A bin that size will produce nearly a ton of compost a year.

One final point which is quite often overlooked in building a compost bin: do make one side removable. Otherwise, you may finish up with a bin full of marvellous compost, but no way of getting it out.

Having built or bought your bin you need to know what to put in it. You can put almost anything of organic origin into the bin; in practice, most people confine themselves to putting vegetable waste into the bin. Meat scraps will compost, but they take longer to do so than vegetable matter and there is always the chance that they may attract animals your neighbours may not welcome: cats, rats, mice, foxes and badgers. So it is safest to stick to vegetable matter.

The main sorts of vegetable matter that should find their way into your compost bin are the outer leaves of lettuces and cabbages; peelings from potatoes, carrots, and other root vegetables; also any discarded garden waste like the outer leaves of cauliflowers which you may remove when you harvest the heads. Quite a lot of household rubbish is organic. A trip to the supermarket will usually result in a large yield of paper bags; these can be added to the contents of your compost bin. So can cardboard cartons and old newspapers, though both of these need to be shredded to compost rapidly. Then there are things like orange peel and apple and banana skins. All these should be added to the normal waste that accrues from your garden: the weeds and the lawn mowings.

The more diverse the ingredients you add to your compost bin the better. You will encourage a wider range of bacteria, and the degree to which they will be able to convert vegetable matter into humus will be greatly increased. The critical thing to avoid is adding only one thing to the compost bin. Some people seem to save their compost bins for one thing only, usually lawn clippings. That is disastrous. All you finish up with is a soggy, slimey and exceedingly smelly mushy mess. But if you mix the lawn clippings with layers of vegetable waste from the kitchen, each will benefit the other, especially if you give the contents of your bin a good shake-up every now and again, to help mix the ingredients.

It used to be the fashion to build up a compost bin rather in the way a large sponge sandwich is made, with a nine-inch layer of compost, levelled off with a three-inch layer of earth, and so on all the way from bottom to top. Some people still do this, and there is nothing at all wrong with it. It simply is not really necessary. You are far better off building the thing up in the natural sequence in which the ingredients come to hand, and shaking them all together occasionally. There are, however, two occasions when it can be a good idea to use the sandwich treatment. One is when you have your first six or eight inches of compost in a fresh bin. Top that off with a three-inch layer of compost from one of the other bins in which the compost is already reaching maturity. By doing this you are simply adding to your new heap some of the bacteria already well-established in your old heap. The other time it is worth using the sandwich treatment is when the bin is full. Top it off with a three-inch layer of ordinary garden soil. It looks tidy and it helps to keep the bacteria in the bin smouldering away.

Some people use things called activators or accelerators in their compost bins. You can use them too, if you happen to like their colour or their smell or their price. But, provided that you have a good mix of ingredients in your compost bin, they really are not necessary. The finest activators of all are animal manures. It is always worth spreading a layer of animal manure across the bin at some stage. If farmyard manure or some such is not readily available to you, try the sweepings from the bottom of the budgie cage, from the family hamster, gerboa, guinea pig or whatever. Failing all else it is worth remembering that among the ingredients that helped to make cottage gardens thrive was good old-fashioned human waste, usually thrown straight out of the window in the morning, and straight onto the garden, accompanied by loud cries of 'gardez l'eau!' or 'Fore!' or some such suitable warning. While it would be unseemly in this modern age to commend the placing of night soil on the compost heap, the fact remains that human urine is one of the finest of all activators. It is most politely applied to the heap by means of a watering can. How you get it into the watering can is your problem.

There are one or two things that are better not put in the compost bin, but saved instead for a bonfire. These are woody prunings, the tough, stringy haulms of vegetables, and hedge clippings. They will compost admirably; the only trouble is that they usually take about eight times as long to compost as the softer vegetable waste. If you prefer not to have a bonfire because it may produce carcinogenic smoke, keep one compost bin especially for slow-composting ingredients. If you do have a bonfire the thing to avoid is a bonfire that billows smoke in all directions. Instead, have a bonfire that blazes with clean, bright flames, and then is over. Apply the ash straight to the vegetable garden: it is rich in potash, which helps to produce vegetables with a good colour and texture. Applying it straight to the garden is important. What is useful in bonfire ash will be washed into the ground with the first burst of rain.

The making of compost is not an end in itself, though

listening to some experts you might well be forgiven for thinking it were. The purpose of making compost is to have an abundant supply of organic matter with which to feed your soil.

There remains merely the question of what you actually do with all this compost once you have produced it. Well, you apply it to the soil. To be precise, you apply it to the top of the soil. You can dig it in if you want to, but it is not necessary to do so. Worms and other soil organisms will mix it into the ground for you anyway. Since we've been conditioned to thinking that digging is good, if not for the soil at least for our souls, do a little digging if the urge is very strong and then put another few inches of compost over the top of the ground you have dug.

You can apply compost to the soil whenever you like. You can apply it in winter, and let wind, rain and frost help work it into the ground. You can apply it in spring as a mulch each side of newly planted rows of vegetables. You can apply it in summer, after heavy rains, to prevent the moisture that is in the soil from evaporating. And you can apply it on the ground again in autumn, or whenever you clear a row.

And you can apply the compost in different stages of decomposition. You can apply it fairly raw, while it is still stringy with the fibres of cabbage leaves; or you can wait until it has decomposed to the point at which it has the fine, crumbly texture of peat. The latter looks neater; the former is probably more effective because the composting process is still going on, so you are adding valuable bacteria along with the compost to the soil.

Of course, all this may seem too much trouble to go to when you can easily buy a bag of fertilizer from your local garden centre. If you feel that way it is worth considering just what it is you are trying to do to your soil.

🎝 Organic or Artificial

It is the custom of those who favour organic gardening, to refer to the sort of fertilisers you can buy in bags from your garden centre as artificial fertilisers, as though the mere mention of the word artificial was sufficient to condemn them forever in all men's eyes.

Those who favour the use of artificial fertilisers claim, quite rightly, that the fertilisers are not artificial at all. They are made up wholly of naturally-occurring substances. Which is true. They are. They are compounded from naturally-occurring minerals such as phosphorus, nitrates, lime and so on. What is artificial about artificial fertilisers is the way they are used. That is, the minerals, which normally occur at some depth in the ground, are applied to the surface of the soil.

In some ways artificial fertilisers have some advantages over organic manures. The greatest of these advantages is that you know precisely what it is that you are applying to your soil in terms of nitrogen, phosphorus and potassium, which you do not if you are applying organic manure. You can buy a packet of high nitrogen fertiliser, and know that you are applying ten parts of nitrogen to the ground for every five parts of potassium and five parts of phosphorus. You can seldom be that precise when you are using organic manures. The proportions will vary according to the source of the organic material. If you are using horse manure the proportions can be affected by such trivial things as what the horse had for breakfast. Artificial fertilisers do not suffer such vagaries.

There is nothing wrong with artificial fertilisers: they are both convenient and expensive. Their main disadvantage is that, while they feed the plants, they do nothing whatever to improve the soil or to maintain it in good heart. All you are doing when you add artificial fertilisers to the soil is adding mineral particles. If you go on doing this for long enough, any humus in the soil will gradually disappear (every time you pull a plant out of the ground you are taking from the ground humus which ought to be put back) and once the humus has gone so too will the soil micro-organisms. Then your soil will be sterile, no matter how much artificial fertiliser you put on the soil.

You may think that all this sounds very alarmist. It would be marvellous if it was only alarmist talk. The fact is that it is happening now. There are places where farmers have abandoned the traditional methods of applying manure to the soil, and have added only artificial fertilisers for years and years – well over two decades in some cases. For a while all seemed to be going well. Then it was found that the soil structure had broken down: put a tractor on wet land and it so compacted the ground that nothing could grow. Come summer and the dry soil particles blew away in the breeze. There are, literally, dust bowls in England's green and pleasant land, in spite of all the rain.

What has happened on these farm lands is a warning we should all heed. We have inherited the earth; we hold it in trust for generations yet to come. It is not ours to abuse or destroy.

It should be very clear that it is not the case that the artificial fertilisers destroy the soil. They do not. They simply do not bring any benefit to the soil if used on their own. The point is not that artificial fertilisers should never be used. It is that they should never be used on their own. If you add an artificial fertiliser to your soil, you must add plenty of organic matter too, whether in the form of farm-yard manure or garden compost. The fertiliser may feed your plants but it can only do so so long as there is plenty of moisture in the soil, and that means having plenty of humus to act as a sponge, both increasing the moisture content of the soil while also increasing the amount of air in the soil.

It is only when you use artificial fertilisers on their own that you are really likely to run into real soil problems in your garden. You could start with a really good loam soil, yet if you use nothing but artificial fertilisers on it for years on end, you could well finish up with a soil that will grow practically nothing.

The best plan is to make it a rule always to apply both artificial fertilisers and organic matter at the same time. That way you can be sure of feeding your soil in the way that will benefit both the plants and the soil best. Put on a thick layer – four to six inches thick – of garden compost or farmyard manure in November, when you have finished digging the garden over, and at the same time add a heavy dose of artificial fertiliser. Then leave them there, on top of the soil, through the winter. In early spring, fork them lightly into the top four inches of the soil, and add another very light dressing of artificial fertiliser, and another couple of inches of organic matter. Fork those over to mix them together, but still leave them on top of the soil.

That way you keep your soil in good heart, and produce bumper crops too. However, while you can add garden compost to any part of the vegetable garden almost any time of the year, there are certain parts of it to which you should never add artificial fertiliser or organic manure at certain seasons. That is part of the mystery of what gardeners call rotation.

❧ Rotation

Rotation is the name given by farmers and gardeners to the practice of moving crops round in time and in space, so that you do not grow the same crops in the same place year after year.

Were one to grow the same crop in the same place year after year, the vigour of the crop would gradually diminish. As the soil became depleted, the yield would markedly diminish and there is every probability that diseases specific to whatever vegetable you were growing there would invade the land or the crop.

Greens, for example, the Brassicas (cabbage, cauliflower sprouts, kale, etc.), make very heavy demands on the soil, and are particularly heavy users of nitrogen. If one were to grow cabbages in the same part of the vegetable garden year after year, plainly the amount of nitrogen in the soil would rapidly be used up; this would result in poorer and poorer yields; the plants would be weaker and weaker, and become increasingly likely to invasion by the dreaded club root disease. Furthermore, once club root invaded the ground, each new planting of cabbages would tend to further exhaust the soil and further encourage club root.

Since the Brassicas draw very heavily on the nitrogen in the soil, it is necessary to replace that nitrogen. If you practise rotation, the way you replace that nitrogen is by growing legumes on the spot where the cabbages grew. The legumes (peas and beans) have strange nodules on their roots which have the unique ability among plants of being able to fix nitrogen from the atmosphere and leave it in the soil in a form readily available to other plants. The legumes, therefore, restore the nitrogen balance in the soil. They can be followed by root crops, which need a balanced diet.

The advent of artificial fertilisers very nearly changed all that. The idea was that if the Brassicas exhausted the nitrogen in the soil – all you needed to do to put matters right was to add masses of nitrogen in the form of a nitrogen-rich artificial fertiliser. When it was found, after some years, that that didn't really work, you merely added twice as much nitrogen-rich fertiliser, and twice as much as that the year after. If pests started becoming a problem, you just added twice the recommended dosage of some pesticide. It sounds as though it ought to work, but somehow it just doesn't.

There are two systems of rotation currently being commended: a three-group system and a four-group system. There is little to choose between them, though probably the four-group system is more adaptable. Both systems are shown diagrammatically at the end of this chapter, and you will note that the only real difference between the two is that whereas in the four-group system you have Legumes isolated as one group, and a group called Floaters, in the three-group system the two are put together in one group. The choice is yours. It is a matter of convenience. The advantage of the four-group system is that it allows you to grow vegetables of which you might need more than usual wherever you like on the plot (so long, of course, as you do not grow them in the same place two years in succession); its disadvantage is that it leaves you with only peas and beans to grow in the area allocated to them, and you will either finish up with too many peas and beans, or not plant enough to keep the soil in balance.

In practice one of the best methods of using a rotation system is to divide the area you allocate to growing vegetables into four areas all of which are the same size. Three of the plots are used in the rotation system. The fourth is then used for permanent crops, things like artichokes, asparagus, leeks, and vegetables you may not want to grow every year, such as sweet corn, or something you want to try out just to see how it does. You can also plant in the fourth plot any extra vegetables you want from any of the other rotation groups.

Because proper rotation of the crops is so essential to the production of good, healthy plants year after year, the vegetables in the section that follows are arranged in groups within their rotation systems, as well as alphabetically in the Contents list of vegetables included in that section.

A THREE-GROUP ROTATION SYSTEM

Brassicas
Brussels Sprouts
Cabbage
Cauliflower
Kale
Kohlrabi
Radish
Savoy
Sprouting Broccoli
Swede
Turnip (grown for greens)

Note: The crops should follow each other in the ground in the order in which they are shown.

Legumes and Floaters
Artichoke, Globe
Asparagus
Aubergine
Beans
Celery
Courgette
Cucumber
Leeks
Lettuce
Onions
Peas
Peppers
Spinach
Sweet Corn
Tomatoes

Root Crops
Artichoke, Jerusalem
Beetroot
Carrot
Chicory
Parsnip
Potatoes
Kohlrabi
Radish
Swede
Turnip

A FOUR-GROUP ROTATION SYSTEM

Brassicas
Brussels Sprouts
Cabbage
Cauliflower
Kale
Kohlrabi
Radish
Savoy
Sprouting Broccoli
Swede
Turnip (grown for greens)

Note: The vegetables shown in this system should follow each other in the land in the order in which they are given, starting with the Brassicas. 'Floaters' can be grown anywhere in the rotation system, or in a permanent bed which is not part of the rotation system.

Legumes
Beans
Peas

Root Crops
Artichoke, Jerusalem
Beetroot
Carrot
Chicory
Parsnip
Potatoes
Kohlrabi

Radish
Swede
Turnip

Floaters
Artichoke, Globe
Asparagus
Aubergines
Celery
Courgette
Cucumber
Leeks
Lettuce
Onions
Peppers
Spinach
Sweet Corn
Tomatoes

🎇 Climate

The Roman historian Tacitus said of the climate of Britain that it suffers from extremes neither of heat nor cold, yet is never pleasant. His statement really seems to sum up remarkably well the interminable dull grey days that are so characteristic of both our summers and our winters. It is, in fact, just because we do not suffer from extremes of heat and cold, and because we have a humid climate, that we are able to grow such a diversity of plants in this country.

Technically, the climate of Britain is a cool, temperate, maritime one. It is the ameliorating influence of the seas that surround us that keeps our summers cooler than they would be if we were landlocked on a huge continent; it also keeps our winters more mild than they would otherwise be.

The benefits of a climate like ours are enormous, and not always appreciated. It is possible to work the land most of the winter: there may be the odd weeks every now and then when the ground is too hard to dig. We can plant vegetables in the autumn and leave them to grow through the winter to harvest in spring. And there are other vegetables that we can sow in summer to harvest in winter. There are relatively few parts of the temperate world where this can be done. In North America or the USSR, for example, the climate is continental, and one effect of that is that once winter has set in and the ground has frozen, it remains frozen right through until spring. It simply is not possible to grow vegetables through the winter in that sort of climate. Sprouts turn to pulp under continuous minus-zero temperatures.

There is however, one advantage to a continental climate which we, with our maritime climate, lack. And that is that in a continental climate, once spring comes, it comes to stay. In our mild, maritime climate, we are never really quite sure when spring is going to come. Most people seem to expect it sometime around April. Sometimes it comes in March and sometimes in August.

Which makes it very difficult to know when to set seedlings in the ground, or to plant out young seedlings that would be damaged by late frosts. To take some of the guesswork out of this, the map in this chapter shows the onset of spring. It should be appreciated that what this shows is a statistical average of when spring is likely to occur. In fact, statistically, the onset of spring may vary by up to plus or minus two weeks. So it helps to know what the lines on the map are actually showing you.

The lines showing the onset of spring are based on what is called isothene datum. An isothene is a line drawn between all those points on which a particular species of plant starts into growth on the same day. If you were to take the isothene for the common primrose, for example, you would find that it starts into growth earliest in the extreme south-west, and starts into growth last in the extreme north-east. From this you could deduce that spring starts in the south-west of the country and moves north-eastwards across the country at the rate of four miles per hour (slowing down for hills, of course).

The most useful isothene from the vegetable growing point of view is that for grass. Grass starts growing at 6°C/43°F. It stops growing in the autumn when the temperature of the soil drops below this temperature again. The space in-between is the period known as the growing season. The great advantage of using the isothene for grass as the measuring point for when spring arrives is that, while the map may tell you when statistically spring ought to arrive, you can observe the grass in your own garden and note for yourself when it actually does start to grow. That will give you the most reliable guide as to when spring has arrived, and when it is safe to sow seed outdoors or to transplant seedlings.

ONSET OF SPRING

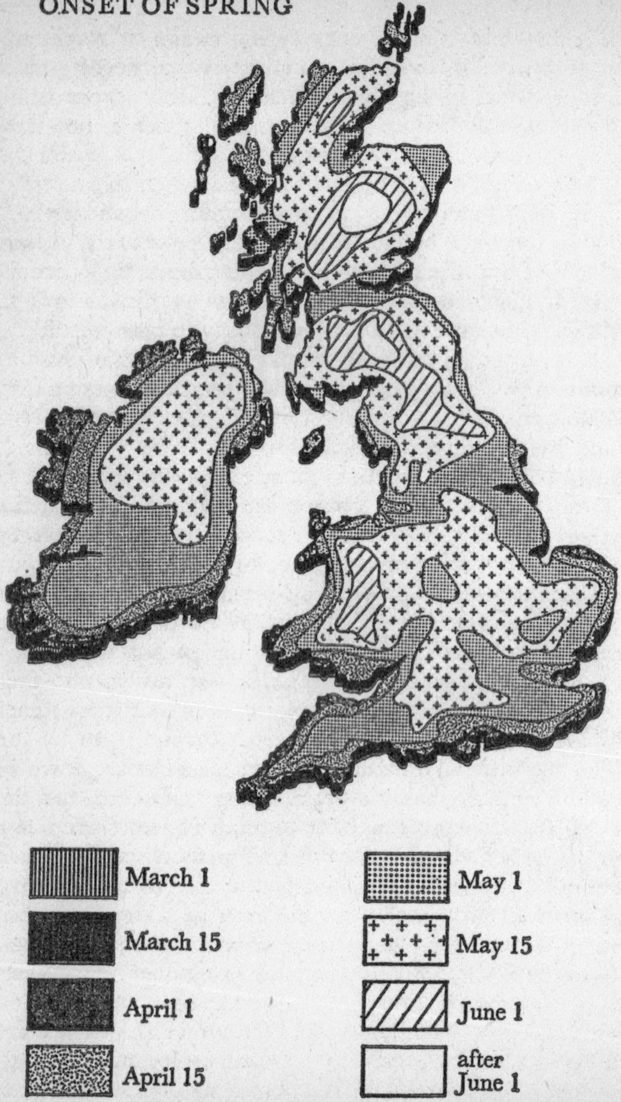

 March 1

 May 1

March 15

 May 15

April 1

 June 1

April 15

 after June 1

The length of your growing season may also be important. This is especially true of crops that need a very long period in the ground if they are to mature. Some crops quite simply will not mature if the growing season is not long enough. With sweet corn, for example, this could be critical.

The other problem you may encounter in some years is whether or not your crops are getting sufficient water. Because our rainfall is distributed surprisingly evenly throughout the year, we tend to rush out and start waving watering cans over our plants whenever the sun comes out for more than a couple of days. If we lived in a country where the rain fell in winter and was not expected to fall in summer we should approach the matter of irrigation in a far more rational way.

What vegetables need to bring them to perfection is neither too much water nor too little water: it is that the amount of water they receive should be applied evenly through their growing season.

Where many people tend to go wrong is in assuming that all vegetables need equal amounts of water, and that the time to start applying it is as soon as the top half inch of soil dries out. Different vegetables have very different water requirements. The simplest way of working out which vegetables need how much water is to group them by the depth to which their roots penetrate. The further down in the soil you go, the longer the soil takes to dry out, and the less you need to supplement the water. However, since water applied to the surface of the soil will always tend to move downwards (allowing for some evaporation at the surface), you could by applying water unnecessarily, actually produce a situation in which deep-rooting vegetables have too much water around their roots, though the soil surface may appear dry and dusty.

Lifting a vegetable gives you relatively little idea of the depth to which its roots really penetrate, since in the process of lifting you tend to break off many of the root hairs, which are the part of the roots which do most of the water absorbing. It might surprise you to know, for example, that the roots of a very average lettuce may penetrate to a depth of 45 cm (18 in), while those of an onion may go down 120 cm (48 in). The actual depth to which roots penetrate depends very largely on the depth of top soil available to them. For this reason the vegetables in the following chart are listed simply as shallow rooting, medium, or deep rooting.

DEPTH OF ROOTING IN VEGETABLES

Shallow (45 cm/18 in)
Broccoli
Brussels Sprouts
Cabbage
Carrots
Cauliflower
Celery
Kale
Lettuce
Potato
Radish
Savoy
Spinach
Sweet Corn

Medium (90 cm/36 in)
Aubergines
Beans
Beetroot
Cucumber
Kohlrabi
Peas
Peppers
Swede
Turnips

Deep (120 cm/48 in)
Artichoke
Asparagus
Courgettes
Leek
Onion
Parsnips
Pumpkin
Tomato

From a chart like this it is quite easy to deduce that, in dry weather, lettuces need watering more frequently than aubergines, and aubergines somewhat more frequently than artichokes. So far so good. There is another factor which is critical in determining how frequently you need to apply water, and that is the type of soil upon which you are growing your vegetables. If you are growing them on a heavy clay soil you will not need to water them so frequently as you will if you are living on a light, sandy soil.

The next chart shows you approximately how frequently you will need to water on different types of soil for any

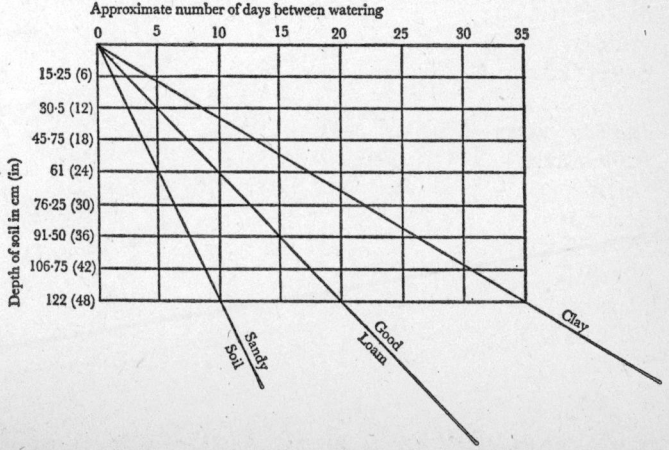

vegetables belonging to the different groups. of rooting depths. The way you use this chart is that you first of all find the type of vegetable you want to water on the depth of rooting chart, and you then follow the depth of rooting line across the lower chart until you come to the diagonal which relates to the type of soil upon which you are gardening. Where the two meet you move vertically upwards to the top of the chart, where you can simply read off the frequency of watering, which is stated in intervals of days. On a light, sandy soil you would need to water lettuce, a shallow rooting crop, every two to three days: on heavy clay you would need to water it every eight or nine days.

By using this frequency of watering chart, you will not only save yourself the time and trouble of watering vegetables that do not need watering, you will actually produce better crops. The chart assumes that there has been no rainfall, and none is expected.

❧ Weeds and What to do with Them

Most of us have a pretty fair idea of what we mean by a weed. We mean a plant we don't want growing in a place where we don't want it. So we get rid of it. We pluck it out and throw it away.

But why?

We probably do this because we have been conditioned to do it. We have been conditioned, for example, to thinking that the presence of weeds in a garden and especially in the vegetable garden, is untidy: perhaps we fear that it shows a slovenly approach to our gardening. And perhaps, too, we have been conditioned to thinking that the weeds in some way compete with the plants that we are trying to cultivate. It may be that there is some truth in some of these things. It may also be true that we have been so conditioned to pulling out weeds that we never stop to consider why we do it.

If one were to accept a different definition of weeds one might look at them in a different light.

The American Ralph Waldo Emerson defined a weed as a plant whose virtues have not yet been discovered.

All weeds are in a way wild plants. But then the plants we cultivate were wild once. They would still be wild plants if we had not discovered some virtues in them. The wild cabbage is still to be found growing on chalk cliffs in southern Britain: if it finds its way into a flower bed it is plucked out as a weed.

Before plucking out our weeds it is well worthwhile pausing to see if any of them have any virtues, and considering what we might do with them if they do. After all, you might as well use them if you can: they are growing in soil that you have put time and energy into tilling, and which you have enriched with manures and fertilisers.

Quite a number of common weeds have only become common as weeds because at some period in the past they were deliberately cultivated. Which means that once upon a time their virtues were well-known. Among these are ground elder, silverweed, yarrow, stinging nettles, fat-hen, dandelion, chickweed and archangels. All of these have been deliberately cultivated in Britain in the past. In some cases their virtues were medicinal, but in many cases they were much more definitely culinary.

Ground elder, for example, also known as herb Gerard, bishop's weed, goutweed, ashweed, goat's foot, dog elder and by one or two more limited local names, was introduced to Britain in the Middle Ages as much for its value as a pot herb as for its value as a medicinal herb. The young leaves, picked green and fresh, make delicious greens, cooked with butter and a touch of seasoning. The mature leaves can be used later in the season to add flavour to more commonplace greens, such as the ubiquitous cabbage.

Silverweed, which is also known as silver fern (though it is not a fern at all) midsummer silver, traveller's ease, goosegrass, fern buttercup and prince's feathers, is one of those plants that naturally grows almost everywhere, from Lapland to the Antartic, and from China to Chile, in almost any soil. In Britain it has been cultivated from prehistoric times into the relatively recent past. The whole plant is full of flavour and rich in available calcium. Probably the best part is its foot-long tap root, which is delicious roasted and eaten like parsnips.

Fat-hen, also known variously as allgood, goosefoot, muck hill, dirty dick, bacon weed, midden styles, lamb's quarters, dung weed and melgs, was long grown for its food value, then passed out of fashion, but is returning to fashion once again now that its virtues have been scientifically proven. It contains more iron and protein than either raw cabbage or spinach, and contains more calcium than both put together. The leaves, plucked with their stalks, can be .

served as greens. Alternatively, they make an excellent soup, especially if puréed.

Chickweed, is another common, cosmopolitan plant, also known as chick wittles, chicklingweed, clucken wort, star chickweed or skirt buttons. It is a slender, overwintering annual, that somehow never seems to be without both flowers and seed pods. For a long time it was cultivated deliberately, but it seeds itself so freely that there is usually little need to encourage it. It is rich in copper (and is one of the few plants that is) and this makes it a valuable item in our diet. It is best eaten as a cress, the leaves and stems washed in cold water, shaken dry in a cloth and then chopped and served as a flavouring in salads or used on its own or together with tomatoes or any other filling in sandwiches. Its flavour can be enhanced by adding a drip or two of lemon juice. The young leaves are also excellent when cooked as greens. So cooked, it tastes much like spinach, and I think rather more pleasant: indeed, many children who will refuse spinach will eat chickweed quite happily.

Stinging nettles are probably about the most useful of our weeds: not only can they be eaten, they can also be put to a multitude of other good uses. The sting in a stinging nettle is actually surprisingly harmless: it is only bicarbonate of ammonia, and as such can be dispelled by heat. If you don't want to get stung while gathering your nettles, wear gloves. As food, nettles are as rich in iron as spinach and rather richer in vitamin C than most more commonplace vegetables. For cooking, use only young leaves gathered in spring, or the tender young tops of the nettles. These can be used as greens, made into a creamed soup or even mixed with barley and made into a porridge or pudding. If something a little stronger is required, it can be used to make a beer or a wine.

Nettles have a number of uses in the garden, too. Chopped nettles allowed to rot down form a very fine, rich humus which can be used as a mulch, but is also of an ideal texture for use as seed compost. Nettles can be placed in a bucket of rainwater and left there for two or three weeks, and then removed: the remains of the nettles can go into the compost bin, where they will help activate the compost, while the liquid can be used both as a liquid feed, poured round the roots of plants, and also as a general purpose spray for use against black fly, aphis, mildew and lice.

All of which may seem to suggest that some of these so-called weeds are not quite so out of place in our vegetable plots as we are accustomed to thinking. It may also suggest that some, at least, of our weeds are not so much plants whose virtues we have not yet discovered, as plants whose virtues we have forgotten.

While it is not actually the intention to encourage you to cultivate your weeds, it should suggest that before throwing them away, you might consider whether you could usefully add them to your diet in season, or give a fresh flavour to something.

As to why we try to rid our gardens, and especially our vegetable gardens of weeds, the reasons are twofold. Firstly, the weeds compete directly with the plants we are cultivating for the available light, air, water and nutrient (and when they compete they very often win); secondly, because they harbour a number of not altogether desirable creatures such as slugs and snails and a number of other greedy grubs as well.

The only effective way of keeping land free from weeds is what is meant by good cultivation, in the old sense. The land should be thoroughly dug, well-enriched with organic materials, and generally kept in good heart. Most of this work is best done in winter, on those parts of the vegetable garden in which no vegetables are growing. Once the winter digging has been done the ground should not be dug again: digging in summer only encourages the ground to dry out. Any weeds that come up on ground that has been properly dug and cleaned are best dealt with by regular mulches of good organic compost. This will smother most weeds, while the few that do come up can easily be dealt with by plucking them out by hand, or chopping the tops off with a knife or with the hoe. Naturally, there are one or two exceptions.

Bindweed and other deep-rooted weeds may persist. While every attempt should be made to dig these out as far down as you can follow the roots, this can only be done in winter on empty land. Any shoots that come to light during the growing season should be plucked off. The golden rule is never to let these weeds see Sunday. That is, make sure you remove the tops at least once a week. The purpose of the exercise is not ritualistic: it is to prevent the leaves photosynthesising; if the plant cannot produce green leaves, it cannot feed its roots, so that persistent removal of the greenery weakens the roots, and, in time, even these persistent weeds give up.

Of course it is possible nowadays to kill almost anything in the way of a weed with one chemical or another. The trouble is that we really do not know enough about the long-term effects of some of these chemicals on the soil or on soil populations. Certainly there is no need to use them on land already under cultivation. Probably the only time when their use would be justified would be on land that is rank and over-run with everything from couch grass to brambles. Even then, whatever weedkiller you use, be sure to use it strictly in accordance with the manufacturer's instructions. Many are very potent, capable of killing large forest trees, so beware!

✿ Bugs and other Bothers

When man brought his food plants into cultivation, he also brought into cultivation the pests and diseases that go with them. So long as man thrives, and his food plants thrive, the pests and diseases that go with them will thrive too. That is how it is. We would do well to accept that.

Of course it is irritating if some bug comes along and starts eating the leaves of your tomatoes, or some disease gives your cabbages club root. It is an inevitable consequence of cultivating these plants that such things will happen.

A lot of people, when they see something creeping, crawling, flying or fluttering in, on or among their vegetables, assume it is there with the sole purpose of stealing their crops, and reach immediately for some deadly aerosol of chemical poison to kill it.

The chances are that the bug was, in fact, perfectly harmless. There are over 1,000,000 species of insect in this world. Less than 1% are known positively to be harmful to man or his plants. Next time you see a bug on a beetroot, it's worth remembering that, statistically, the chances are less than 1 in 100,000 that its motives are malicious.

It is far more likely that the innocent bug was looking for a friend or for food. If it was looking for food the sort of food it was looking for was rather different from the sort of food you and I tend to eat. Its food would be the pollen or nectar in flowers, even in the flowers of vegetables. We tend to forget once we get in the vegetable garden, the glories of the decorative garden. The big, brightly-coloured flowers with which we fill our flower gardens did not evolve for man's benefit. Man is very much an accidental bystander.

Flowers evolved the way they did partly for their own benefit, and partly for the benefit of insects of many types. The relationship between insects and plants is exceedingly intimate. Most plants need to be pollinated by insects if they are to produce fertile seed, and for this reason, plants and insects have evolved hand in hand in the most intimate relationship over the vast, slow eons of evolution.

Most insects can be trusted to get on with their intimate relationship with plants: it is only a tiny handful of wayward ones that have taken to eating the plants instead. Man has exacerbated the situation somewhat. When he cultivates a plant he increases the number of individuals within the species. That also increases the number of individuals within any species that happens to like that plant.

It is just those few that cause the problems. Some of the others are actually predators on the bugs that eat our vegetables. Ladybirds, for example, eat aphids, and aphids eat our plants. Whatever remedies we propose to use against the aphids, we do not want to kill the ladybirds too.

When considering ways of dealing with the bugs that eat your vegetables, it is worth considering their role in an ecological sense. The purpose of the bugs that eat our plants is to act as scavengers: the plants they feed on are the weak and the sickly. If they feed on them effectively they prevent them from seeding, which in turn prevents the perpetuation of a weak strain. However, while plant-eating pests are part of nature's scheme to keep weaklings down, she has her own checks on the scavengers. For every ugly bug that eats your vegetables, there is at least one other bug that will eat that one. And so on.

Essentially prevention is better than cure. If the bugs that eat our plants go for the weak ones, the answer is to have no weak ones. And the way to minimise your chances of having weedy vegetables is to have a healthy, humusy soil. Even then some bugs will still come, having started on your neighbour's weak plants.

When a bug does turn up on your vegetables, deal with him and his friends by the gentlest methods first, only doing him violence in the last resort. The simplest way of dealing with any bug is to crush him between finger and thumb. If you don't like getting your hands dirty, use a water cannon technique, squirting him off your plant and onto the ground with a fine jet of water. Slightly more effective is the use of vegetable oils (cooking oil, olive oil, and so on) which can be applied in the same way. Not only will it knock the bugs off the plants, but by smothering them in a thin film of oil, it clogs their pores and prevents them from breathing. Milk used in the same way does much the same thing.

Only if pests really seem to be getting out of hand should you resort to materials that are in themselves deadly. The best two to use are derris and pyrethrum, both of which are naturally occuring insecticides, derived from vegetable sources. Both are fairly effective against most garden pests, safe for man and his pets but deadly to fish. Never stick with just one of these: use first one and then the other, alternating their use through the season.

Diseases of cultivated crops, like the bugs of cultivated crops, usually attack weak plants first. Again, you are least likely to have problems with diseases in your vegetable garden if you cultivate the ground well, and keep it liberally supplied with humus. The more humus there is the better: because then there will be a wide range of micro-organisms, and that in turn will decrease the chances of any one of them becoming dominant. The other effective preventive measure is a proper rotation of your crops.

With the diseases of plants, even more than the bugs that attack them, prevention is better than cure. The only real cure for most of the diseases of cultivated vegetables is to dig the vegetables up and burn them.

❧ Good Companions, Bad Companions

The idea that some plants are good friends, as it were, and that others are not, stretches back into the remote past and is somewhat surrounded by mystery and magic. Which is perhaps a pity, since it discourages people from taking seriously the findings of modern science about which plants encourage or hinder the growth of other plants; and that there really are plants which discourage pests and diseases in other plants.

Certainly this whole idea of companion plants has intrigued people down the ages, so much so that certain companionships, and certain antipathies, have become incorporated into folklore. In the days when gardening was an oral tradition, which plants you grew together, and which plants you avoided growing together, was everyday knowledge.

Alas, much of this knowledge has been lost with the spread of education, which tends to encourage us to think that we are 'above' the old superstitions. What few companion plants remained common knowledge in spite of education, were wiped out with the emergence of modern pesticides, insecticides, herbicides, and almost everything else-ci-cides after the second war.

The chemicals which then became available seemed to enable one to control almost any pest, disease or problem with the sprinkling of a powder or the squirting of an aerosol. Sadly, many people still think that this is the case. The achievements of the modern generations of garden chemicals are quite substantial: if you list only their positive virtues, they seem almost miraculous. There is no doubt that modern artificial fertilisers can increase crop

yields by 50% or more, if they are used on fields on which
they have never been used before; modern insecticides
certainly kill insects; and modern herbicides are powerful
enough not merely to clear corn fields of poppies, but
literally to wipe out forests (for which purpose they have
been used). The other side of the coin is that if you go on
using the artificial fertilisers indefinitely the gain in yield
levels off after a while and, because chemical fertilisers add
no humus to the soil, a time comes when crop yields
actually decline: if you use modern insecticides you not only
destroy the target insect, you also destroy its natural predators; and if you use the modern weedkillers you may find
that you are not only killing the weeds, you may well be
killing the worms as well, those worms whose role in keeping
soil aerated and well-drained is so vital. Of course modern
chemicals have their place in the modern world: but there
are more enlightened ways of killing an aphid than with a
sledge hammer.

Those more enlightened ways are not new knowledge. On
the contrary, they are old knowledge, long forgotten. But
what is really fascinating is that the giant multi-national
chemical companies, who pour literally millions of pounds
into intensive research programmes before they launch any
new product, are now spending that money not so much on
messing about with the molecular structure of the powerful
pesticides that have come into being since the last war, but
in investigating the natural checks and controls which,
without man's interference, control pests and diseases in
plants. And many of the plants at which they are looking
turn out to be the companion plants of folklore.

The sledge hammer approach is to use something like
endrin, one of the chlorinated hydrocarbons, to kill an
aphid. You will also kill the ladybirds that naturally prey
on the aphids, and much else besides, including some of the
birds that eat the insects that eat your plants. Endrin, like
the other persistent economic poisons, is a broad spectrum
killer, totally unselective. Chemically it is very complex. It
is in fact 1,2,3,4,10,10-hexachloro-6,7-epoxy-1,4,4a,5,6,7,8,

8a-octahydro-1,4-endo-endo-5,8-dimethanonapthalene. It is very closely related to dieldrin, but a tiny twist in its molecular structure makes it about five times as poisonous. So powerful is it that the universally known forefather of this group of chemicals, DDT, seems almost harmless. Endrin is 15 times as poisonous to mammals, 30 times as poisonous to fish and 300 times as poisonous to birds. Quite how any of us ever came to use anything as deadly as that against a tiny little aphid is hard to understand.

Natural checks are, by comparison, sophisticated in the extreme. The North American Balsam fir, for example, synthesises certain terpenes which serve to keep them remarkably free of pests. It seems that how these terpenes work is that they activate the juvenile hormone in the larva of insects feeding on their needles, and that hormone, once activated, prevents the bug ever maturing or reproducing. The firs, it is worth remembering, are a very ancient race of plants: the insects are a very ancient group too. It seems that at some stage of evolution the firs had to learn to protect themselves against insects. Whatever the insect was, against which the Balsam fir learned to protect itself, is apparently either extinct or has learned to avoid Balsam firs.

Other plants are known to be very specific in the spectrum of bugs they kill. Nature never elaborates systems that are not essential to survival. No plant would manufacture a chemical to deter a pest that never visits it.

Which is why it is the plants themselves that are the best of all possible pest and disease controls.

One of the main pests of the carrot, is carrot fly. The maggot or larva of this fly often attacks young roots. It seems that what attracts the larvae to the carrots is the smell of the carrots. When you thin a row of carrots, you damage the roots of the little plants as you pluck them out. Plainly you would be less likely to have a serious invasion of carrot fly if you did not thin them. If you must thin a row of carrots, put onions or leeks beside the row, so that their smell will disguise the smell of the carrots. Better still, actually grow carrots and leeks together. Sow, and sow thinly, a seed mix of two parts leek seed to three parts carrot seed. The carrots will be ready to harvest early, and still give the leeks plenty of time to mature. And you won't have problems with carrot fly.

The cabbage white butterfly is a common enough pest of most of the Brassicas. Our forefathers used to alternate the Brassicas with rows of celery, and they had far less problems with the cabbage white than we do. Research carried out in Germany over 20 years ago shows that statistically where cabbages are growing close to celery, the incidence of attack by pests and diseases is very substantially less than when they are not grown near celery.

Tomatoes growing near gooseberries seem to keep the gooseberries free from pests and diseases.

Apart from plants acting as insecticides for one another they can also act to promote growth. Beans for example, grow faster, larger, and crop more heavily if grown close to carrots. If beans and beets are grown close together, both do better than they would otherwise. Radishes seem to encourage the growth of most other vegetables, and are particularly helpful to peas. If intercropped with lettuces, the radishes will be more tender than usual; if grown together with chervil, the radishes will taste stronger than usual.

While there are many other mutually beneficial companionships, there are also some plantings which are mutually harmful. Radish and hyssop, for example, seem to dislike each other, and neither will grow so well close to the other as it would well away from the other. Dandelions tend to inhibit the growth of neighbouring plants, and to rush neighbouring plants into flower prematurely. It is known that dandelions give off ethylene gas, and the observable effects of dandelions on surrounding plants are exactly what one would expect from this gas. Dill inhibits the growth of carrots, while chives makes them grow better than average.

If all of this seems outrageously improbable to our edudated modern minds, it really should not. Most of us know that there are desert plants which exude poisons from their roots to keep down competition (including their own seedlings). And most of us know that the legumes (peas and so on) have nodules on their roots that fix atmospheric nitrogen, thereby leaving the soil richer in nitrogen than it was before. No one doubts the efficacy of these things. There is no reason to doubt the efficacy of other plant companionships. These things are easily proven by experiment and careful record keeping in one's own garden.

Because of the pesticidal effect of some of these plant companionships, as well as the mutually beneficial effects, or mutually inhibiting effects, which plants help or hinder which are listed under each vegetable. If you don't believe they'll work, try them: you may be surprised.

⚜ Brassicas

BROCCOLI

Broccoli is one of the many monstrous forms of the common cabbage that mankind has developed for his own delectation. It is very closely related to the cauliflower (another and even more monstrous form of common cabbage), but differs from the cauliflower in that whereas the cauliflower is eaten mainly for the compact and bulky, fleshy flowers, it is the flower stalks that form the bulk of the edible matter in broccoli, the degenerate flowers having very little substance.

No one seems quite sure where or when broccoli originated: it is generally presumed to have originated in Italy. Certainly it has been cultivated in Italy for very many centuries.

In fact, two forms of broccoli are grown. There is heading broccoli, which looks rather like cauliflower and is treated rather like cauliflower, and sprouting broccoli, which is the form normally grown. The sprouting flower heads may be either green or purple, hence one can grow either purple sprouting or green sprouting broccoli. Both are grown the same way.

The land on which broccoli is to be grown should be in good heart, having been thoroughly prepared and well manured during the winter before the sowing is made. Seed should be sown 1·5 – 2·5 cm (0·75 – 1 in) deep, the seeds spaced about 35 cm (14 in) apart, with 60 cm (24 in) between the rows, any time from mid-April till mid-May. The ground into which the seed is sown should be firm, and should not have been dug since the previous crop was removed, especially if the crop is to be grown to maturity where the seed is sown. If you are going to transplant the crop, seed can be sown in a prepared seed bed, and then transplanted to firm ground. Transplants should be placed 60 cm (24 in) apart in rows about the same apart, and transplanting should be done in June or July, when and as ground becomes available through clearance of earlier crops. Little cultivation is needed, beyond some hoeing to keep weeds down. When harvesting, always pick the terminal flower head first, as this encourages the lesser side-heads to develop.

Broccoli grows particularly well in ground previously occupied by potatoes, and its growth is encouraged by dill and camomile. It is definitely not happy growing close to strawberries, or on land recently occupied by strawberries.

BRUSSELS SPROUTS

The sprout is yet another monstrous form of the common and ubiquitous cabbage. Where it differs from the common cabbage is that, instead of bearing one huge terminal bud, it bears masses of lateral buds, in place of the side shoots. The first record of the sprout occurs in 1587, and it seems that it was developed in the fifteenth century in that part of northern Europe that is now Belgium. Certainly it continued to be grown in that part of Europe for many centuries, but it is only comparatively recently that it has become popular in other parts of Europe. It was not until after the first war that it became popular in Britain.

Sprouts, like broccoli, grow best in ground in which a previous crop has grown, and which has not been subsequently dug. Mature plants are relatively top heavy, and have far too small a root system in relation to their top weight. In some seasons it may be necessary to stake them to prevent them falling about in the wind. The ground should be in good heart, having been manured for a previous crop. Nutrient content can be topped up by dressing the ground with superphosphate and sulphate of potash and forking this in very lightly before planting. Seed should be sown in prepared beds, in mid-March or April, and the seedlings transplanted to their permanent positions in May or June, the plants being set about 60 cm (24 in) apart in rows 60 cm (24 in) apart. To avoid damaging the roots when transplanting, always water the seed bed the night before you lift the seedlings. Transplants should be set in the ground firmly, and firmed regularly. About a month after transplanting it is worth drawing a little extra soil about the stems of the plants, to help them form adventitious roots which in turn will help to keep them stable. As the plants continue growing, the lower leaves will gradually turn yellow. These should be removed once they are evenly yellow, usually in the autumn, to make room for the developing sprouts. The sprouts should be harvested from the bottom of the plant upwards. The terminal bud is sometimes harvested as well, though this is seldom done in Britain. It is of looser structure and has a less pleasant taste than the lateral buds, but it can be cooked and eaten in just the same way as the sprouts.

Sprouts grow well in ground close to that occupied by potatoes or tomatoes, and thrive when grown together with dill or camomile. They definitely dislike growing near strawberries.

CABBAGES

Cabbages are in many ways the most monstrous of all the vegetables we grow. The wild cabbage, which can still be found growing on cliffs along the south coast, is a biennial or perennial plant with an erect stem, a well developed tap root and large leaves. It has perfect flowers. In its way it is an attractive wild plant. In the cultivated form the normal flowering raceme has been supressed at the cost of a huge, densely compacted, leafy, terminal bud. As terminal buds go, the cabbage bud is, by any standards, extraordinarily large. No one seems quite sure where the cabbage as we know it today was developed, but, because it will tolerate cold, it has been widely grown in Eastern Europe, particularly Poland, Bohemia, Germany and Austria, as well as in Russia, where it is used for stuffing cakes, as well as a vegetable.

There are now well over 200 named varieties of cabbage, but these fall into various groups. The first grouping is according to whether the leaves are green, in which case you have a white cabbage; or purple, in which case you have a red cabbage. From a cultural point of view they are divided into three groups, and if you grow cabbages belonging to all three groups you can have fresh cabbage at any time of year.

The first group are those cabbages sown in spring for harvesting in summer. Seed should be sown in prepared seed beds in early April, the seed being placed about 2 cm (0·75 in) deep. Seedlings should be transplanted to their final positions in June.

The second group are those cabbages sown in summer for use in autumn and winter. Seeds of these are sown, again on prepared seed beds, in May, and the seedlings transplanted in July.

The third group are those cabbages sown in early autumn for spring harvesting. Seed of these should be sown in July or August in prepared seed beds, the seed being sown about 2 cm (0·75 in) deep. Seedlings should be transplanted between mid-September and mid-October.

The basic cultivation for cabbages is the same for each group. Spring cabbage benefits from having the ground deeply dug and thoroughly prepared, but the others are less demanding. Plants should be set between 45 and 60 cm (18 and 24 in) apart in the rows, the rows 60 cm apart. The ground should be hoed regularly when the plants are growing, or alternatively mulched with garden compost to suppress weeds.

All the problems relating to the cultivation of cabbages are concerned with the pests and diseases or cabbages – which are many. However, generally there is less incidence of pests and diseases where cabbages are grown in ground that is rich in humus. The pest problems start with the seedlings: the seed leaves and the first true leaves are much liked by flea beetles and turnip flies. The traditional remedy is to spray or dust the seedlings with gamma BHC as soon as the seedlings show, and to continue doing this at weekly intervals until the plants are well into the rough leaf stage.

Having survived that stage the cabbages then become liable to invasion by caterpillars, especially those of the cabbage white butterfly: the attacks, which occur during late summer, can be quite devastating. The caterpillars themselves are best removed by carefully examining each plant regularly, and removing the caterpillars by hand. The caterpillars can then be fed to the goldfish, or simply crushed. Egg clusters are easily destroyed by crushing between thumb and finger. Plants can be dusted with gamma BHC or derris, but these remedies should not be applied within two weeks of harvesting.

The next pest is cabbage root fly, and this is less easily dealt with. It is in fact the legless white maggots that do the damage, eating the roots and tunnelling through the stems. Preventive measures consist of dusting round the plants with a 4% calomel dust, but once plants have become infested the only thing to do is to dig them up and burn them.

Cabbage aphids and cabbage whitefly can be a nuisance, but do not really do all that much damage. They are easily got rid of by using a spray of milk or cooking oil, but more traditional remedies include such lethal economic poisons as malathion, dimethoate, formothion or nicotine.

In some areas pigeons are a pest, doing an immense amount of damage. Sparrow-hawks are the only effective remedy: provided you have time to train the sparrow-hawk, and are prepared to spend a series of sleepless nights manning it.

The most troublesome disease of cabbage is club root, sometimes known as finger and thumb. This is a soil borne infection, and the best measures to take against it are the preventive ones, particularly ensuring a regular rotation programme and the addition of copious quantities of organic matter to the soil. Where the disease becomes a real problem the ground should be treated with hydrated lime applied at the rate of 12·4 kg (28 lb) per sq. rod, with a dressing of 6·2 kg (14 lb) per sq. rod in succeeding years. Ultimately, the most effective remedy is simply not to grow cabbages on the ground for several years: the organisms, having nothing to feed upon, die.

If it seems that cabbages are prone to an inordinate number of diseases and problems, it is worth remembering that the more widely grown a plant becomes, the more the pests and diseases that are natural to it become disseminated too. When you bring any plant into cultivation, you bring its problems into cultivation too. But take heart, the English oak is prone to over 1,000 diseases, and there are plenty of fine oaks around.

There are a number of companion plantings which not only encourage the cabbages to do well, but also discourage some of their pests and diseases. Late cabbages and early potatoes are beneficial to each other. Cabbage grows better when grown in proximity to dill, camomile, sage or rosemany, and does especially well if one of the mints is allowed to run through the rows or between them. They actively dislike growing near strawberries or in ground that has been occupied by strawberries. The cabbage white butterfly, and its attendant caterpillars are repelled by tomatoes, sage, rosemary, thyme, mint or hyssop growing nearby. The ideal thing is to grow the cabbages next to the tomatoes, and use some plants of thyme as ground cover between the cabbage plants.

CAULIFLOWERS

The cauliflower is yet another of the monstrous cabbages bred by man to satisfy his own appetite. While from the purist-botanist point of view, monstrous it may be, it is certainly one of the most delicious monstrosities ever raised. The plant is native to Asia Minor, but it seems to have been developed in cultivation only relatively recently. It was not introduced to Britain until the seventeenth century, though it was known in continental Europe at least a hundred years before that. Its first mention is a description in a book by the Dutch botanist Doddeus, published in 1559. John Parkinson, the English herbalist, describes the cauliflower, already characterised by its dense, globose head, but in his day the edible head was about the size of a golf ball: an American golf ball at that.

The very large-headed cauliflowers we eat today are extremely recent in origin, some of the finest varieties having become available within the last thirty years. The edible part of the cauliflower is an overgrown and abortive flower-head. The inflorescence is totally degenerate, and consists of numerous fleshy flowers (which are so abortive they lack any of the reproductive organs proper to a flower) and numerous stalks, both of which are usually white or whitish in colour.

Though cauliflowers are easily grown, they are not quite so easily grown well. The seeds of summer cauliflowers should be sown either in boxes under glass in January or in prepared seed beds outdoors during March or April. Autumn heading varieties should be sown in prepared seed beds in May. Seed should be sown 2 cm (0·75 in) deep. Land for the cauliflowers should be in good heart, deeply dug and well manured. This should be done during the winter before the cauliflowers are to be planted out. A couple of weeks before putting out the transplants the ground should be fertilised with superphosphate applied at the rate of 60 g per sq m (2 oz per sq yd) hoed in. The summer varieties should be transplanted to their permanent positions during March, April, May or June, the plants being set about 45 to 60 cm (18–24 in) apart, in rows 60 cm (24 in) apart. Autumn heading varieties should be set out rather futher apart, about 60 cm (24 in) each way, the transplanting being done during June or July. Cultivation consists of little more than keeping the hoe moving between the plants and ensuring that the plants suffer from neither extremes of wet nor dryness. In some seasons plants seem to make very slow growth, and when this happens the maturing process can be speeded-up by adding a dressing of nitrate of soda or sulphate of ammonia at the rate of 30 g per sq m (1 oz per sq yd). Once the curds have formed it is best to break a leaf or two over them, to protect them from weather. The finest, whitest curds are produced by blanching, which involves breaking the outer leaves of the plant and bending them closely over the curds so that no light reaches the centre.

Plants are subject to the same wide range of pests and diseases as the cabbage, which are scarcely worth repeating here. The same preventive and remedial measures may be resorted to, according to one's faith in chemicals or more natural controls.

❦ Legumes

BEANS, BROAD or FAVA

Broad beans, still known as horse beans in some parts of the country, are not beans at all. Come to that, they're not peas either. They belong to the vetch family, which tends to suggest that they would make good cattle fodder. In fact, they were the only beans known to the Old World, until the Old World discovered the New World. They were cultivated by the Egyptians, the Greeks, the Romans, and every civilised European nation since. They are reputed to have been introduced to China as long ago as 2822 BC, and they have been found among the remains of Bronze Age Lake Dwellings in Switzerland. In most countries the beans are eaten when mature, but in France they are eaten immature, the whole pod being steamed till tender.

Broad beans need a deep, rich, well-worked soil – so they are not a good crop to grow on new land. Seed should be sown as early in the season as possible, preferably February or early March, with successional sowings made through till late April if you want them. The large seeds should be sown 5 cm (2 in) deep, 20 cm (8 in) apart, in rows 45 cm (18 in) apart. Where double rows are used, and this practice can increase your yield per sq m (yd), the rows should be 20 cm (8 in) apart, with 60 cm (24 in) between the double rows. Plants are often encouraged to grow erect between taut wires stretched between short stakes at the ends of the rows. The practice is a good one since, although the beans are not climbers and produce no tendrils, they have a very weak habit, and tend to flop on to the soil.

The two most important cultural considerations are to

keep the land free from weeds by hoeing regularly, and to keep blackfly under control. Indeed, the main importance of keeping the weeds down close to this crop is to prevent them harbouring blackfly. This pest will infest almost every part of the plant, but is particularly partial to the tender tips of the growing shoots. Once the plants are in full flower the growing tips should be pinched out, since these are usually the part of the plant most affected by blackfly. Apart from that the pest can be dealt with by squirting milk or cooking oil on the blackfly. There is a whole arsenal of chemicals available for those who believe in such things, including derris, dimethoate, formothion and nicotine.

The beans are best picked while they are still fairly young, and repeated pickings of young beans will give you a larger total yield than fewer pickings of larger beans; besides, the younger beans taste better. Try to avoid being too violent with the beans when you pick them: the plants have only the feeblest of root systems, and are very easily dislodged from the soil.

Beans are encouraged in both health and vigour if grown close to carrots and cauliflower. Their growth is inhibited by onions, garlic or leeks.

BEANS, FRENCH, COMMON, KIDNEY, STRING or SNAP

Any plant that manages to collect as many common names as this one must have been pretty popular at some time. The reason for its popularity is simple: it produces more edible matter per unit area than any other vegetable we can grow. French beans, which are natives of Mexico and were introduced to Spain by the Portuguese in 1594, are twining annuals capable of growing to as much as 3 m (9·8 ft), but usually rather less. They have been cultivated in Mexico for thousands of years, and radiocarbon datings show that remnants of these beans found in caves at Tehuacan are some 7,000 years old. During the time they have been under cultivation a number of forms have been selected, of these four are of major economic importance. The first group contains the snap beans, of which the unripe pods and beans are cooked and eaten. They are called snap beans because when in perfect condition for picking, the pods should give a clear and distinct snap if bent sideways. They are also known as string beans, because of the bundles of fibrovascular matter running along the seams of the pods: modern plant breeding has, however, virtually eliminated the string. The second group contains varieties of which the immature green seeds are eaten, these having to be shelled first. The third group, which is economically the most important, is grown for the dry, mature beans, known as haricot beans. It is from this group that the beans used in baked beans are derived.

The plants grow best in a well-worked soil, and in one which has been manured for a previous crop. The first sowing of seed should be made in early May, with a second sowing about three weeks later. The seed should be sown in drills, the seeds being planted 5 cm (2 in) deep and 12 cm (4·5 in) apart in rows 45 cm (18 in) apart. Once the seedlings are through, thin out to 25 cm (10 in) apart in the rows, and insert twigs between the plants to support them later: plants in full crop are very heavy and easily beaten to the ground by wind or rain. Hoe regularly and water when necessary.

Harvest the beans while they are young and tender. Not only does this ensure a virtually stringless bean, with a good flavour, it also encourages the proper formation of further beans. If you want beans for winter use, set a few plants aside for this purpose and do not pick any of the beans until they are fully ripe at the end of the summer.

These beans make good companions for carrots, beets, cucumbers and marrows, as well as maize. They do not get on well with chives, leeks, onions or garlic.

BEANS, RUNNER

These are probably more widely grown in home gardens than any of the other beans. Indeed, almost everyone seems to grow them, and most people usually finish up growing too many. Perhaps, in these days of freezing and drying, that is no longer such a waste as it used to be. The plants are natives of South America, and were introduced from there to Britain in 1683. Although often known as scarlet runner beans, the flowers may be red or white, while the pods may be green or black, and can vary enormously in length, some varieties being grown specifically for their yard-long beans. Plants were originally grown in Europe for ornamentals, for the curiosity of both the flowers and the pods, the latter being considered inedible. In America, of course, they still are considered inedible. In Continental Europe the beans are used in the same way as French beans, that is, it is the beans which are eaten, while in Britain it is the young pods complete with the immature beans that are used.

Plants are easy enough to grow, either on land that has been manured for a previous crop, or on land that has been prepared for the beans during the previous winter. Where this is necessary a trench should be taken out a spade's depth deep, and half a metre across, and a liberal dressing of well-rotted manure or compost worked into the soil. Seed should be sown where the plants are to grow from mid-May till the end of June, the seed being placed in parallel drills 30 cm (12 in) apart with 15 cm (6 in) between the seeds, the seeds being sown 5 cm (2 in) deep. Seedlings should be thinned to 30 cm (12 in) apart, any gaps being made good with surplus seedlings. As soon as the first pair of true leaves show, you should hoe between the rows, and then add stakes for the beans to run up. Once that is done the plants should be given a good thick mulch of straw matter or compost, and should be watered only if the ground becomes dry. Once the flowers begin to colour it pays to give the plants a good soaking. When the plants reach the top of the stakes the growing tip should be pinched out. The plants can be grown without stakes, and if you want to do this, what you do is pinch out the tips as soon as the plants start to run, and keep on pinching out any shoots that start to run. In this way the plants can be kept compact.

The beans are best if picked when young, usually about two-thirds of the length to which the seed packet claims they will grow. Heavy picking encourages more beans to mature. If you want to save your own seed, and many people used to do this, leave a plant or two at the end of the row, and do not pick any of the beans until they have ripened thoroughly, which is usually in late summer or early autumn. Store the beans in a cool, dry place through winter.

Blackfly can be something of a pest but can be kept to manageable proportions if you grow nasturtiums beside the rows or even among the beans. The point is that blackfly finds nasturtiums even more tasty than runner beans and, if given the chance, will go for the nasturtiums in preference. More conventional methods of dealing with this pest is a spray or dust of such deadly things as malathion, dimethoate, formothion, nicotine or derris.

Runner beans make excellent companions for maize, especially if grown all round a bloc of maize, thereby protecting it from excessive winds. They add nitrogen to the soil, which the corn can exploit. They are also good companions for beets, cucumbers and cabbages. Onions, garlic and shallots inhibit their growth.

PEAS

Peas are leguminose annual climbing plants, natives of Asia. From Asia, they have spread both westwards into Europe, and eastwards into Tibet and China. As early as the fourth century AD they reached Abyssinia, and from there moved southwards into eastern and central Africa. Although essentially temperate region plants, there are varieties which thrive in the tropics, even at low altitudes.

For anyone growing peas in Britain a fundamental choice has to be made. You can either opt for growing the round-

seeded varieties, which have the advantage of being very
hardy and highly tolerant of cold, wet soils; or you can go
for the wrinkle-seeded varieties, which are sweeter and have
a finer flavour, but are not so hardy. Your soil may well
dictate your choice. The plant breeders are hard at work
trying to bring the best qualities of both types of pea
together into a Superpea, but until they succeed, the choice
is yours.

All peas need to be grown in is ground that has been well
manured in the winter, and mulched with garden compost
in spring. Seed of wrinkle-seeded varieties should be sown
through April, May and June in successional plantings, each
made about a fortnight apart. Seed should be placed in a
broad, flat-bottomed drill about 5 cm (2 in) deep, covered
and firmed. Seed should be sown fairly thickly, as one is
aiming to get about seven plants in each square 30 cm (foot) of
soil. The growing plants will need the support of pea sticks
(traditionally elm, field maple or hazel twigs cut during
winter), or of wire or plastic netting stretched between
posts at the ends of the rows. Harvesting should begin while
the peas are still quite small, since this encourages further
pods to fatten up. Keep picking till the plants are exhausted.

Round-seeded sorts should be sown in single rows in
October or November, or in very early spring. Seed should
be sown about 4 cm (1·5 in) deep and fairly close, the aim
being to produce about eleven plants per sq 30 cm (ft). Plants
can also be sown indoors in peat pots during January or February for planting out in March. Plants will need some support
in the form of pea sticks or wire netting. The peas should be
harvested relatively small, and again harvesting should
continue until the plants are exhausted.

Slugs can be a nuisance, and can be dealt with either by
sprinkling slug pellets or by trapping: mice are inclined to
eat the seeds in the ground, but are generally not too
troublesome; while sparrows enjoy eating the growing tips
of all peas – where this happens the rows should be protected
with plastic netting.

The best companions for peas are radishes, carrots,

cucumbers and beans. Onions, shallots and garlic all inhibit the growth of the peas. Potatoes are a particularly good crop to plant where peas have been grown, since they can make full use of the nitrogen left behind by the peas.

❧ Root Crops

ARTICHOKES, JERUSALEM

This is one of the most decorative of vegetables in flower since it is, in fact, a perennial sunflower. Indeed, it is from this that it derives its name, Jerusalem being, apparently, a corruption of the Italian name for a sunflower, *girasóle*. It is a native of North America, where it grows from Nova Scotia to Minnesota and Kansas.

The plant is cultivated for its tubers, which may be as much as 10 cm (4 in) long and 7 cm (2·5 in) across. They are generally used much like potatoes, though are vastly superior in flavour. In place of the starch which potatoes contain, Jerusalem artichokes contain inulin, which is a polysaccharide consisting of residues of fructose, for which reason they are often recommended to diabetics.

Although by nature a perennial growing to 2 m (6 ft) or more, it is usually cultivated as though it were an annual. If cultivated is the word. For the Jerusalem artichoke will grow on any rough bit of ground, and in places where the soil would not be considered good enough for other vegetables, though it will repay good cultivation. It is started, much as are potatoes, by planting seed tubers, 15–25 cm (6–19 in) deep (deepest on light, sandy soils), in rows about a metre apart, with about 0·5 m (1·5 ft) between the tubers. Plants grow very fast, and make an excellent summer screen. They can be planted on the side of the vegetable plot to break the force of prevailing winds.

They need little in the way of cultivation, beyond hoeing between the rows to keep the worst of the weeds down. In early winter the stalks should be cut down to ground level, and the tubers left in the ground to be lifted when and as they are needed. A few tubers should be put on one side to provide tubers to start the following season's crop. These can be planted at the same time as the lifting operation is being done.

Some people simply leave the artichokes growing in the ground from year to year, lifting what they need, and leaving the rest. While the plants will go on producing tubers grown in this way, the tubers get smaller year by year as they crowd each other, and the result is tubers that are scarcely worth the trouble of lifting.

BEETROOT

Beetroot is just one of the many forms of beets which we cultivate. It is derived from the wild *Beta vulgaris*, or *Beta maritima* (depending which botanists you believe), which used to grow wild from the west coast of Ireland right through Europe and into Asia, its range extending to the east coast of India; the wild plant is still to be found in some coastal regions of India. The plant has been grown as a vegetable for a very long time; certainly records of it reach back to 300 BC, but it was not until the sixteenth century that improved forms were evolved, forms that are more or less recognisable as the vegetable we eat today.

Although beetroot is classed as a root vegetable, it is not in fact the root that is eaten. It is a part of the plant called the hypocotyl: that is the section below the seed leaves or cotyledons, and above the soil. The swollen part that is eaten is the result of secondary swelling of the vascula cambia, and if you cut a beetroot transversely you can see quite clearly the concentric rings which cause the swelling. The red colouring of most beetroots is caused by a glucoside called betanin. The edible part contains an exceptionally large amount of sugar – up to 8%.

Beetroot grows best on land manured for a previous crop. Seed of early varieties such as 'Boltardy' and 'Early Bunch' should be sown in March or April (or in succession). Varieties such as 'Crimson Globe' and 'Detroit Red' are better sown in April. The main sowing of all varieties is best done in mid-May while seed can be sown in July to produce plants ready for harvesting in late winter. Seed should be sown 3 cm (1·5 in) deep, 5 cm (2 in) apart in rows 30 cm (12 in) apart. Seedlings should be thinned to 10–12 cm (4–5 in). Keep the hoe moving between the rows to discourage weeds, and try not to let the crop suffer extremes of wet or dryness. Plants should be harvested as soon as they are large enough to eat: seed packets sometimes claim phenomenal sizes at maturity. A large beetroot is a coarse beetroot, full of woody matter and singularly tasteless. As a rough guide, most beets are best harvested when about 7 cm (2·5 in) across. For pickling, baby beets are best. The late beets can be left in the ground until they are needed: they will make little growth in the ground in winter.

Beetroot grows well near onions and kohlrabi, but is definitely harmed if grown near charlock or field mustard.

CARROTS

The carrot is an ancient vegetable, known and grown by both the Greeks and Romans, and the habit of eating carrots was spread through Europe by the Romans. The plant is native to Europe, as well as to Asia and North Africa. There are carrots native to other lands, but they are of little importance. An Australian native species is cultivated only as cattle feed, while the North American native species are of no known importance. Curiously, the carrot was first introduced to America in 1607 by settlers in Virginia. It was promptly taken over by the native Americans, who spread its cultivation throughout the whole of the new continent. Meanwhile the European settlers in North America more or less ceased to bother with it. Even now it is grown in America only as a very minor crop.

The edible part of the carrot is part root and part hypocotyl. These together form the conspicuous swollen part we eat. The tap root passes through this swollen section and may continue on into the ground as a very thin, almost thread-like root, to a depth of as much as 60 cm (24 in), sometimes more. The edible part of the carrot contains carotenes, which are the precursors of vitamin A. It is these carotenes which give the carrot its distinctive colouring. Indeed, so strongly coloured are these carotenes that they are often used for colouring other foodstuffs, not only soups and sauces, but even things like butter.

Carrots, like most root crops, are best grown on soil that has been manured for a previous crop. The presence of fresh manure or fertiliser in the soil produces malformed carrots, which may be comical but are not really to be encouraged. The ground should be left rough until sowing time, when it should be broken down into a fine tilth. Carrot seed should be sown very thinly in March then at fortnightly intervals till the end of July, with a good 5 cm (2 in) between the seeds of the stump varieties, and nearly 10 cm (4 in) between the seeds of the intermediate or long varieties. If you are used to sowing carrot seed very close and then thinning, seriously consider changing your practices. The advantage of sowing carrot seed thinly is that you do not then have to thin the carrots. And that in turn makes it much less likely that the rows will be attacked by carrot fly, which can be a real menace. The fly is attracted to the carrots by their distinctive smell. This smell is emitted very strongly when you are thinning seedlings, since the tender little carrots get damaged as you pluck them out. It has been found that where carrots are grown together with onions, salsify, leeks, or close to strong-smelling herbs like sage or wormwood, carrot fly is very seldom a problem. Even laying fresh-plucked leeks, shallots or onions alongside the bed if you do have to do any thinning, can help to deter carrot fly.

The traditional cultural technique of hoeing between the rows is not really to be recommended. Unless you are a very good shot the chances are that sooner or later you will slice into a carrot or two, and then along will come the carrot fly which you have been so clever in deterring till now. A good mulch of garden compost will suppress the weeds adequately. In good soil the carrots can simply be plucked from the ground when they are large enough to eat, but late-sown varieties which may remain in the ground till winter are better lifted with the aid of a fork. Most varieties will withstand frost provided that the ground in which they are growing is covered with a few inches of bracken or straw whenever severe frosts are promised. They can then be lifted when needed, leaving room in the freezer for vegetables that will not stand in the ground.

KOHLRABI

This is the old English cole, and it seems rather a shame that we have come to use a German name for a vegetable which has a perfectly good English name in its own right. Though people tend to think the vegetable, under its new name, is a new vegetable, it is very far from that. It was certainly known to the Romans, and is mentioned in Pliny. It was known to Charlemagne, who mentions it in 794, which makes its recorded history in modern Europe rather older than many of the vegetables we cultivate.

In spite of its ancientness it is still not as widely cultivated as it might be. It is grown for its swollen hypocotyl, and its cultivation is essentially the same as for turnips.

Kohlrabi grows well in the company of beets and onions, but has a stunting influence on tomatoes. It does not grow well near beans.

PARSNIPS

The parsnip is a biennial native to Eurasia, where it has been known and grown for many a long century. The parsnip as we know it, however, was probably developed during the Middle Ages.

Since parsnips are cultivated for the long, thickened tap root base, they grow best in a deep and well-worked soil, preferably free from stones or rocks: where these are a hazard the variety 'Offenham', which produces a more or less round parsnip, is the best choice. The best soil is one that has been manured for a previous crop. It should be dug deeply and left rough until sowing time, when it should be worked into a fine tilth. Seed can be sown as early as March, as soon as the ground becomes workable, but sowing can be left until as late as May. Seed should be sown in drills 30 cm (12 in) apart, the seed being covered by about 2 cm (1 in) of soil. Once the seedlings are large enough to handle they should be thinned to leave plants growing 15 cm (6 in) apart. They need little cultural attention, beyond an occasional hoeing to keep weeds down. The plants can be left in the ground to be lifted as required. However, any plants still in the ground in March should be lifted and stored in sand or soil in a shed or outhouse to prevent them from breaking into growth again.

POTATOES

The plant is a native of the High Andes, being found originally at altitudes of over 2,000 m. Although the potato is now grown all over the world, the finest crops are produced in areas in which the summers are relatively cool and that, as you might expect, includes Britain. The sad thing is that potatoes grow so readily in this country that we tend to eat them as a staple of diet: were they somewhat more difficult to grow, and somewhat more of a rarity on the table, we might appreciate their fine flavour rather better than we do.

Potatoes are an excellent crop to grow in virgin land, since the operations involved in their cultivation, as well as the action of the roots themselves, work the soil to a good texture. On land already in use potatoes should be grown on land that has been manured for a previous crop, but it should be treated with a good general fertiliser before the potatoes are planted, the fertilizer being lightly worked into the soil. Potatoes are normally grown from 'seed' potatoes, which are small tubers, weighing on average 60–85 g (2–3 oz). The potatoes are started by placing them on trays of damp peat in a light, airy, and frost-free place in February. This starts them into growth, the young shoots coming through whitish or pale green; they should not be allowed to become too etiolated. The sprouting tubers are then planted in rows 60 cm (24 in) apart, the tubers being placed about 10 cm (4 in) deep, and 30 cm (12 in) apart, during April. Tubers of later varieties should be planted slightly further apart, with the rows slightly further apart, from April onwards. The young growths of early varieties sometimes need to be protected from late frosts by placing straw over them. Keep the hoe moving between the rows, but do not worry about small annual weeds that occur between the plants: the leaves of the crop will smother these. Earthing up should be done with care, and may be done either at one go, heaping the earth up into ridges no more than 15 cm (6 in) high, or in two or three goes, but still to roughly the same height. The harvesting of the early varieties usually begins in July, but is sometimes delayed by weather till August. Later varieties are not lifted till September and October. It is best to do the lifting with a flat-tined potato fork. The proper way to judge when potatoes are ready for lifting is by observing the top growth: once this turns yellow and starts to dry, then the crop is ready.

The potato is subject to all sorts of pests and problems, but generally these are little trouble if a regular pattern of rotation is followed. Wireworms can cause havoc when potatoes are grown on newly converted pasture land. There is little that can be done to prevent such attacks, but they are generally least damaging if early varieties are grown, and if main-crop varieties are lifted a little prematurely. Potato blight is the main enemy of main-crop varieties, especially in wet seasons: the rows should be sprayed with maneb, zineb or Bordeaux mixture as a prophylactic. If the disease appears on the potatoes at the end of the season, the haulms should be burnt.

Potatoes grow particularly well in the company of beans,

sweet corn, cabbage and peas. Combinations to avoid are potatoes with sunflowers or with tomatoes.

RADISH

Radishes are another of the ancient vegetables, having been eaten by not only the Egyptians but also the Babylonians, not to mention the Greeks, Romans and sundry others. Indeed, for so long have they been in cultivation that no one seems quite sure where they originated, though it is presumed that it was within the Fertile Crescent.

Radishes are cultivated for the swollen hypocotyl, which has a pleasing 'hot' taste due to the presence of mustard oil which is produced by the breakdown of a glucoside. All cultivated varieties possess this characteristic, though they belong to several different species. Those cultivated most frequently in the UK are *Raphanus sativus* var. *radicula* or *R.s.* var. *esculentus*. The edible part of the former is usually spherical or nearly so, while the edible part of the latter is somewhat elongated. Another variety, *R.s.* var. *longipinnatus* is cultivated in both China and Japan, and is slowly, but very slowly, finding its way into Britain. This is distinct in having a cylindrical fleshy red root up to 20 cm (8 in) long (as opposed to about 7 cm (2·5 in) with the varieties more usually grown). Some of the Japanese varieties make even this seem a dwarf: they have varieties which commonly weigh 25 kg (55 lb) or more.

Radishes are something one does not really cultivate. You just sow them and they come up if you leave them alone. It is, perhaps, the only crop whose sowing you can safely trust to a child. Radishes will grow well in any good soil, and though it is usual to grow them in rows (probably because one grows everything else in rows) they can just as well be broadcast. The seed needs only the lightest covering with soil, and will usually germinate even if not covered. Successional sowings should be made from March till May, at intervals of a couple of weeks. Sowings made in summer are a disaster, since the plants rush into seed, and the edible part is dry, woody and excessively hot. Sowings can be made in autumn for early spring picking, but since the plants take only a couple or three weeks from seed to harvesting, it is scarcely worth the bother.

Radishes do particularly well if grown near nasturtiums or lettuces, and are supposed to encourage most other vegetables to excel themselves.

TURNIPS and SWEDES

The turnip is an ancient vegetable, having been cultivated in Asia Minor for at least 4,000 years. The swede, by contrast, is a relatively modern vegetable, having first cropped up in Bohemia in the seventeenth century. In both cases, the part that is eaten is the swollen hypocotyl which is united with the swollen stem base and the upper part of the taproot. The swede, in passing, is of hybrid origin, and is probably the only hybrid normally eaten as a vegetable.

The cultivation of both is virtually identical. Like other root crops, they should be grown in ground that has been manured for a previous crop, dressed with a general fertiliser applied at the rate of 85 g (3 oz) per sq m (sq yd). Late varieties can be grown in ground that has been just cleared from a previous crop, in which case it is particularly important to ensure a good top dressing. In both cases the top dressing should be lightly hoed in. Seed should be sown where the plants are to grow, in drills 2 cm (0·75 in) deep. Germination rate is very high, so the seed should be sown thinly. The first sowing for turnips should be made in April, the first sowing of swedes about mid-June. Once the first rough leaves appear, you should start thinning. The first thinning should leave the plants about 10 cm (4 in) apart; a second thinning should leave them 20 cm (8 in) apart. The plants need an even supply of moisture while in growth. Plants should be pulled while they are still young, since full-size plants tend to be tough and woody and coarse in flavour.

Flea beetles tend to be troublesome on both crops,

especially in dry weather. They can be deterred by watering the plants at dusk.

Turnips and swedes both grow better in proximity to peas.

❧ Floaters

ASPARAGUS

Asparagus is one of the relatively small number of vegetables which are monocots – that is, plants whose seedlings produce only one seed leaf, instead of the more usual two. It is, perhaps surprisingly, a member of the lily family, though neither its growth, its foliage nor its flowers seems at first glance to suggest such exotic kinship. Perhaps its fruits, which are very similar to those of some of the other members of the lily family, are the only thing that give its relationship away.

Asparagus is an herbaceous perennial growing to about 3 m. It has been cultivated as a vegetable since Greek and Roman times, and possibly much earlier. It is a native of Eurasia, so could well have been known to the Persians too. It was considered one of the most delicious of vegetables in ancient times, and is still so considered by its devotees.

The parts of the plant used as a vegetable are the young shoots, just as they emerge from the ground. These shoots spring from a complex crown of roots which is usually planted quite deep, and the shoots are harvested before the first leaves appear, while the shoot is no more than 25 cm (10 in) long.

There is something of an argument as to whether the shoots should be blanched, or harvested when green. Those who favour blanching claim that the white shoots are more tender and subtly flavoured than those which are allowed to go green. Those who favour green shoots claim that the shoots do not become tender or attain their full subtlety of flavour until they have been exposed to sunlight. Probably the answer is to try both green and white, and make up your own mind. In the UK and the US, the green shoots are traditionally preferred, the blanched shoots being considered fit only for canning. Throughout continental Europe it is the blanched shoots which are preferred, the green ones being considered fit only for canning.

The finest asparagus is said to come from the Argenteuil region of France. The soil imparts a particular subtlety to the flavour. Unless you live at Argenteuil, it is difficult to grow Argenteuil asparagus, though quite a number of different areas of the world grow asparagus which turns up in the shops under that name.

World demand for asparagus far exceeds production, which tends to make this delightful vegetable expensive and, therefore, well worth growing in the home garden. Indeed, by so much does demand exceed production that a number of asparagus substitutes are sold. Leeks, harvested when very young, are one widely used substitute; the blanched shoots of the mid-ribs of the cardoon are also sometimes offered for sale as asparagus, as are the blanched young shoots of blackberries. Perhaps the most widely sold asparagus substitute, often sold as Cape asparagus, is a South African water plant, *Aponogeton distachium*, which is now naturalised in parts of Europe and the US. Such substitutes not only emphasise the demand for asparagus, but should also give you some ideas of asparagus-like plants you might like to try yourself.

Asparagus is dioecious, which means that male and female flowers are borne on different plants. The female plants give a higher yield, and are to be preferred to male plants.

Plants may be grown either from seed or from crowns.

If you are starting plants from seed, be sure the seed is fresh. If it is, you should get about 70% germination. One-year-old seed will give only 25% germination. If it's older than that you'll be lucky if anything comes up at all. Sow seed outdoors in early April in well prepared seed beds, about 4 cm (1·5 in) deep. Seedlings should be thinned to

15 cm (6 in) apart, and left to grow on for a further year before transplanting. If you want to select females only, grow on in the beds for an extra year, and select only those that bear fruit.

If you start with crowns, which you should be able to buy from most good garden centres, you will get a crop at least a year earlier than you will from seed-grown plants.

Whether you start from seed or with crowns, the secret of success with asparagus lies in the preparation of the asparagus bed. The best asparagus beds are double trenched, with plenty of manure dug in a full year before the asparagus is to be planted. Then when the time comes to plant, trenches 30–45 cm (12–18 in) wide and about 25 cm (10 in) deep should be opened, and the bottoms of these covered with a few inches of really old farmyard manure or garden compost. This organic matter should not be flattened: it should lie at the bottom of the trench with a hump in the middle. The crowns or young transplants are then set astride this hump, the roots being spread well out on both sides. At this stage only cover the plants with about 5 cm (2 in) of soil. Fill the trench back with the soil that came out of it as the young shoots grow, always leaving the young shoots a little above the soil level.

Routine cultivation is really a matter of keeping weeds out of the way, and feeding the plants regularly. A twice-yearly regime seems best. Feed the plants with a mixture of organic manure and artificial fertiliser, and feed them once before growth starts in spring, and again as soon as you have finished harvesting the sticks. This second feed ensures that the plants build up plenty of 'fern', which is what the growers call the top growth. The more top growth they make, the stronger the roots will become, and that is the best way to ensure plenty of sticks the following season. Keep the plants regularly watered through the growing season, and ensure an even supply of moisture to the roots by mulching with compost, peat or forest bark.

Don't harvest a single stick until the plants are three years old. At the first harvest, don't take more than three sticks from any one crown. Let the other shoots grow on. The first sticks appear as soon as hard frosts are over. Once you start harvesting on mature plants, keep harvesting every three days for six weeks, then stop and let the fern grow. The most tender shoots are harvested when the sticks are some 15–20 cm (6–8 in) tall. Either pluck the sticks by bending them towards you, and snapping them, or use a proper asparagus knife. Always take care not to damage young and oncoming shoots.

If you want to blanch your asparagus sticks, earth the rows up as soon as you see growth beginning in the spring, making mounds to 15 or 20 cm (6–8 in). Once you see the tips pushing the soil aside, the sticks are ready to harvest.

The most important cultural point is to keep the plants well fed. Asparagus that is well grown and well fed will remain productive for 15 to 20 years.

Growing asparagus and tomatoes together is beneficial to both, and asparagus grows well if parsley is planted with it. Asparagin, a substance isolated from asparagus, is known to be effective in controlling some of the soil-borne pests of tomatoes.

ARTICHOKE, GLOBE

Normally thistles are something which one leaves for the goats or donkeys to eat, so there is, perhaps, something slightly comic about the fact that the globe artichoke is, after all, only a thistle. But a very special thistle. Very special indeed. It has been regarded since classical antiquity as one of the most delightful of all vegetables, and is still so regarded wherever civilised people gather to eat.

The plant is perennial, growing a metre or more tall. It is a marvellous plant, with bold, architectural grey leaves which spread out, arching from a central rosette. It has a suckering habit, and, while it may be readily propagated from these suckers, more vigorous plants are usually achieved by dividing the crown into several pieces. The practice of dividing the plants is a good one, since the plants produce their crop during their second and third years, the fourth year crop being tolerable but not brilliant, so that division and renewal are beneficial in any case.

The part of the artichoke you eat, the globe, is in fact the flower bud, which consists of a fleshy receptacle, from which on a mature flower spring masses of small, bluish sessile flowers, completely encased in a defensive armament of fleshy green scales. Both the scales and the receptacle are eaten, but it is the receptacle that is the really delicious part.

In theory you would expect to be able to buy artichokes from any good garden centre; in practice they seem to be in rather short supply. Probably the best way of getting a plant or two is to beg one from a friend who is lifting and dividing his plants. If one cultivates the plants properly there comes a time when one has so many pieces one doesn't know what to do with them. The young plants, however acquired, should be set in rows, with the plants about a metre apart, and the rows a little further apart. What artichokes need in order to thrive is a rich, well dug but perfectly drained soil, especially one which will not become excessively wet during winter. If you have a heavy soil and suspect that it may get too wet in winter, raise the level of the soil in the area where you want to grow the artichokes, and add plenty of coarse grit or sand, or even old-fashioned cinders, to the soil. And feed the plants well, using organic manure. This increases the humus content of the soil, and that in turn helps the soil to warm up quickly in the spring, as well as improving soil aeration and drainage. It is important to firm the plants well in the ground. Young plants are easily rocked by the wind; water collects in the hole they make when they rock, and rots the roots.

Cultivation is not difficult at all. The plants should be given a good mulch of manure in spring as growth begins, and another in about May, to help retain soil moisture and suppress weeds. Old and unwanted flower stems should be removed in autumn, along with any decaying outer leaves.

The heads should be harvested before there is any sign of blue coloration: the top bud is taken first, and the others in succession. Secateurs are used. Heads that are too small for the table, can be preserved in oil and served as an appetiser.

If you find that you have so many plants that you are having difficulty in eating all the heads, try blanching the mid-ribs of the leaf-stalks and the central, summer shoots. To do this, you simply draw the crown together, folding the outer leaves over the top, and tie it in that position, wrapping it all round with corrugated card. After three weeks the summer shoots should be well blanched and ready to be used.

AUBERGINE

The aubergine or egg-plant is a tropical vegetable, which explains why it has been little cultivated in Britain in the past. However, modern plant breeding has produced varieties which no longer need such high temperatures and which, moreover, are relatively fast-maturing. This makes them quite a tempting proposition for anyone who wants to be a little more adventurous than growing merely mustard, cress and cabbages.

The aubergine is a member of the same family as both the potato and the tomato, but bears little resemblance to either. The plant is a big grower, and something of a sprawler: it seems never to have made up its mind whether to become a climber or not. It has large, felted leaves, showy lavender flowers and brightly coloured fruits, so that if you cannot find room for it in the vegetable garden, it will always be an asset in the ornamental garden: lovely in a pot on a patio. The part of the plant that is eaten is the fruit, which is technically a berry (in the sense that botanists use that term). Though very low on nutritional value, the fruit has a flavour that is totally unlike that of any other vegetable we can grow.

The plants need a light, sandy, well-drained soil. If yours is not like that to start with, dig in plenty of coarse river sand, clinkers, perlite, vermiculite or something similar to open the soil. Alternatively you can grow the plants on hills, as one grows marrows, to ensure good drainage. However, nutritional requirements are not high, so you do not need to make the hills of pure manure.

Egg-plants need the longest possible growing season you can give them, so start the plants from seed sown indoors in mid-March. Sow the seed in a soilless growing mix in peat pots, one seed to each pot. That way you can pot them on or plant them out without any check. Put the plants outdoors in early May, and cover them with cloches until they are re-established. Alternatively, grow them in frames, but leave the lights off once the plants get too big for the frames. In colder areas you can get a good crop from plants grown on in 30 or 38 cm (12 or 15 in) pots in the greenhouse.

The most important thing to remember when cultivating egg-plants is that they need an even supply of moisture through the growing season, never too little, never too much. The best way of ensuring an even supply of moisture is to give the plants a thorough watering when you put them out, and then put a thick mulch round them, 8 or 10 cm (3 or 4 in) deep. Mulching is important in another way too: it keeps the weeds down. If you want a good crop, the one thing you never do is disturb the roots, so there's no chance of hoeing round the plants.

When it comes to harvesting, use secateurs. If you've never grown egg-plants before you'll be surprised how woody the stalk is. Test the fruits for ripeness by pressing the side gently – but gently – with the ball of your thumb. If the fruit is ripe, this will leave a slight indentation. If it is not ripe, it'll leave no mark. Handle the fruits very gently: they bruise extremely easily. And never be afraid of picking too many fruits off a single plant: they always produce more flowers than they can turn into ripe fruits, and by harvesting heavily you encourage other fruits to fill out and follow on.

CELERY

Celery, like the beets, is one of those vegetables which have been developed in two quite different directions; one line

of development has led to the root crop, celeriac, the other
has led to the celery grown for its etiolated leaf stalks. In the
wild the plant is a biennial growing up to 1m (1 yd) tall,
and is native to Eurasia, South Africa, South America and
New Zealand – which gives it a somewhat discontinuous
distribution. It was first recorded being deliberately cultivated as a vegetable in France in 1623.

Celery used to be thought of as a somewhat 'precious'
vegetable, needing particular skills in cultivation. It is not, in
fact, in the slightest difficult to grow well, but it does require
just a little more attention than some other vegetables.
The most important thing is to ensure that the ground is
very thoroughly prepared for the celery. The ideal way to
prepare the ground is to take out a trench about the depth
of two spades, and about two spades in width, and to work
copious quantities of well-rotted farmyard manure into the
bottom of the trench. If you cannot obtain animal manure,
use garden compost, but enrich it with an artificial fertiliser,
used at the rate recommended on the pack. Once the
bottom of the trench has been prepared, the soil that came out
of it should be put back, but not all of it. The trench should
only be back-filled to within 6 or 7 cm (2·5 in) of the level of
the soil. The trench should be prepared during the winter.
Seed should be sown under glass in pots during March, the
seedlings being hardened in frames. If you can't treat seed
and seedlings this way, buy transplants from your garden
centre. The plants should be set out in the prepared trench
or trenches in late May or during June, in double rows
25 cm (10 in) apart, with about 20 cm (8 in) between the
plants. The plants should be watered in thoroughly, and it
is particularly important to ensure that at no time does this
crop suffer a shortage of water to the roots. The blanching
process should begin when the plants are about 30 cm (12 in)
tall, perhaps a little more. The stems should be tied loosely
just below the leaves, and earthed up in three stages. The
first earthing up should only cover the lower third of the
leaf stalks. A week should be left before the next earthing up,
which should come two-thirds of the way up the leaf

stalks. The final earthing up should be done a week later, leaving only the tops of the plants showing. Soil removed from the trench when it was being prepared should be kept on hand to use for earthing up. Plants can be unearthed and harvested when and as required. Since celery is a particularly precious crop in winter, the earthed-up rows should be covered with bracken or straw to keep the worst of the frost off, and to carry the crop on as late as possible.

The general cultivation of the self-blanching types of celery is very similar. A trench needs to be prepared in the same way. Seed should be sown in pots in March, the seedlings pricked off into boxes, and finally set out in the rows in late May or June, the plants being spaced about 20 cm (8 in) apart. The plants will not need earthing up, but seem to grow best when planted in square blocs rather than in rows.

Of the pests and diseases that trouble celery, the celery fly or leaf miner is probably the most annoying. It causes brown blisters to appear on the leaves from May onwards. The bugs are easily detected and should be removed by hand and crushed. The sledge-hammer treatment is to blast the things with malathion, dimethoate or trichlorphon.

The leaf miner is less likely to trouble the celery if the celery is growing close to cabbages, and its growth is promoted by leeks or tomatoes growing nearby. Dwarf beans demonstrably keep the plants free of diseases and encourage their growth. The best results are obtained where one dwarf bean plant is grown for every six plants of celery. The same 1 : 6 relationship is also beneficial if leeks are used.

COURGETTE and MARROWS

Courgettes are, in fact, simply one of the multitude of types of vegetable marrows in cultivation. The marrows themselves are merely a part of a larger group, known as gourds, some of which are edible. The edible sorts were discovered by Columbus on his first voyage, and later it was found that they grow from one end of the Americas to the other.

Gourds, in Red Indian mythology, play much the same role as the primal egg of Orphic and Hindu mythology. Of the edible species, different ethnic groups seem to have opted for just about every possible option. In Asia the plants are grown for their oil-yielding seeds, while in Africa the leaves and flowers are used as vegetables, and also dried and stored for use as pot herbs.

Marrows were introduced into Britain round about 1700. Their origin and cultivation is the same as for courgette, except that the marrows are usually harvested when rather larger than the courgettes, though not too much larger or they lose their flavour. It seems to have been a peculiarity of the British to acquire a singularly large-fruited variety, then breed it so that it grows even larger, and then to boil it down to a virtually tasteless pulp. Fortunately, after some two and a half centuries, it seems that the British are finally acquiring a proper taste for marrows, harvesting them when they are small enough to be a delight, and cooking them with some sense of proper decency as well.

The finest of all the vegetable marrows are the courgettes, which is a special variety, whose marrows are meant to be picked when no more than 10 or 20 cm (4–8 in) long: if other varieties are picked when as immature as this they will be found to be unbearably bitter. Courgettes are also known as Italian smalls or zuccini.

Essentially they are cultivated in the same way as any other vegetable marrow. The ground should be thoroughly prepared well before the seeds are sown. A site for the courgettes should be selected that is in full sun for as much of the day as possible, and the place selected should be dug over thoroughly, copious quantities of organic matter being incorporated at the same time. Alternatively, the plants can be grown on hills, the hills being made from rings of heaped-up soil whose centres have been filled with the entire contents of the previous year's compost bin.

Seed should be sown outdoors towards the end of May, the seeds being inserted in groups of four or five, about 15 cm (6 in) apart, with the seed being covered with about

2 cm (0·75 in) of soil. Once the seedlings are up, the strongest two from any seed group should be selected to grow on, the others being discarded. It is important to keep the plants growing well: if they suffer a set-back they never seem to catch up with their projected rate of progress again. The most important thing is to ensure that the plants have an even and steady supply of water at the roots at all times. They need pollinating to ensure a good crop, and this is done firstly by noting the differences between male and female flowers: the female flowers have tiny, immature 'marrows' immediately behind them, whereas the male flowers do not. What you do is you take a male flower, pluck off the petals, and then go round prodding it into the female flowers. The courgettes should be harvested when no more than 10 or 15 cm (4 or 6 in) long, 20 cm (8 in) at most.

The one thing to watch for with courgettes is infection by cucumber mosaic virus: this causes stunting of the growth, and puckering and mottling of the leaves. The worst disaster is that it causes the fruits to become distorted. There is no effective cure or control, and infected plants should be burned, before the infection spreads.

CUCUMBERS

Cucumbers have been cultivated for so long that no one is really sure any more where they came from in the first place. Some authorities say that they came from India, other authorities from Africa or Asia or both. Certainly they had reached China, to which they are not native, at least two and a half thousand years ago. More puzzling is that the French found them being cultivated in what is now Montreal, and de Soto found them being grown in Florida, yet they are not native to America. It is one thing to cross the Himalayas from India to China, but no one really seems to have any idea how they got to America before the Europeans.

Two types of cucumbers are grown in the UK: ridge and frame. The ridge type can be successfully cultivated out of doors, but the frame types need to be grown in a cold green-house or in frames. The cultural requirements are much the same, apart from that. The soil in which ridge cucumbers are to be grown should be rich in humus. You can grow them on hills or in rows, but in either event the soil should be raised by making a heap or ridge of rich garden compost, and covering this with no more than 7 cm (2·5 in) of fine garden soil. Seed should be sown where the plants are to grow in May or June, the seeds being sown in groups 60 to 120 cm (24–48 in) apart, each seed being covered with about 3 cm (1 in) of soil. Once the seedlings are up, select the strongest in each station, and discard the others. Frame cucumbers can be started rather earlier, in March, the seed being sown in peat pots so that when the plants are put out in frames there is no check to their growth. Both types need ample moisture at the roots during the growing season. With the ridge types it is not necessary to pinch out the growing tips, but it is necessary with the frame types. Fruits should be harvested young, to encourage continued production.

Cucumbers grow most happily when grown together with lettuce or radish, and these can be used as catch crops while the cucumbers are getting themselves established. Cucumbers and beans are mutually helpful, while sunflowers have a beneficial effect on the cucumbers.

LEEKS

Leeks are one of our most ancient vegetables, having been cultivated in Egypt in the time of the Pharaohs. They are natives of the Mediterranean regions, and were distributed throughout Europe by the Romans, who took them wherever they went. The Welsh relationship with the leek began very early in their history. Tradition has it that the Welsh, led by their king, Cadwallader in AD 640 to a victory over the Saxons, wore leeks in their hats to distinguish themselves from their enemies, the leeks having been stolen from a nearby garden.

Leeks, which are very closely related to onions, differ

from them in that whereas in the onion it is the fattened underground storage organ that is eaten, in the leek no such storage organ is formed, the part eaten is the fleshy bases of the broad, strap-like leaves.

To grow leeks well it is worth the trouble of preparing the ground thoroughly. The ground should be turned over as soon as the previous crop is lifted, and manure should be incorporated in the soil at the same time. Many people prefer to grow leeks in permanent beds, so that the soil goes on getting better year by year. However, leeks should not be planted in freshly manured ground, so that the incorporation of manure should be done in the autumn or early winter. Seed can be sown as early as February, but is more generally sown in March or April in a small prepared seed bed. The earlier the seed is sown the larger the leek will be when the time comes to transplant it. The seed bed should be thoroughly soaked before the leeks are lifted for transplanting, which is best done during May, by which time the plants should be about 15 cm (6 in) long. The leaves should be slightly trimmed before the leeks are set in their rows, the plants being set about 20 cm (8 in) apart in rows 45 cm (18 in) apart. Planting should be done with the aid of a dibble, the plants being dropped into the dibhole. The hole need not be filled: a good watering usually firms the plants sufficiently. Hoe between the rows to keep weeds down, and ensure that the plants are evenly moist throughout the growing season. Once the plants have almost reached full size, heap earth round the bases to blanch the sticks. Leeks are extremely hardy and can be left in the ground, to be lifted as and when needed; there is really little advantage in lifting them earlier unless the ground is desperately needed for another crop.

Leeks are singularly free from pests and diseases, and for this reason they are often grown between rows of other vegetables, acting as a deterrent barrier to the spread of the pests and diseases of other plants. Leeks and both celery and celeriac are mutually beneficial while leeks tend to discourage carrot fly if grown with carrots.

LETTUCES

This is an almost ubiquitous salad crop, and it seems to have
been around for a very long time: there are plants depicted
on the tombstones of Egyptians dated about 4,500 BC
which would appear to be lettuces, and they were certainly
known to the Persians, and later to the Moors, who bred
many new varieties. It was introduced into China in the
seventh century, and the Chinese have developed it in more
diverse ways than the Europeans: they have lettuces which
they cultivate for their stems, a practice quite unknown in
Europe.

Lettuces grow best in ground that has been well prepared,
preferably ground which has been well dug and into which
a good quantity of manure has been dug in early winter.
The ground should be left rough-dug until spring, when it
should be raked into a fine tilth. The earliest sowings of
lettuces should be made under cloches or in frames in mid-
October, the seedlings being transplanted but still grown
under glass from the middle of December onwards. For
later crops, sowings can be made from mid-January on, the
seedlings being transplanted in late February. Another crop
can be raised by sowing seed in the open in August, and
transplanting the seedlings to grow on under cloches or in
frames in mid-September. This will produce a crop that can
be picked in late autumn and early winter.

For outdoor crops the first sowing can be made in early
March, with successional sowings at fortnightly intervals
till August. Seed should be sown where the plants are to
grow, in drills 2 cm (0·75 in) deep, 30 cm (12 in) apart, the
seedlings being thinned to about 20 cm (8 in) apart.
Thinnings can be used in salads, as garnishing or to flavour
soups and stews. A further planting can be made in August
for growing through the winter for spring use. Seed should
be sown as before and the seedlings lightly thinned in
October, the thinnings being planted up to make another
row.

The greatest problem disease of lettuce is grey mould,

which is a fungal infection that attacks the lettuces at ground level. It can be guarded against by ensuring that the soil is rich in humus and well worked, and by careful planting. If the fungicide Quintozene is raked into the soil before planting, the virus can be kept under control.

One of the most important cultural points is to be sure that you plant the right types of lettuces at the right season. If you plant a lettuce intended to be over-wintered for use in the spring, in early summer, it will run amok for you: it may be an amazing sight, but it is scarcely edible.

Lettuces grow happily in combination with radish, carrots and strawberries. Sometimes lettuce, radish and carrots are grown together in a mixed planting from which all partners seem to benefit.

ONIONS

The onion, in one form or another, has been around for a very long time indeed. It is known that it was in cultivation in ancient Egypt as long as 5,000 years ago, and that it was grown by the Jews before their exile from Israel. A native of Asia Minor, its use by Europeans was learned from the eastern nations, and there is now no Western civilisation where it is not in use.

The edible part is the bulb, which can vary vastly in size, and somewhat in shape and colour, the colours ranging from whitish to brownish, reddish or purplish. When intact the bulb is completely odourless: it is only when it is cut that its very distinct smell becomes apparent. The smell carries with it a lachrymatory substance called allicin, which is produced from S-allyl-L-cystein sulphoxide by the action of the enzyme allinase.

There is now a vast number of different sorts of onion, each with its own merits. Shallots are one of the group known as multiplier onions: these produce numerous small bulbs instead of a single large one. Several other bunching onions are widely grown. The so-called tree onions produce clusters of bulbils in place of flowers, these bulbils then being used to start another generation of onions. The Welsh onion has nothing whatever to do with Wales: it is native to Siberia, is cultivated mainly in Japan, and gets its name from the German *welsche* meaning foreign.

For cultural purposes there are three main groups of onions: there are those which are sown under glass in January, there are those which can be sown outdoors in spring, and there are those which can be sown outdoors in autumn for spring harvesting. It is useful to grow some from each group. Onions can also be grown from sets, which are simply small bulbs.

Onions need to be grown in ground that has been thoroughly prepared. It should be dug deeply in winter and have plenty of organic matter incorporated. The land should be left rough through winter, and only worked to a fine tilth in February or whenever the ground becomes workable. The earliest sowing of onion seed should be made under glass in January, the seedlings being planted outdoors in April, set 15 cm (6 in) apart in rows 45 cm (18 in) apart. It is important to plant onions with a trowel, and to make certain that the base is at least 1 cm below soil level.

The second sowing of onion seed should be made outdoors in mid-February or until the end of March. Seed should be sown in drills 30 cm (12 in) apart, and the seeds only just covered with soil.

The third sowing should be made in August, the seeds being sown in a seed bed and planted out in their rows in early March.

Where sets are being used these should be put in the ground during April, the practice being to plant them in drills 30 cm (12 in) apart, the sets each 15 cm (6 in) apart in the rows. The sets should be planted so that only the tip of the bulb is above the soil.

To ensure good crops the ground should be kept well hoed between the rows, and the weeds between the plants should be removed by hand. Two thinnings should be made of seed-grown onions, the first thinning the plants to 5 cm (2 in) apart, the second thinning them to 10 cm (4 in) apart.

About mid-August the green tops of the onions should be bent over to speed the ripening of the bulbs. Two weeks later the bulbs should be lifted carefully and laid out where they were growing to finish ripening. After that they can be stored in ropes or bunches.

The most serious pest of onions is the onion fly. There is no effective cure, nor really effective preventive treatment. The infected bulbs should be dug up and burned.

Onions grow well in company with beets, and if grown in rows with carrots, not only deter the carrot fly, but also tend to suffer less with onion fly. Onions should never be grown near peas or beans, whose growth they inhibit.

CAPSICUMS or PEPPERS

Capsicums are one of America's gifts to mankind, having been cultivated by the native Americans from prehistoric times. They became popular with the Latin races of Europe, long before the British discovered their virtues. They are known variously as capsicums, peppers, pimento (which is the Spanish name) or paprika (which is the Hungarian name). Under whatever name, they are members of the potato family, and are probably most closely related to tomatoes.

They are not the easiest of crops to bring to perfection in the dull grey climate of Britain since, even when grown under glass, they really need rather more sunshine than the average British summer provides. Even in a good summer, they are still quite a challenge. If you're going to try peppers outdoors, choose the sunniest position you can, and grow them on a hill of specially prepared, very sandy soil. They need the same sort of soil if you are going to grow them in the greenhouse, or better still, grow them in 30 cm (12 in) pots in the greenhouse: that gives you greatest control over watering and feeding. Seed should be sown as early in the season as possible, but it won't germinate at a worthwhile rate unless the temperature is above 15·6°C/60°F. If you've got a propagator, use it. Seed should be sown shallowly and scarcely covered, preferably in a soilless growing mix in peat pots. Plants should be moved on to jumbo flower pots or tomato bags in the greenhouse in late May or early June, or planted outside from mid-June onwards. At the slightest suggestion of cold weather or chilling winds, cover the young plants with cloches. Once the plants are in position, don't disturb them. Feed and weed them at the same time by applying a thick mulch of good garden compost. Keep the plants always moist but never wet. Flower drop is a problem with capsicums in some seasons: it is usually caused by the temperatures being too low, but dryness at the roots is another common cause. Plants will turn yellow, stop growing, and never really recover if night temperatures drop much below 13°C/55°F. On the other hand if day temperatures go over 32°C/90°F, that will produce blossom drop too. It may sound tricky, but you can win. Certainly you'll never win if you never try. Once you have a good set of blossom on the plant, don't worry about subsequent blossom drop: that is just the plant's own way of ensuring that it doesn't set more fruit than it can mature. Harvest peppers when they are green or yellow, depending on variety, and always harvest them with secateurs: the fruits bruise very easily, so it is no good trying to rip them off the plants.

SPINACH

There was a time when spinach was a sort of joke vegetable, really rather too revolting to contemplate. However, things have changed for the better, and new varieties as well as an improved understanding of how to cook it, mean that spinach is now a worthwhile crop. The wild plant is probably a native of Persia, but it is now cultivated throughout the civilised world, including Britain.

It is an easily grown crop, doing best on ground that is in good heart, but which has not been freshly manured. Sowings should be made at fortnightly intervals from February till May, using summer varieties. A further sowing can be made from late August into September, using winter varieties. In both cases seed should be sown 2–3 cm (1 in) deep, in rows about 30 cm (12 in) apart. The plants should be thinned when large enough to handle to 8 cm (3 in) apart in the rows, and a second thinning should be done later taking every other plant out: these thinnings should be large enough to be used. Hoe, and water regularly. Discard plants as soon as their usefulness is over, otherwise they continue taking goodness out of the ground, without giving any return.

Downy mildew is probably the worst of the problems encountered with modern spinach varieties. It can be most effectively prevented by ensuring a well-drained soil, and ensuring proper thinning: plants are most prone to mildew if they are grown too crowded.

Spinach and strawberries are good companions, each being beneficial to the other.

TOMATOES

The tomato, is, as someone once rather quaintly put it, the fruit of a vegetable. It counts as a vegetable because it is used as a vegetable. It is only when it is drunk as tomato juice, that it counts as a fruit. The wild plant is a native of South America, scarcely recognisable as the plant we cultivate today. It is a spineless thing, that creeps and crawls along the ground, producing a few tiny little tomatoes. It was introduced to Europe in 1523, and was for a long time grown as an ornamental; the fruits were thought to be poisonous. The Chinese, however, realised that the fruits were edible long before the rest of us, and it is from the Chinese *koe-chiap* that tomato sauce gets its name ketchup.

Tomatoes are probably the most widely grown home crop of all, and the ways of cultivating them are numerous. Probably the most successful methods are those in which tomatoes are grown in bags of specially prepared compost, usually sold as tomato bags. These should be placed in a sunny position, and the tomatoes inserted through a cross cut or rectangular opening on the upper side of the bag.

Similar composts are available for growing tomatoes in large flower pots, indoors or out. Tomatoes can be grown successfully in the ground, but it is most important that they are never grown in the same ground two years in a row: if they are, soil sickness is liable to develop. However they are grown, the essential cultural points are the same. Seed should be sown indoors in boxes or trays in March or April, and the seedlings pricked off into peat pots as soon as the true leaves appear. They should be gently hardened in a cold frame, and are ready for setting outdoors when the stem at ground level is about the thickness of a pencil. Plants are usually ready to be set out in early June, and should be placed about 45 cm (18 in) apart with 76 cm (30 in) between the rows. A good strong stake should be placed beside each plant when it is planted. Pinch out side shoots as they appear, and pinch the tops off the plants once they reach the tops of the canes, or when four to five trusses have set. At this stage the plants usually benefit from a dose of liquid tomato fertiliser, after which a thick mulch of straw should be placed around the plants: this is partly to retain the moisture in the soil, but also to prevent the lower fruits from being damaged by mud splashes in wet weather. Fruits should be harvested when ripe, but frequently there are still many unripe fruits on the plants in September, when frosts begin to be likely to occur. The plants should then be cut loose from their stakes, and laid out on the ground, keeping the fruits off the ground by means of short Y-shaped sticks. If the stakes or canes are removed, and the plants covered with cloches, the fruit will ripen well and quickly. If you don't have any cloches, take the fruits indoors to ripen in the warmth.

Tomatoes grow best when planted near asparagus, and with parsley growing between the plants. If tomatoes are grown near gooseberry bushes, the bushes seem to remain quite remarkably free from attack by insects. It has been scientifically proved that tomatoes give off a volatile oil that is lethal to some insects.

❧ Pot Herbs

The term 'herb' is a rather imprecise one. Properly speaking, a herb is any plant that is not a tree or a shrub: it embraces those plants which we now call annuals, biennials and perennials, as well as a number of bulbous or tuberous plants. A perennial, for example, is, in the strict usage of the language, a perennial herb.

In fact, probably the earliest plants known by man to have specific health-giving properties, and possibly the first to be cultivated, were those plants which we would now call medicinal herbs. The term 'herb' itself was first used of those plants grown in monastery gardens in the more or less Dark Ages, either to heal or to hide the revolting flavour of meat that had to be preserved by salting through the winter. It is in this latter sense that we now use the term herb – as any plant which either adds its own distinctive flavour to a dish, or draws out the flavour of the dish itself. Properly, such herbs should be called pot herbs, to distinguish them from the medicinal herbs.

The herbs we grow in our gardens today are very much the same as those that were grown in monastery gardens in the Middle Ages. They have changed very little, except that perhaps the range of herbs that we cultivate now is rather narrower than it was some centuries ago.

Most of our pot herbs are plants that are natives to the Mediterranean: they are sun-loving plants, used to poor soil and abundant sunshine. Through cultivation most of them have become more adaptable, both to soil and climate, but one or two still seem to miss the sunshine of their native lands, and need some cosseting over winter.

While there is some passing interest in growing herbs in

deliberately designed herb gardens – which can look extremely attractive – by and large herbs are best grown wherever they are convenient – near the back door, near the vegetables, among the flowers, or to advantage among the vegetables themselves, just so long as the situation in which they are growing is sunny enough for them to thrive.

BASIL

This is one of those herbs with which strange magical stories are connected: such as that scorpions breed in it, or even from it. Fascinating idea. It is more tender than most of our pot herbs, originating in the tropics, in places like Asia, India, Africa and the Pacific Islands.

There are two forms of this frost-tender annual: the common form, which grows to 90 cm (36 in); and a dwarf form which grows to only about 20 cm (8 in). There is also a purple basil, though it is not often grown. Plants are raised from seed sown in the protection of a greenhouse in March. Since the plants resent root disturbance, the seed should be sown either in peat pots or directly in the container in which they are to be grown. By and large, basil does best in pots with good drainage, stood in the shelter of the sunniest wall you can find. In September the pots can be brought into the greenhouse and, if cut hard back, will produce a further harvestable crop. Old plants should be discarded, and new ones started each season.

The leaves are strongly and sweetly aromatic, somewhat similar to cloves in flavour. They should be used sparingly since the flavour is very powerful. It is much used in continental Europe in salads and soups.

BAY

This is the laurel with which the ancients crowned their conquering heroes. In the hey-day of the herbalists it was used in cases of hysteria, and also to relieve flatulent colic. Nowadays its uses are almost entirely culinary.

The bay, unlike most herbs, is a small tree. It has a reputation for being somewhat tender, but seems hardy enough once established, at least in the southern half of Britain. It makes an attractive plant against a wall. If you want to grow it on a single stem, any suckers should be removed: grown in the open garden the suckers really do not matter much and afford a ready means of propagation. It grows happily in most fertile soils, or can be cultivated in a large pot or tub. Plants are readily increased from cuttings taken between late July and Christmas. There is a form in which the leaves are bright golden yellow if the plant is grown in full sun; they have the same flavour as the leaves of the more usual form with green leaves.

CHIVES

Chives are a somewhat anomalous member of the onion family, being grown not for their bulbs but for the hollow, rounded leaves, which impart a most distinctive flavour to anything in which they are cooked. Chives are readily raised from seed sown outdoors in spring, but once you have plants, they can be increased by division in the spring. In fact, chives really ought to be lifted, divided and replanted every spring, otherwise they loose much of their flavour. They are happy in any soil, but must be planted in full sun. The flowers need to be removed, partly because if they are allowed to set seed, you will find chives coming up all over your garden, but also because the removal of the flowers promotes the growth of good, tasty leaves.

DILL

This is one of the annual umbellifers that throws up a single stalk and then rushes into flower. The first leaves are finely divided, but later leaves are really whispy. The plant, though not a native to Britain, is native to many other parts of Europe. It is easily raised from seed sown during March or April where the plants are to grow. They grow best in a moist soil, but in a position in full sun. The best way to achieve this is to grow the plants in an area that has been really heavily mulched, year after year. Spring-sown plants will flower about August: it is also worth making a sowing in July to ensure a supply of dill for the autumn. Once you have dill in your garden, it may well sow itself. If you want it to do that, grow it well away from fennel: the two cross readily, and the flavour of seedlings of such crosses, while curious, is seldom as pleasant as either dill or fennel.

FENNEL

There are in fact two fennels, not one. The one most usually grown as a herb is sweet fennel; the less common one is Florence fennel, which has swollen leaf bases. These are sometimes used much as celery is used, while the leaves can be used like the leaves of sweet fennel. The seeds of both can be used for flavouring.

Both fennels are best raised from seed sown outdoors in late spring, where the plants are to grow. Plants of sweet fennel should be placed about 60 cm (24 in) apart: they are perennials and will go on producing good crops for many years. Tall growing, they need staking otherwise they are inclined to drag their leaves in the mud. Florence fennel is an annual, and seed is best sown a little later than that of sweet fennel. The stem bases should be earthed up once they start swelling, to blanch them. Plants can be lifted, potted up, and grown in the greenhouse through winter.

GARLIC

Like chives, garlic is really an onion, but a very special onion. It is a native of the Mediterranean region, and has been cultivated since a very remote period in history. Usually you will find that you need only a relatively small number of plants.

Garlic is grown from small bulbs called cloves, in much the way that onions may be grown from small bulbs called sets. In Britain it is usual to plant the small cloves in the spring, but in fact a far better crop can be achieved if the cloves are planted in November. They need a situation where they get sun all day long. A spring planting can be made to harvest in autumn. The plants should be kept growing well: while they need ample moisture they will not tolerate wet feet. Once the greenery starts to turn yellow, it should be bent over. Once it has dried off lift the cloves, wash them clean, and store them. Garlic can also be grown in pots on a patio or on a kitchen window sill. Plant four cloves to a 20 cm (8 in) pot: once the leaves turn yellow, lay the pot on its side and allow to dry out completely.

HORSERADISH

Think well before you decide whether you really do want to cultivate horseradish. Though not a native of Britain, it has become widely naturalised, and is known in gardens where it has long been cultivated, and in many allotments, as a pestilential weed, almost impossible to eradicate owing to the enormous depths to which its roots penetrate.

One of the peculiarities of horseradish is that you do not grow it from seed, or from divisions: you grow it from thongs, which are root cuttings. These should be planted 7 cm (2·5 in) deep and about 30 cm (12 in) apart, in deep, rich soil, and kept well separated from other crops. They are safest grown in some sort of container, a giant pot, a tub or even a barrel. One of the problems of growing them in the open ground is that of digging deep enough to get the whole root out. You need only leave the tiniest fragment of root behind to have a plague of horseradish on your hands a year or two later.

MARJORAM, POT

Two marjorams are commonly cultivated: marjoram itself (sometimes delightfully known as 'Joy of the Mountains'), or sweet marjoram, which is a bushy plant with green or golden leaves and is best grown in the garden; and pot or winter marjoram, which is a semi-shrubby perennial best grown in the greenhouse or the kitchen through winter so that its leaves can be used fresh. Both are natives of the warmer parts of Europe.

Pot marjoram is easily grown from seed, but is so inexpensive you might just as well buy it from a garden centre. Plants should be grown in $12\frac{1}{2}$ cm (5 in) pots in the greenhouse or the kitchen. For a fine crop of leaves for winter picking, prune the plant hard in the autumn. Cuttings can be rooted quite easily if taken in December and stuck in a frame or in the greenhouse. While plants will go on from year to year, the leaves have more strength of flavour in young plants, and this is the reason for starting afresh from cuttings each year.

MINTS

There are mints and mints and mints. One university botanic garden grows some thirty plants, each with a quite distinct flavour. The two kinds most widely grown for cooking are spearmint, with long narrow, dark green leaves, and apple mint, with furry rounded leaves.

All mints need very similar cultivation. They are best started from runners or cuttings (which root very readily). Young plants should be put out in spring or autumn, but not in the dead of winter. They like their roots in a damp soil, but their heads in sun. Generally, they are plants which need curbing rather than encouraging. For this reason they may be grown in large ornamental terra cotta pots, or contained in a bottomless bucket sunk in the ground.

PARSLEY

According to folklore, this is a herb that will only thrive when it is sown by whoever is the real head of the household. It is an annual herb so needs to be started afresh from seed each season. For best results the seed should be sown where the plants are to grow, in moist, fertile soil, in sun or shade. Though most people only make one sowing each season, it is really better to make two sowings, since it is the leaves produced by vigorous plants that have the best flavour and the highest content of vitamin C. Make one sowing in March or April for harvesting through summer, and another sowing in July for harvesting into autumn. Thinnings can be used in soups or salads, while the old plants are useful in the compost bin.

ROSEMARY

This is another of our herbs which originates from the countries bordering on the Mediterranean, and so is slightly tender. It is a woody plant, a true shrub, with grey, peeling bark and tiny leaves which look hard and sharp but in fact are very soft. While it will survive many years out of doors in Britain, it seldom lasts more than a decade before succumbing to a winter which does not take its fancy, winter wet seeming as much to its dislike as severe frosts. The plant is not long-lived, even in its native countries. Young plants can be bought from most garden centres from spring through summer and should be planted in a sunny, well-drained position, preferably against a warm wall or at the foot of a large rock. Tip cuttings taken in March root readily, and it is always worth having a few coming on, either to give away, to hand round to sales for charitable causes, or simply to replace your own plant when it dies. There are several forms of rosemary besides the type usually grown, including a prostrate one, which is most attractive but more tender than the one usually grown, and a relatively dwarf plant with a much stronger flavour than usual.

SAGE

This is another tender, shrubby labiate from the Mediterranean, which should be treated in the same general way as rosemary. There are several forms around, including both narrow-leaved and broad-leaved forms. One excellent form has purple leaves, and another has golden variegations to the leaves. The most striking is the variety properly known as 'Tricolor', in which the leaves are relatively narrow, a rich, deep purple, with a broad margin of white – a most striking garden plant, but decidedly more tender than the other sorts. Most sages will survive British winters if grown against the wall of a house or greenhouse, but they can equally well be grown in large pots, and moved into a light but frost-free place for the winter.

TARRAGON

Tarragon has a taste all its own, though it is apparently chemically similar to anise. However, you do have to be sure you get the right tarragon. The right tarragon is French tarragon, which is highly aromatic. The wrong tarragon is Russian or English tarragon, which has no flavour to speak of.

French tarragon is a semi-shrubby perennial, and again, is a native of the Mediterranean regions. It needs a light, sandy soil, and all the sun it can get. It will grow well even in relatively dry soil. Plants are best obtained from a garden centre, though seed can be purchased: cuttings will root taken any time when the plant is in active growth. Otherwise increase it by lifting and dividing the roots.

THYME

This is a herb whose medicinal uses would seem to go back to long before mankind started to lead a settled life or had any pretensions to being civilised. Its medicinal qualities include phenols, thymol, carvacrol as well as cymene, pineme, menthone, borneol and linalol. It is antiseptic against some staphylococci and basilluscoli, and is helpful in some types of stomach upset, as well as in sore throats, bronchitis and whooping cough.

Its culinary uses would appear to be every bit as ancient as its medicinal uses, for the flavour is most distinct. Several thymes are cultivated, each varying somewhat in flavour. All need the same basic treatment. Young plants should be put out in spring in a sunny position in a light, sandy soil. Plants can be increased easily, either by division in spring or by layers, or by cuttings taken in early summer. Plants grow well in pots, and where space is limited, this is an ideal herb to grow in a pot on a windowsill in the kitchen. Spring or early summer cuttings should be well enough established to move into the kitchen in autumn, so that the leaves can be used fresh at a time when the plants out of doors will virtually have stopped growing.

❧ Fruit

There was a time when no self-respecting gardener would have considered his garden worthy of the name if he didn't grow some fruits. But times have changed: gardens have got smaller; and fewer and fewer people seem to bother to grow fruits any more. Yet they are not difficult, need not take up much space, and really, the joy of picking and eating your own fruit is worth the little time and trouble it takes to get the plants growing well.

In modern small gardens one has to think in terms of combining fruit trees and bushes with other plants. Some will mix well with vegetables, while others may be better grown among the miscellaneous flowers and shrubs of the ornamental part of the garden. The cane fruits, blackberries, raspberries and the other cane berries, can be grown in one place, tied to wires stretched between strong posts. Used in this way they could hide a compost area or be used as a hedge to break the force of the wind across the vegetable garden. Some fruits do not mind shade: you could grow a quince as a standard, surrounded by bush fruits such as redcurrants or blackcurrants. Strawberries will grow in shade, and these can be grown under gooseberry bushes provided that the gooseberries are grown up on a short, single stem. Blueberries and newberries are probably best grown among flowers or shrubs, rather than in the vegetable garden, while the large growing plants like apples and pears can be grown as espaliers or oblique cordons, in which case they take up very little room.

Really, if you want to grow fruit in your garden, there are dozens of different ways in which you can fit it into the general scheme of things, and even use some of your fruit trees or bushes to benefit other crop plants.

CANE FRUITS

The cane fruits embrace all those fruits which throw up long, vigorous new growths in one season, these being tied in to produce fruit the following year. Best known among these are blackberries, raspberries, and loganberries, but there are several new hybrid berries coming on the market, whose general cultivation is the same as for the other cane fruits.

Cane fruits all need similar cultural conditions. A good deep, well-worked soil, with plenty of humus added in. More humus can be added on top of the soil in the form of a mulch each year. All cane fruits need a strong framework on which to be trained. Raspberries are best grown in a single or double row, with really stout stakes at each end, each stake being topped with a cross bar (to form a letter T) with strong wires held taut between them. The canes are simply tied into an upright position on the wires. Any canes that stray from the straight and narrow should be chopped off with a side-cut from a spade. Old canes should be cut out once they have fruited, partly because they will not produce much fruit a third year, but also because they hinder the flowering and fruiting of younger canes. Canes should be removed with secateurs as close to the ground as possible.

Blackberries, loganberries and the new hybrid berries need a similarly humus-rich soil, but are better trained in a single plane. Again, if two stout stakes are driven into the ground each side of the plant, and wires are stretched between these, the canes can be tied into the wires when and as needed. Old canes should be cut back to ground level once they have fruited. New canes need to be tied in as they grow, otherwise they will sprawl and root all over the place.

BLUEBERRIES and NEWBERRIES

Although these have been cultivated in America for years, both as commercial and home garden crops, it is only relatively recently that anyone has taken much interest in them in this country. They are not difficult to grow, provided one has an acid soil, and they take up very little space.

What they need is a really acid soil, one with a pH of between 3·5 and 5·0. They also enjoy all the humus they can get. They are natives of peat moors and heathlands, and those are the sort of conditions they need in the garden. If you don't have a soil sufficiently acid, they can be grown in a peat mixture in raised beds or tubs. When planting, the shoots should be cut back to about one-third of their length. No further pruning is required, except perhaps the removal of exhausted wood from long established plants.

Blueberries, cranberries, bilberries and the other berries in this group all have a long season in fruit, and the fruits are best protected from the birds by covering the bushes with plastic netting once the fruits start to ripen.

BUSH FRUITS

The bush fruits, which include red-, white- and black-currants, as well as gooseberries and quinces, will grow in sun or shade, though the best crops are obtained in sun. If you have nowhere in your garden to grow them in full sun, they are still worth cultivating, even if they only get sun for a part of the day.

The most important thing with any of these fruits is to make sure you buy good, strong, healthy young plants. These are best purchased and planted in the autumn, though spring planting is successful provided that you water the plants well and mulch them thoroughly. The soil should be deeply dug and liberally enriched with organic manure or compost.

Blackcurrants should be planted about a hand's depth deeper than they were growing in the nursery, but the other bush fruits should be planted at the same depth as that at which they were growing in the nursery. In general, all currants should be pruned immediately after harvesting. The old wood should be cut hard back to encourage young shoots to grow vigorously in the spring.

With gooseberries, however, there is some debate as to whether or not these should be pruned. The old practice has always been to remove old or unproductive wood, and to cut all other shoots back to about half their length. However, it has recently been discovered that bushes that are left unpruned very seldom suffer from diseases, while those that are pruned unfortunately tend to become diseased.

When buying gooseberries, it is worth remembering that gooseberries do not have to be grown as sprawly, spiny shrubs. It is possible to buy standard gooseberries, which have a clean stem of about 1 m (1 yd). This is achieved by grafting the gooseberry onto a stock of yellowcurrant. Such bushes give one room to grow other crops under and around them, as well as being far easier to pick.

It is also possible to buy fan-trained gooseberries which can be grown flat against a fence, making them a practical proposition in even the smallest garden.

APPLES, PEARS and CRABS

There is really no longer any excuse for people not growing apples or pears in their gardens. The days have long gone when one could, with justification claim that they were too big for all but the largest gardens. You no longer need an orchard to grow apples. They are available on dwarfing rootstocks, and this makes them small enough for even the smallest gardens.

Apples grow best in a sunny, south-facing position, sheltered from north winds by a wall or even a hedge or fence. Apples should not, however, be grown in too hot a place: they should not actually be grown against a south wall, for example; it is simply too dry for them to thrive.

Pears, on the other hand, demand all the heat and warmth they can get. Really, they enjoy a rather warmer climate than ours, so they do best when planted against a south or west wall, or against a south-facing fence. Beautiful though the trees are when grown on their own, the best fruit is produced on trees trained flat against a hot wall so, if you want to grow a pear, make sure you have a wall for it. There are dwarfing rootstocks, which mean that it is now possible to buy pears which are small enough to grow even on the walls of a bungalow.

Crab-apples are probably the best bet if you have only enough room for one tree in your garden. They are every bit as beautiful as flowering cherries when they blossom, many have purple or purplish leaves, and they are a joy to behold in late summer, their branches weighed down by the weight of the colourful crabs.

While crabs are normally grown as small trees, with a single, clean stem, both apples and pears can be grown trained in a number of different ways. They can be grown as standards, half-standards or bushes, and the bushes can be trained as pyramids, inverted pyramids, as cordons or espaliers, which makes them eminently suitable for growing along a fence or beside the drive or the vegetable garden.

Your best bet really is to make up your own mind which of these fruits you want to grow, and how much room you are prepared to give over to them. Then go along to a nurseryman who specialises in fruit trees and ask his advice. He is also the best person to consult about pruning. The pruning of apples and pears is important: a well-pruned tree is far more productive than one that has not been pruned at all; while one pruned badly is the worst of all possible worlds. If you buy, for example, a fan-trained tree, the nurseryman who sells it to you knows the right way to prune it to make it most productive: and if you think you have gone wrong, you can always go back to him for more advice.

PLUMS and RHUBARB

The two may seem an odd combination, but in a way they are not. Both enjoy a deep, rich, well-dug soil, and an annual mulch of good, strawy old manure.

Plums are usually grown as half-standards these days,

presumably because it makes them easier to pick. They are easy enough to grow, provided you have room for them. The big bugbear is having to spray them frequently against silver leaf disease, and if you have a plum tree you will amost certainly have silver leaf disease too. This disease is a fungus infection, and it gains entry into the trees through wounds in the stem or bark. The wound does not have to be a large one: the damage done by the snapping of a twig when you're picking the plums is quite enough. For this reason the greatest care should be taken not to damage the tree: if any damage is done it should immediately be repaired with a pruning compound. The other thing to watch for is dead wood. The fungus can only fructify on dead wood so keep your plums clean of dead wood at all times, whether the dead matter is merely a twig or a much larger branch.

Plums will grow happily in any open position, and in any fertile soil, but do best when the soil is well-enriched with humus.

Rhubarb counts as a fruit because it is used as a sweet and not as a vegetable. Which may seem odd, but that's how it is.

Rhubard needs a deep, rich, well-dug soil, and a situation in full sun. The crowns should be bought in spring and planted firmly, well-watered and then given a good thick mulch. No sticks should be culled for cooking during the first year of growth, and preferably none in the second year. In the third year you can start culling lightly, and after that settle down to a good harvest every year.

Rhubarb should be plucked, not picked and not cut. What you are plucking is the leaf and the whole of its stalk, and this will come away from the rootstock quite readily provided you have the confidence to give it a good sharp tug.

It used to be the fashion to force rhubarb, but few people seem to bother any longer. The rhubarb is far better if it is forced; the sticks are longer and the flesh far more tender. It is still possible to buy clay forcing pots from one or two old potteries, or to pick them up second-hand at auctions. Nowadays most of us have to make do with home-made forcing jars. The most usual substitute is a chimney pot, but it is possible to use a dustbin, or anything else that will force the plants to grow upwards.

PEACHES, NECTARINES and APRICOTS

These are some of the most delicious fruits that can be grown out of doors in Britain, but they are not always satisfactory in the crops they produce. All three are very closely related botanically, and need the same cultural conditions.

They need the warmest, sunniest place you can find for them. A south-facing wall is ideal, and a west wall will do. The ground should be prepared before planting by digging deeply and incorporating a good quantity of organic manure or compost in the soil. It is said of all these trees that they must never be allowed to put down a tap root, and though most of the marvellous old gardeners who preached these things have sadly long ago disappeared, if you ever see an old house being pulled down, you'll nearly always find that there was a paving slab placed about three feet down in the ground right under the tree. If you want your peach, nectarine or apricot to fruit freely, do what the old-fashioned gardeners did: put a paving slab under it.

Some of the old gardeners went further: they encased the roots in what amounted to an underground sarcophagus, for not only did they put a paving slab under the tree, they surrounded the roots on the three sides away from the house with paving slabs set vertically in the ground. And it worked.

Just as effective, but far more labour, is to root prune the trees every few years. You do this by digging a trench in a semi-circle round the tree on the side away from the wall – in a radius of about five feet from the stem. This should reveal the active growing tips of the roots, which you then leave exposed to air and elements until they are thoroughly dead. You then refill the trench and repeat the same exhausting operation a few years later. Paving slabs really repay the work you put into them far better.

The main problem with these trees is that they blossom

before there are enough bees about to pollinate them. To overcome this it is worth dusting pollen from one flower to another with a camel-hair brush. Late frost can kill blossoms which have set, thereby depriving you of a fine crop. So watch the weather closely, and if frosts are threatened, even light ones, cover the whole plant up with fine gauge plastic netting or muslin: this will keep frost off very effectively. Later in the season, you will need some sort of netting to keep birds away from the fruits. To cope with all the various contingencies needed to bring these fruits to a good harvest, buy a fan-trained tree, and keep it as flat against the wall as you can. And arrange a row of vine eyes in the wall a couple of feet above the tree so that you can use these to hang the frost-proofing or bird-proofing materials on.

THE KITCHEN

by Robin Howe

❧ Globe Artichokes

General Instructions

A native of Europe and North Africa, globe artichokes thrive in many parts of the world, including California where some of the finest artichokes are grown. It has been a favourite vegetable for centuries. Pliny, however, had no use for it, crossly asking people, why pay so much for a dish of thistles, and indeed artichokes are the buds of a thistle. In the seventeenth century in France artichokes enjoyed the reputation of being an aphrodisiac and strolling baskers along the Pont Neuf in Paris had only to mention the name artichoke to evoke a snigger.

Globe artichokes are also called leafy artichokes because of the pointed 'scales' which cover the head-like petals but which are part of the edible plant itself. Artichokes with dark green, sometimes almost purplish, heads vary in size from very large, 10–13 cm (4–5 in) in diameter, to the really tiny. In the larger artichokes there is a choke and this needs some explanation. It is a fine, almost hairy-like growth which would develop into a flower if allowed to do so. It is not edible but it is not at all difficult to remove, either before or after cooking. The really small artichokes are chokeless and are eaten in their entirety. These are usually preserved in oil and used as part of an hors d'oeuvre.

The flavour of the globe artichoke is delicate, almost nutty, but it is an odd fact that it does not go with certain beverages, namely tea and wine. Both lose their flavour altogether when taken with artichokes, indeed, wine takes on a harsh flavour. Ask me not the reason why, I do not know but it is so. I live in an artichoke belt.

To Prepare Globe Artichokes

One large artichoke serves one person but most people can manage two medium heads. Handle with care, many types of artichokes have some nasty prickles. Pull off the really small lower leaves that obviously are not fleshy. Clip off the hooked sharp tips of the leaves with scissors and cut off the top with a sharp knife, this will give the artichokes a neat, rounded appearance. Cut off the stalk close to the base so that the artichoke will rest well on a plate.

Large artichokes, either hot or cold, are served with a sauce and eaten with the fingers. Each leaf is pulled off and dipped in the sauce and the tender, green fleshy end of the leaf eaten. Have a bowl or two on the table to put in discarded leaves. When all the leaves have been stripped off you are left with the fond, plus the choke. Lift up the choke with a fork and discard. Then eat the fond or base with a fork and with a little extra butter poured over it. Some might, like Pliny, think eating artichokes is a tedious operation but it becomes almost a ritual as one progresses.

How to Cook Globe Artichokes

Give the artichoke a good wash under running water. Put with the stalks uppermost into a large pan with boiling, salted water. Add a little lemon juice, not too much or you will ruin the flavour of the artichokes. Cook them from 20 to 45 minutes, according to their size. They are ready when a leaf pulled off comes away easily. Take from the pan with a perforated spoon, make sure all the water has drained off. If to be served hot with a hot butter sauce, serve on individual plates, tilted away from you so that the sauce forms a pool. Or they may be served cooled or even cold with a French dressing or a Hollandaise sauce but made with lemon juice, not vinegar.

In parts of Provençe, also in Liguria, artichokes often are cooked in very little water to which both garlic and olive oil is added. Or, before cooking, olive oil is poured between the leaves. Artichokes take kindly to pressure cooking: small ones take 6 minutes; large 8 to 9.

There are numerous recipes for stuffing artichokes but I feel that artichokes have such a delicate flavour they should be cooked in the most simple way possible.

Boiled Artichokes Cold

Prepare and cook the artichokes as directed. While still hot, separate the leaves a little from the stalk and press down lightly so that when the artichokes are served they have a flower shape. Serve with a Hollandaise sauce.

❀ *Jerusalem Artichokes*

These are members of the sunflower family and it is said they were named 'jerusalem' from the Italian word *girasóle*, meaning sunflower. But this now seems not to have been correct and the reason for its name is as obscure as ever. It was not known in Britain until after Columbus discovered the Americas, for it is a native of Canada and the Mississippi basin. It was cultivated by the natives for its sweet flavour. It has no relationship to the globe artichoke.

Jerusalem artichokes are misshapen tubers with a pleasant flavour and make an interesting change from potatoes, which they resemble although they are much more warty. They are best cooked in their skins after being washed and scrubbed, then the skin peels off easily. Peeling before cooking is a long and tedious business.

Boiled Jerusalem Artichokes

4 servings

1 kg (2¼ lb) artichokes
30 g (1 oz) butter
juice 1 lemon

2 tablespoons finely chopped
    parsley
salt, pepper and cayenne pepper

Wash and gently scrub the artichokes. If young, put into a pan with boiling water (stock or milk if preferred); if old, put into cold water; cook until tender, 20 to 30 minutes. Drain and peel. Return the artichokes to the pan, add the butter, lemon juice, parsley, salt, pepper and a good pinch of cayenne pepper and cook for 5 minutes longer over a gentle heat. Serve hot.

Over-cooking toughens Jerusalem artichokes.

Jerusalem Artichokes au Gratin

4 servings

1 kg (2¼ lb) artichokes	salt and pepper
butter or margarine	finely chopped parsley
fine breadcrumbs	juice ½ lemon

Wash the artichokes, scrubbing well with a soft brush. Cook covered in boiling water, 20 to 30 minutes or until tender. Drain, peel and cut into medium-thick slices. Rub a baking dish generously with butter and sprinkle with breadcrumbs. Add the artichokes, cover with breadcrumbs (if liked, mixed with grated cheese), sprinkle with salt, pepper, parsley and lemon juice, dot with butter and bake in a hot oven (220C, 425F, Mark 7) for about 15 minutes, or until the top is brown.

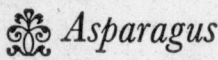 *Asparagus*

General Instructions

Exactly when and how asparagus developed from being a wild vegetable is not precisely known. It is said to have originated in Asia and was an established vegetable in the second century BC. The Greeks, we are told, were the first to use it as a vegetable and its present name stems from the

Greek. The Romans, in their usual manner when they discovered something good to eat, took it over enthusiastically
and cultivated asparagus with much success at Ravenna in
Italy (still today one of the main asparagus producing
centres of Italy). It is claimed they produced stalks weighing
some three pounds each, and we are asked also to believe
that the African variety grown in Libya reached a height
of 3·60 m (12 ft). Whether it was edible is not recorded. In
those days asparagus was considered a cure for several ills
and a preventive for others, especially internal diseases,
although some pronounced it as bad for the eyes.

Before being cultivated, asparagus was a wild plant and
indeed still is in many parts of the Mediterranean where
today it is much appreciated. A variety of wild asparagus
called sprew-grass was found in the woods of the West
Country in recent years and was hawked by peripatetic
costermongers in the streets. But asparagus was not well
known in Britain until some time before the middle of the
eighteenth century. Charles Lamb wrote of asparagus: 'it
still seems to inspire gentle thoughts'. But does it? There is a
fierce controversy between the producers of the green and
white stems, anything but gentle. The white's argument
briefly is that since their asparagus is brought to maturity
underground and prevented from becoming green, its
flavour is milder. Whereas the green's ask, how can anyone
prefer white asparagus to the green which has gained its
delicate flavour from the sun and thus is far more tender?

Asparagus is the stem or shoot of a plant covered with
little scales which are really unopened leaves. As one of my
favourite culinary writers wrote: 'it has got its name among
the lower classes of "sparrow-grass", sometimes even
abbreviated into "grass" and the wild kind is a greater
favourite with them than the cultivated stuff'. Which I
think shows their good taste. As a point of minor interest,
my cook in India who had served many British memsahibs
in his day, always talked of sparrow-grass.

How to Cook Asparagus

Fresh asparagus is brittle with close compact tips. Cut off the woody ends of the stalks leaving 5–8 cm (2–3 in) before the actual tips start; and with a sharp knife scrape the stalks, working downwards. Make certain that all the stalks are of the same length and the tips of an even size. If the asparagus is not even-sized when the stalks are cooked some will be under-cooked, others over-cooked. Carefully wash the asparagus in warm water and gently brush the tips with a soft brush. It is very important that the asparagus should be cooked upright in a pan with the tips at least 2·5 cm (1 in) out of the water to let them cook only in the steam, as asparagus tips require less cooking than the stalks. There are special steamers for cooking asparagus, tall and narrow, containing an inner cylinder into which the asparagus is placed, held as it were in a sort of cage with no danger of falling and, therefore breaking. Water is poured into the main pot, brought to the boil and the cylinder holding the asparagus put into the steamer and hitched on at the sides. The pan is covered and the asparagus cooked for 15 to 20 minutes. By this time the stalks are tender, the tips soft but still firm. If in doubt, test by piercing the tines of a fork into the stalks; if they go in easily, the asparagus is ready. Failing an asparagus pan, tie the stalks into neat bundles and cook them in a tall narrow pan with the tips just above the water. Always handle with care as the tips break off easily.

When serving asparagus hot it must be drained and served the moment it comes from the pan. Serve melted butter separately. Other sauces, such as a *suprème*, Hollandaise or Normandy, also can be served with hot asparagus; cold asparagus, which must be really cold, is served with a salad dressing or a mayonnaise.

It is not easy to say how much asparagus makes one serving. With us greed creeps in and, when in season, we make it a main dish. Asparagus is eaten with the fingers, the tips being dipped into the melted butter or sauce. Only the tips are eaten.

Other methods of serving asparagus are as follows, they do not require precise quantities.

Asparagus with Cheese

A recipe from Milan. Place the stalks of cooked asparagus in a shallow fireproof dish. Cover the tips only with grated cheese and pour melted butter over the top. Brown quickly under a grill and serve at once. Parmesan cheese is the best.

Asparagus and Ham Casserole

Make a thick Béchamel sauce and mix this with finely chopped parsley and chives. Dice some cooked ham and cut cooked asparagus into short lengths. Put a layer of diced ham at the bottom of a casserole, add a layer of sauce then one of asparagus and another of ham, sauce, asparagus and a final layer of sauce. Sprinkle this with fine breadcrumbs or soft breadcrumbs fried in butter and bake in a moderate oven (180C, 350F, Mark 4) until the top bubbles and the crumbs are browned.

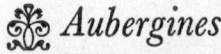 *Aubergines*

General Instructions

Aubergine, eggplant, eggapple, garden egg, *melanzane*, *patliçan* and *brinjal* are some of the names of a fruit which is native to southern Asia but whose exact history is not known. It has been on record for centuries and probably India was its natural habitat although it was known to the Egyptians. The aubergine, one of the great vegetables of the world, can be long and thin like a sausage, pear-shaped, or completely round like a football. It varies in size from the very small to the enormous; in colour from an almost purple black to the palest mauve, or mauve and white striped, even completely white and yellow, although the more usual are the purple varieties. I have only met the white egg-shaped and sized aubergine in India and found them rather dull eating, although piled on a silver dish in a pyramid they made an unusual and attractive centrepiece for the dining table.

The aubergine is one of the most popular vegetables in the Middle East, the Balkans and the Far East, also in France and Italy. It is the subject of many stories, many coming from Turkey, where the aubergine to the Turk is what the potato is to the Britisher, bread to the Frenchman and pasta to the Italian. However, despite this, for a long time the British and Americans would not eat aubergines, claiming they were poisonous or caused insanity. Aubergines are related to the deadly nightshade and thus calumny was poured on them, although no one seemed to have taken into account the fact that thousands of Asians and others, even the Spaniards, had been eating them for centuries without ill effect. In Europe it was the French who, as always intrepid when it came to cooking something new, began to cultivate aubergines in the seventeenth century and it was they who gave them their name, corrupting the Arabic *al-Badindjan.*

How to Cook Aubergines

Augergines can be cooked whole, in their skins, or peeled, or chopped or sliced. They can be boiled, fried and baked.

Because of the aubergine's reputation as a poisoner, began the custom of soaking them in cold water before cooking, or, after slicing, sprinkling the slices with salt and leaving them for about an hour on a tray well covered and weighted. After this the liquid which poured out from the slices was discarded and, it was assumed, the poisons as well. Well, this was not so but it did rid the aubergine of its rather bitter liquid and a considerable quantity of water as well and this was a good thing for, when frying aubergine slices, they then fry crisp on the outside and soft inside, a result which is not achieved when the surplus liquid is allowed to stay in the slices. But the salting is not required for all aubergine recipes as the following recipes will show. Do not use metal with aubergines, it discolours them.

Fried Aubergines

This is a general recipe and preferably oval aubergines should be used. They can be peeled or left with their skins intact. Wipe the aubergines, cut into rounds or slices lengthwise, sprinkle with salt, cover and weigh down and leave for about an hour. Pour off the bitter juices and wipe the slices free of salt. Fry the slices in deep hot oil until brown. Serve hot or cold.

The aubergines can be served with a tomato sauce and sprinkled with grated cheese, or in a favourite way of the Turks, with a garlic-flavoured yogurt sauce, i.e., chilled natural yogurt well laced with crushed garlic. Serve as a main dish at the beginning of a meal, as an hors d'oeuvre.

Stuffed Aubergines

6 servings

6 *large round aubergines*

Stuffing:
450 g (1 *lb*) *minced lamb or mutton*
1 *onion, finely chopped*
85 g (3 *oz*) *uncooked rice*

1 *teaspoon each, finely chopped dill and mint*
1 *tablespoon tomato purée*
salt and pepper

Sauce:
280 ml (½ *pt*) *natural yogurt tomato purée*

Cut off one end from each of the aubergines, scoop out the insides leaving the skins intact. Make the filling. Combine the stuffing ingredients in a bowl and knead well. Push some of this into each aubergine. Put these in an upright position in a baking pan and add enough water to almost cover them. Cook on top of the stove, or in a hot oven (220C, 425F, Mark 7) for about 1 hour, or until the aubergines are soft. Just before they are ready, make a sauce. Combine the yogurt with just enough tomato purée to lightly colour it then add about ½ cup of the liquid from the aubergines.

Serve as a main dish, hot or cold.

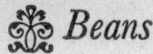 # Beans

General Instructions
It was Alexander the Great who found the bean in India while campaigning. A worthy pupil of Aristotle, he went botanising and came across a field sown with haricot beans. His cook prepared a dish with this, to him, new vegetable and Alexander was so impressed he brought back seeds to Macedonia where it flourished. From here it spread throughout Europe and the rest of the world.

How to Prepare Broad Beans
Broad beans, also called Windsor beans, can be delicious when correctly cooked. In Italy they are often served in their pods and eaten raw, together with a glass of wine. And good they are too. There are three stages when broad beans are edible. First, when the pods are so small the flower has only just withered. At this stage they can be cooked whole and eaten, pod and all. Secondly, when the beans are not much larger than a pea, when they can be cooked in their pods and shucked before serving. Finally, when their pods are really large, when they should be shucked before cooking as their pods have a rather unpleasant flavour.

How to Cook Broad Beans
Broad beans can be cooked in three main ways.
1. Blanch the beans in boiling water for 5 minutes. Drain, pull off the pods and return the beans to the pan in just enough boiling salted water to cover. Continue cooking until tender, about 10 minutes.
2. Cook the beans in their pods in boiling salted water until they are quite tender and the pods begin to show definite signs of loosening.
3. Shuck the beans before cooking.

All three methods have their fierce adherents. However, it is generally agreed that broad beans, like so many vegetables, should not be prepared until just ready to be cooked as they lose flavour quickly, hence the reason for cooking them in their pods.

Broad beans are usually cooked and served with their skins or envelopes, but many cooks are emphatically against this. Perhaps a compromise is the best. Certainly, when the beans are young they need no shucking for much of the flavour lies near the skin. When the beans are elderly and shucked, drop them for a minute or so into boiling water, drain and their skins will come off as easily as almond skin.

Then put them into boiling water and cook until tender, time depending on their age, 15 to 20 minutes. Drain well and return to the pan to dry with a knob of butter; when this has melted, serve the beans in the butter with, if liked, a sprinkling of finely chopped parsley, but better still with summer savory. You can also add a squeeze of lemon juice immediately before serving.

Purée of Broad Beans

3–4 servings

heart 1 *lettuce*	1 *onion, chopped*
450 g (1 *lb*) *broad beans, after shucking*	30 g (1 *oz*) *butter or margarine*
	salt and pepper
450 g (1 *lb*) *peas, after shucking*	1 *teaspoon sugar*
	2 *tablespoons cream (optional)*

Wash the lettuce, separate the leaves and break into small pieces. Put the beans, peas, lettuce and onion into a pan and cook in a little boiling salted water until very tender. Drain and rub through a vegetable mill. Dry the pan, return the vegetable purée to it and, stirring all the time, cook until it begins to thicken. Cut the butter into small pieces and add to the pan together with the salt, pepper and sugar. Stir and cook until the butter is blended into the purée. Just before

serving, add the cream, give the purée one good final whisk
and serve hot with sippets of fried bread.

This recipe is suitable for old broad beans and peas, thus
it is easier to shuck them before cooking. Ingredients are
approximate: it is really a recipe for using up small quantities and can be adjusted at will.

Boiled and Buttered Broad Beans

4 servings

2 *teaspoons salt*	*finely chopped parsley or other*
2 *kg (4½ lb) young broad beans*	*sweet herb*
60 *g (2 oz) butter or margarine*	

Put the salt into a pan with enough water to come up about
4 cm (1½ in) and bring to the boil. Stir to dissolve the salt,
add the beans and cook until tender, if young they will take
only 10 to 15 minutes. If still in their pods, peel these off.
Drain well, their liquid can be used in a stock or a sauce.
Return the beans to the pan, add the butter, cut into small
pieces, and continue cooking only long enough to allow the
butter to melt. Add salt and parsley, or other green herbs
such as summer savory, but if the latter it must be very
finely chopped.

Broad Beans with a Wine Sauce

4 servings

2 *kg (4½ lb) young broad beans*	15 *g (½ oz) butter*
60 *g (2 oz) butter or margarine*	15 *g (½ oz) flour*
1 *small onion, chopped*	*hot stock or water*
a little diced ham	140 *ml (¼ pt) sweet white wine*
finely chopped summer savory	2 *tablespoons sugar*

It may seem extravagant to use wine for cooking beans (one
could use cider instead) but tender fresh broad beans do
deserve special attention.

Blanch the beans in slightly salted water, drain, and pull

off the pods. Melt the first quantity of butter in a large pan, add the onion and simmer until it changes colour. Add the beans together with the ham and savory. Cook gently. Knead the second quantity of butter with the flour and add this to the pan bit by bit until it has blended in. Add the stock and continue cooking for 10 minutes, then add the wine and sugar and stir gently until the beans are very tender and the sauce hot.

Serve as a main dish.

How to Prepare French Beans

French beans are also called dwarf, kidney or snap beans and should be picked when very young, 8–10 cm (3–4 in) in length. If kept too long on the plant they are usually tough and stringy. Smaller and more delicate in flavour than the runner bean, they need only to be topped and tailed, and snapped in the middle, although beans 8 cm (3 in) long can be served whole. When young, French beans can be eaten pods and beans together, but when mature the pods should be shucked and the beans cooked alone. To be eaten with the pods they should be round and not show much, if any, of the bean inside. A really good bean is crisp, fleshy and practically without strings.

How to Prepare Runner Beans

Also called scarlet runners and string beans, runner beans are by nature larger, longer, wider and stronger in flavour than the French or haricot beans and, oddly, sometimes grow as long as 30 cm (1 ft) without becoming tough and still make good eating. Young beans should be rather flat without showing much sign of the beans inside, fleshy and without strings, firm and crisp. To prepare, it is enough to snip off tops and tails, as with French beans, and either cook whole or broken into suitable lengths. When beans are large and rather coarse, they must be topped and tailed and run down each side with a sharp knife to remove the strings, then sliced diagonally (there are many types of bean slicers which do this job rapidly and well) and cooked in boiling salted water. In this way their flavour loses some of its strength which, to some people, is unpleasantly strong. Instead of boiling beans, they can be steamed.

Fresh runner beans hardly need more than just salt and pepper for seasoning, plus a knob of butter and a sprinkling of chopped fresh herbs such as parsley, summer savory or tarragon. A sliver of garlic cooked with the beans also adds an intangible extra flavour. However, when there are beans in plenty and they are getting a little older, other methods of cooking are welcome if only to avoid monotony.

Boiled Runner or French Beans

6 servings

1 *kg* (2¼ *lb*) *runner beans*   30 *g* (1 *oz*) *butter or margarine*
1–2 *teaspoons salt*

Wash the beans, top and tail and cook them whole or snapped into halves if young, slice diagonally if old. Bring 3 cm (1 in) of water to the boil in a pan, add salt, then the beans, cover the pan and cook rapidly until the beans are just tender. Drain thoroughly, return to the pan with the butter, continue to cook until the butter is melted and toss gently. Serve hot.

Steamed Runner or French Beans

4 servings

30 *g* (1 *oz*) *butter or margarine*   450 *g* (1 *lb*) *runner beans*

Melt the butter in a pan which has a tight fitting lid. Trim the beans as directed, keep whole, add them to the pan, cover tightly and cook over a low flame until tender, 15 minutes or so, shaking the pan from time to time to prevent sticking.

French Beans in a Parsley Butter Sauce

4–6 servings

1 *kg* (2¼ *lb*) *French beans*   1 *tablespoon finely chopped*
85 *g* (3 *oz*) *butter*   *parsley*
salt and pepper

For this recipe the beans are best left whole, but if too long they can be broken into halves. Top and tail the beans and cook in boiling salted water until tender, about 20 minutes. Drain well and pat dry. Heat the butter in the same pan, return the beans and cook for a few minutes. Shake the pan from time to time to coat the beans with butter. Add salt, pepper and parsley to taste and serve the beans hot in their butter sauce.

This is a French method of cooking beans and usually they are served as a separate dish.

French Beans in Cream

4–6 servings

1 *kg* (2¼ *lb*) *French beans*   280 *ml* (½ *pt*) *single cream*
85 *g* (3 *oz*) *butter*   *salt, pepper and nutmeg*

Prepare and cook the beans as directed in the previous recipe until drained and dried. Heat the butter in the same pan, add the beans and simmer for 5 minutes. In a separate small pan scald the cream, do not let it boil, pour this at once over the simmering beans, add salt, pepper and nutmeg to taste, stir gently to blend in the cream and serve at once, preferably as a separate dish.

French Beans Portuguese Style

4–6 servings

1 *kg* (2¼ *lb*) *beans*	2 *tablespoons olive oil*
340 *g* (12 *oz*) *peeled and de-seeded tomatoes*	280 *ml* (½ *pt*) *hot stock*
	salt
85 *g* (3 *oz*) *diced fat bacon*	*finely chopped parsley*

Wash and prepare the beans as directed. Cut the tomatoes into chunks. Cook the bacon in a casserole with the oil for a few minutes, add the beans and tomatoes, stir well, then add the stock. Add salt and cook slowly for about 20 minutes, or until the beans are tender. Serve very hot as a main dish, sprinkled with parsley.

The beans look their best if served in a rustic-style pottery dish. Crisp young runner beans, snapped into halves, can be cooked in the same manner.

Runner Beans with a Mustard Dressing

4 servings

450 *g* (1 *lb*) *runner beans*	140 *ml* (¼ *pt*) *milk, scalded*
1 *egg yolk, lightly beaten*	2 *teaspoons mild vinegar*
1 *teaspoon prepared English mustard*	15 *g* (½ *oz*) *butter or margarine*
	salt and pepper

Older beans can be cooked in this fashion. Top, tail and string the beans and slice diagonally. Cook in a little salted boiling water until tender. Make the sauce. Beat the yolk with the mustard in the top of a double boiler, add the scalded milk, stirring all the time. Place over hot but not boiling water and cook, stirring constantly until the mixture thickens. Drain the beans thoroughly, add to the pan, stir in the vinegar, butter, salt and pepper and continue to cook for a minute or so. The sauce should be slightly curdled. Serve very hot, either as an accompaniment to meat or with fried bread sippets as a main dish.

Runner Beans au Gratin

6 servings

1 kg (2¼ lb) young runner beans	salt and nutmeg to taste
butter for greasing	2 egg yolks
420 ml (¾ pt) milk	140 ml (¼ pt) single cream
60 g (2 oz) butter or margarine	3 tablespoons grated cheese
60 g (2 oz) flour	

Prepare and cook the beans as directed, either whole or snapped into halves. Drain when tender and leave to cool. Rub a baking dish generously with butter, add the beans and put aside until required. Scald the milk. Melt the butter, add the flour and stir well to make a roux. Gradually add the milk and stir fairly vigorously until the sauce thickens. Add salt and nutmeg, stir well, lower the heat and cook gently for 10 minutes, stirring frequently. Lightly beat the yolks into the cream. Take the pan from the stove and beat the egg and cream mixture into it, then return to the stove and, stirring gently, continue to cook gently for a minute or so. Add the cheese, stir well and pour the sauce over the beans, spreading it all over. Put into a hot oven (220C, 425F, Mark 7) and cook until the top is browned.

French beans can be cooked in the same way.

 *Beetroots*

General Instructions

This homely and generally popular vegetable, which seems to be with us all the year round in some form or other, was well known to the ancients and we find considerable mention of it in Greek and Roman writings. Apicius gave a number of recipes for its cooking, usually combining it with leeks and cooking it in a gravy with raisin wine and strong flavourings. Beet leaves were said to have been served on a silver platter to the god Apollo by the Greeks when paying him homage. But the type of beet leaves used were not quite the same as those we know today.

The beetroot is a member of the plant of the genus *Beta* of which there are several varieties including the mangel-wurzel, an unpopular vegetable if ever there was one, white beet, which is used for the manufacture of sugar, and the so-called sea-beet, the leaves of which are cooked as spinach.

How to Cook Beetroots

Beetroots can be boiled or baked, the latter produces the best flavoured beetroot but it is a long expensive process unless you own a solid fuel stove. To bake beets they must be carefully washed and put into a moderate oven (180C, 350F, Mark 4) on a grid. Bake until tender; time will depend on their size but even the smallest take quite a long time. In Italy they bake beets in hot embers and they develop a thick ash-encrusted skin and have an earthy flavour. Beetroots lose their colour if peeled before cooking. To boil, they must be washed carefully in order that the skin is not broken, the tops removed leaving about 5 cm (2 in) of the stems, and dropped into fast boiling water, lightly acidulated with lemon juice or vinegar, and cooked until tender, 30 to 40 minutes for small beetroots, up to 2 hours if really large. Or they can be cooked in a pressure cooker in 10 to 40 minutes, again depending on size. To make sure the beetroots are tender before removing them from the water, pinch the skin with your fingers; if it comes off easily, they are ready. Do not on any account test with a fork as this will make them bleed and lose colour. When tender, take the beetroots from the pan, plunge into cold water and peel them with the fingers, not with a knife.

Beetroot tops

When young and garden fresh these tops have a mild and agreeable flavour which is lost when the leaves are older, when their flavour is too strong for most people. They should be washed and cooked like spinach, that is, cooking them only in the water which adheres to their leaves after washing.

Beetroots in an Orange Sauce

4 servings

3 tablespoons grated orange rind
2 tablespoons lemon juice
salt, pepper and nutmeg
1 dessertspoon flour
3 tablespoons sherry

30 g (1 oz) butter or margarine
½ cup warm stock or water
450 g (1 lb) cooked beetroots, cubed
finely chopped parsley

Mix the orange rind and lemon juice, add salt, pepper and nutmeg then stir in the flour. Blend to a smooth paste then add the sherry. Cook gently in a shallow pan until the mixture thickens. Add the butter. When this has melted, gradually stir in the stock, add the beetroots and reheat, coating them with the sauce. Serve in a hot serving dish sprinkled with parsley.

Serve with duck, hare or other game meats. Small whole beetroots also may be cooked in this fashion.

Beetroots in a Piquant Sauce

4 servings

60 g (2 oz) butter or margarine
1 coffeespoon dry mustard
3 tablespoons tarragon vinegar
½ teaspoon sugar
blade of mace
2 tablespoons minced onion

1 tablespoon finely chopped parsley
2 teaspoons Worcestershire Sauce
450 g (1 lb) cooked hot beetroots, cubed
finely chopped chives or dill

Heat the butter, add the remaining ingredients (except the beetroots and chives) and bring gently to the boil. Add the beetroots, stir well until coated with the sauce. Discard the mace and turn the beetroots into a hot serving dish. Sprinkle with chives.

Beetroots with Horseradish Sauce

4 servings

450 g (1 *lb*) *small beetroots*
15 g (½ *oz*) *butter or margarine*
280 *ml* (½ *pt*) *white or Béchamel sauce*

1 *tablespoon freshly grated horseradish*
salt and pepper
1–2 *tablespoons double cream*

Prepare and cook the beetroots as directed. When they are cooked, plunge for a moment or so into cold water and pull off the skins with the fingers. Return the beetroots to the pan with the butter and gently reheat. Mix the sauce with the horseradish, salt, pepper and cream. Put the beetroots into a hot serving dish and pour the sauce over them. Finely chopped parsley may be sprinkled over the top.

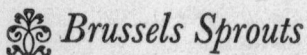 *Brussels Sprouts*

General Instructions

'Sprouts', as they are popularly called in Britain, are among the green vegetable favourites, not only in Britain but also in France and Belgium. They are a variety of cabbage and were introduced into Britain by the Belgians in the nineteenth century and have flourished in kitchen gardens ever since. Like miniature cabbages, sprouts have neither a heart, like the cabbage, nor a head, like the cauliflower. In France sprouts are tiny, of a quality and delicacy not always found in Britain where there is a tendency to grow them

larger. However, if allowed to become too large they become
rather coarse both in texture and flavour but still can be
made into a very acceptable dish of purée (p. 158). Brussels
sprouts have a pleasant nutty flavour and when picking
them try to choose sprouts all of approximately the same
size so that they will cook in the same time.

Quantities. Allow 225 g (8 oz) sprouts per serving.

How to Cook Brussels Sprouts

Cut off any spoiled or discoloured outside leaves. Make a
small incision in the stump of each in the shape of an x or v.
This ensures that the leaves and stump will cook in the same
time. Wash the sprouts in plenty of cold water, put into a
colander and pour boiling water over them. Then cook in
fast boiling, salted water for 10 minutes. They must never
be over-cooked. Drain thoroughly. Return to the pan, add
salt, pepper and a small knob of butter or margarine, mix
well and serve as soon as the butter has melted. Or drain
and serve in a hot dish and pour melted butter over the top.

Brussels Sprouts with a Cheese Sauce

4–6 servings

1 kg (2¼ lb) cooked sprouts   grated cheese
280 ml (½ pt) white sauce   paprika pepper to taste

After cooking and draining the sprouts as directed, pile them
loosely in a fireproof vegetable dish, mask with the sauce,
sprinkle generously with grated cheese and brown under a
hot grill. Just before serving, sprinkle with paprika pepper.

Choose a hard piquant cheese for this recipe.

Brussels Sprouts Sautéed in Butter

4–6 servings

1 kg (2¼ lb) cooked Brussels   30 g (1 oz) butter or margarine
  sprouts   salt and pepper

Melt the butter in a pan large enough for all the sprouts to lie on the bottom. Add the sprouts and cook quickly, turning them occasionally until they are lightly browned. Add salt and pepper. Serve very hot with the remainder of the fat sprinkled over them.

To serve as a main dish, garnish with fried bread sippets.

Brussels Sprouts with Bacon

4–6 servings

30 g (1 oz) *butter or margarine*
1 kg (2¼ lb) *cooked Brussels sprouts*

110 g (4 oz) *fairly fat bacon rashers*

Melt the butter in a pan, add the sprouts and cook until they are lightly browned. Fry the bacon until crisp. Pile the sprouts on to a hot serving dish (it must be very hot), surround with bacon and, at the last moment, pour the butter from the sprouts over the top.

Fried triangles of bread may be served as a garnish.

Purée of Brussels Sprouts

4–6 servings

450 g (1 lb) *Brussels sprouts*
250 g (9 oz) *floury potatoes, mashed*

15 g (½ oz) *butter or margarine*
1 *egg yolk, well beaten*
fried bread sippets

A useful recipe for large, over-blown sprouts. Prepare and cook them as directed. Drain thoroughly and finely chop. Cook and mash the potatoes as directed on page 221. Combine the two ingredients and return to the pan. Add the butter, blend this well into the purée, then, beat in the egg yolk. When the purée is thoroughly reheated, pile on to a hot serving dish and serve at once, garnished with fried bread sippets.

❧ Cabbages and Kale

General Instructions

The cabbage, a most common vegetable, belongs to one of
the hundred varieties of *Brassica oleracea* and therefore is
related to Brussels sprouts, cauliflower, spring greens,
turnips and kohlrabi. It is a reliable vegetable and one of
the oldest known. It was probably cultivated in Britain in
the Middle Ages by the monks in monastery kitchen gardens,
and in a fifteenth century manuscript we read: 'Take
cabaches and cut hom on foure . . . and let hit boyle'. But
the cabbage is far more ancient than this. The ancient
Egyptians so adored the cabbage they raised altars to it and
then made this odd god a first dish to a meal. The Greeks
and Romans ascribed to it the quality of preventing drunkenness, while Erasistratus, founder of a school of medicine on
Samos, was certain it cured paralysis. Apicius included a
number of cabbage recipes in his book and it is reported
that the Emperor Tiberius chided his son for not eating
enough cabbage. Cato was convinced that not only did
cabbage prevent drunkenness but also saved his family from
the plague. The poor cabbage down through the centuries
had come to a pretty pass as when, given as an example of
Beau Brummell's wit, asked why he did not marry a girl to
whom he had been more than attentive, replied: 'My dear
fellow, the thing was impossible. What could I do? I found
that she actually ate cabbage'. Ah well, maybe if the Beau
had eaten cabbage, and married, he would have come to a
better end.

A keen gardener, Sir Arthur Ashley of Dorset, in about
1510 introduced cabbage into his own garden and, therefore, into England; it was a hard cabbage and came from
Holland. Incidentally, the cabbage was taken to Scotland
by Cromwell's soldiers.

There are several types of cabbage and recipes for them

can be applied to all. But generally cabbages fall into two main classes, those with smooth and those with curled leaves. There are spring, summer and winter cabbages. They are versatile in the extreme and can be eaten raw, cooked or pickled.

In Britain the cabbage is one of the most maligned and badly cooked of our vegetables, which is a pity for when correctly dealt with it is most palatable indeed. By nature the cabbage is a watery vegetable and care must be taken in its cooking.

How to Cook Cabbage

Remove the coarse outer leaves and thick stump and cut the cabbage into quarters. Cut away any excessively thick stalks and wash the cabbage thoroughly. Have ready a pan with fast boiling salted water, add the cabbage, one chunk at a time otherwise the water will go off the boil, and cook the cabbage until tender, 15 to 20 minutes. It must still be crisp. Drain well. The cabbage is now ready for serving or for further treatment. It can be returned to the pan and gently simmered for a few moments in butter, either in its chunks, or cut into serving portions, or coarsely chopped.

Some people complain that cabbage smells when being cooked. Well, you can try putting slices of stale bread on top of the cabbage while it is cooking, or tie bits of stale crusts in cheesecloth and put in the pot. I am not sure that these remedies really help but then I do not find cabbage smells enough to fuss about.

To cook cabbage ahead of time, cook as directed but, after draining, leave the cabbage in the colander, put aside and let it become cold. It can be reheated in butter later and to advantage. If the cabbage is kept for any length of time, then it really will develop an unpleasant odour.

Gross weight per portion: as an average, allow 225 g (8 oz) of spring cabbage and 170 g (6 oz) of winter.

Small Spring Cabbages Cooked Whole

There are no set quantities for this recipe.

Wash the cabbages, remove any bruised leaves and trim the stump end. Make a cross on the stump end with a knife, drop into boiling salted water and cook until just tender, even slightly underdone. Drain well. Return the cabbages to the pan with just enough water to cover the bottom, put a small knob of butter on each. Cover with buttered paper, then the lid and cook over a low heat until the cabbages are warmed through and tender. Turn out on to a hot dish, sprinkle lightly with finely chopped parsley or chives.

Savoy Cabbage au Gratin

4–6 servings

1 *savoy cabbage* – 1 *kg* (2¼ *lb*)   *salt and pepper*
butter   *sour cream or yogurt*
chopped cooked pork or other   *fine breadcrumbs*
  white meat

Prepare and cook the cabbage as directed. After draining chop coarsely. Rub a deep baking dish with butter and spread with a layer of chopped cabbage, sprinkle with meat, salt, pepper and sour cream (quantities to taste). Repeat these layers, making the top layer cabbage. Sprinkle lightly with breadcrumbs and slivers of butter. Bake in a moderate oven (180C, 350F, Mark 4) for about 30 minutes.

Any type of cabbage can be cooked in this manner.

Braised Cabbage

4–6 servings

1 *kg* (2¼ *lb*) *cabbage*   1 *small onion, finely chopped*
15 *g* (½ *oz*) *butter or margarine*   *salt, pepper and paprika pepper*
a few rashers streaky bacon,   ½ *cup stock or water*
  chopped   *fried sippets of bread*

Prepare the cabbage as directed. Cook in boiling salted water for 10 minutes. Drain thoroughly and chop. Put aside.

Heat the butter in a casserole, add the bacon and onion and fry until the onion begins to change colour; then add the cabbage, seasonings and stock. Cover and bake in a moderate oven (180C, 350F, Mark 4) for about 20 minutes, or continue cooking on top of the stove. Serve in the dish in which it has been cooked, garnished with the fried sippets of bread.

Creamed Cabbage

4–6 servings

1 kg (2¼ lb) cooked cabbage   salt, pepper and paprika pepper
60 g (2 oz) butter or margarine   2 eggs, well beaten
½ cup cream or top of milk

A good way in which to use up cold cooked cabbage.

Make sure the cabbage is completely drained. Heat the butter in a shallow fireproof dish, add the cream, salt, pepper and paprika pepper. Stir well, add the cabbage and stir over a moderate heat until the mixture is well blended. Add the eggs, stir lightly and either put the cabbage into a hot oven (220C, 425F, Mark 7), or under a grill to brown the top.

Serve hot with cold meats.

'Instant' Sauerkraut

4–6 servings

1 kg (2¼ lb) hard white cabbage   280 ml (½ pt) clear stock or
5 tablespoons oil   water
salt and pepper   140 ml (¼ pt) mild vinegar

Prepare the cabbage as directed and shred. Heat the oil in a large pan, add the shredded cabbage, salt and pepper, stir well and cook over a low heat until the cabbage is very tender, adding stock from time to time. Towards the end of cooking time, add the vinegar, stir well, cook for a further 5 minutes and serve hot.

This 'instant' sauerkraut recipe comes from northern Italy and usually is served with boiled meats and sausages. It has a pleasant, milder flavour than the usual sauerkraut.

Cabbage Alsacienne

4–6 servings

1 *hard white cabbage* – 1 *kg*   140 *ml* ($\frac{1}{4}$ *pt*) *dry white wine*
  (2$\frac{1}{4}$ *lb*), *shredded*   *salt and pepper*
30 *g* (1 *oz*) *butter or margarine*   *finely chopped parsley*
1 *small head celery, shredded*

Drop the cabbage into a pan of boiling salted water and cook for 3 minutes. Drain well. Melt the butter in a small pan, add the celery and simmer for 3 minutes. Add the cabbage, stir to mix, then add the wine, sprinkle with salt and pepper, cover the pan and cook gently until the cabbage is tender, 25 to 30 minutes. Add parsley when serving.

Serve with frankfurter sausages, also with boiled pork, etc. Failing wine, use dry cider or wine vinegar combined with a clear stock.

Cole-Slaw

6 servings

This is an American recipe and I am giving the measurements in cups. Whether a British or American cup is used is of no matter provided the same cup is used throughout. It is simpler when measuring small quantities. This salad, which owes its name to the Dutch from the time they took over Manhattan Island (*Kool*, cabbage and *sla*, salad), is now popular throughout the world and has numerous variations. It is easy to prepare and can be used as an accompaniment to many cold dishes.

1 *medium-sized hard head
  white cabbage*
⅓ *cup tarragon vinegar*
2 *tablespoons vinegar*
*salt, pepper and paprika pepper
  to taste*

*diced red and green sweet pepper
  (optional)*
¼ *cup each double cream and
  mayonnaise*

Prepare the cabbage as directed, shred it finely and leave in iced water for 30 minutes. Drain and dry thoroughly. Drop into a bowl, add the vinegar, sugar, salt, pepper and paprika pepper. Toss well then leave for 1 hour. Drain again and gently squeeze to remove any surplus liquid. Add the sweet pepper. Whip the cream and mix into the mayonnaise. Pour this over the cabbage, toss lightly but thoroughly and serve.

RED CABBAGE

General Instructions
A variant of the cabbage family, grown in Britain but usually prepared and eaten as a pickle. On the Continent and very much so in Holland, Germany, Austria and Hungary, however, it is cooked and served as it should be, as a vegetable in its own right. In the USA it is also served as a vegetable, either to accompany meat dishes or as a main dish.

Cooked Red Cabbage
4–6 servings

1 *kg (2¼ lb) red cabbage*
60 *g (2 oz) lard, pork or other
  fat*
2 *medium-sized tart apples*

salt and pepper
1 *tablespoon brown sugar*
nutmeg
2 *tablespoons vinegar*

Trim the cabbage, removing any bruised leaves and wash in salted, acidulated water. Cut into four and trim off any hard stalks or stumps. Drop the cabbage into a pan of boiling water and cook for 10 minutes. Drain, rinse in cold water, drain and shred. Heat the fat in a large saucepan. Peel and coarsely chop the apples. Spread a layer of shredded cabbage in the pan, then a layer of apples, sprinkle with salt, pepper, sugar, nutmeg and vinegar. Repeat these layers until all the ingredients are in the pan. Cook over a low heat until the cabbage is very tender, 1 to 1½ hours. Stir well from time to time. The cabbage can be served at once or left and reheated next day – many people prefer the reheated cabbage as it gains in flavour by being left.

Serve with boiled bacon, fried sausages or frankfurters, boiled or roast pork, goose, duck, hare, ham or pork chops.

KALE

General Instructions

A hardy member of the *Brassica* family, often known as winter greens, also borecole, which is the anglicized version of the Dutch *boerenkool*, or peasant's cabbage. It is one of the earliest vegetables known to the British and has always been popular with country people, especially the curly kale with its curled, crimped leaves. The kales have recently taken on a new turn with the cultivation of new varieties, as those with purple or silver leaves. These, although edible, also are used for floral decoration. Although kale is considered mainly as a winter vegetable, the young and tender shoots which branch freely in spring are much more delicate in flavour and more tender. Kale can be used in much the same manner as spinach or cabbage.

How to Cook Kale

Kale is cooked by stripping the leaves from the stems. Young leaves can be cooked whole, older leaves should be chopped. It is important not to over-cook kale as this destroys its flavour. It can be plainly boiled with salt and pepper, creamed, or cooked with salt pork and bacon, as are turnip tops.

Buttered Kale

4 servings

1 *kg* (2¼ *lb*) *kale*
420 *ml* (¾ *pt*) *boiling salted water*

45 *g* (1½ *oz*) *butter or margarine*
nutmeg, salt and pepper

Trim off the roots, pick over the leaves and wash thoroughly. Drop into a pan with the boiling salted water, cover and cook for 25 minutes, or until tender. Drain well, as you do for spinach, and finely chop. Return to a dry pan, add the butter, nutmeg, salt and pepper and cook until the butter has melted.

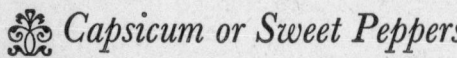

❧ *Capsicum or Sweet Peppers*

General Instructions

Capsicums or sweet peppers are of tropical American origin although they were widely cultivated in Europe before they became cultivated in the United States, having been left in their wild state. Botanically they are not related to the pepper we grind. The species include many assorted peppers, some which grow up to 25 cm (10 in) long and correspondingly swollen. The fruit varies also in shape, from long to narrow and to almost spherical; they also differ widely in colour, from green, which are the more immature peppers

although ready for eating and cooking, through to brilliant
reds and bright yellows and even variegated colours. Most
of the large peppers are indeed sweet, although from time
to time one can get a shock. Sweet peppers of all colours
can be used in salads, casseroles, stews, stuffed, used in
sauce and pickled.

How to Prepare Sweet Peppers

Cut off the stem ends and then cut through the ribs with a
sharp knife and remove the core and seeds. These are hot
and should you get any on your fingers don't put them into
your mouth, you will get a nasty shock. If you want sweet
pepper rings, cut across the peppers; if strips, cut into half
and again in half and slice lengthwise to the size required.

Peppers for Salads

Wipe the peppers with a damp cloth, spear on to a long
fork, i.e., toasting fork, and hold over a gas flame until the
outside is burnt and blistered. Take from the heat, pull off
the thin skin and as quickly as possible wipe lightly, cut into
slices and drop into a salad dressing. The peppers also can
be burnt in a very hot oven, or under a grill. Serve cool or
chilled.

Stuffed Peppers

4 servings

4 *sweet peppers*	2 *cloves garlic, finely chopped*
225 g (8 oz) *cooked minced*	1–2 *sprigs parsley, chopped*
meat	1–2 *eggs*
85 g (3 oz) *sausage meat*	*salt and pepper*
2 *tablespoons grated cheese*	*oil*

Choose well shaped, medium-sized peppers for this dish.
Slice off the stem ends and discard cores and seeds as
directed. Put the tops aside. Combine the two meats, cheese,
garlic and parsley, bind with the egg(s), add salt and pepper
and fill each pepper with some of the mixture. Sprinkle

with a little oil, cover the tops and bake in the oven (180C, 350F, Mark 4), or cook on top of the stove in a baking pan with enough hot water to come half-way up the sides of the peppers. With a moderate heat they will take about 45 minutes to cook until tender but firm.

Peppers with Bacon

4 servings

4 *sweet peppers*	1 *small onion, sliced*
85 g (3 oz) *pork fat or lard*	85 g (3 oz) *lean bacon, diced*

Prepare the peppers as for salads, cutting them into wide slices. Heat the pork fat, add the onion and fry until a golden colour, add the bacon, let this brown, add the peppers and cook over a moderate heat until they are soft.

Sautéed Peppers

Prepare the peppers as directed and cut into rings. Heat a little olive oil in a heavy pan, add some slivers of garlic and fry until they begin to change colour. Take from the pan before they brown, otherwise they will give the oil a bitter flavour. Add the peppers, stir well, lower the heat and simmer until they are tender and crisp, 10 to 15 minutes. To test, pierce with the tip of a small sharp knife. Serve hot sprinkled with salt and pepper.

Can be served with grilled meats, also with cold meats.

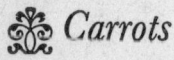 *Carrots*

General Instructions

One of our brightest looking and commonest vegetables, the carrot is of ancient lineage, originally coming from the East. It first emigrated to Europe in France in the days of

Charlemagne where it flourished, but did not reach England until the end of the sixteenth century, coming via Flanders and France. It is an attractive vegetable with a sweet flesh and a pretty foliage. We read that the ladies of the Court of Charles I used to wear the foliage as a decoration instead of feathers. Pliny wrote of the carrot: 'They cultivate a plant in Suri like wild carrot and of the same properties which is eaten raw and cooked, and is of great service as a stomachic'. Its properties linger on, for in the days of the last war it was said to assist pilots to see better in the dark. There are ancient Chinese and Japanese references to carrots but curiously no Indian records until 1826. Apicius mentioned carrots in his Roman cookbook and gave recipes for fried carrots, as well as carrots cooked with parsnips, which is surprising for today neither the Italians nor the French consider parsnips as food for humans.

Carrots are grown for their roots which vary in size, some are long and tapering, others short and rounded; some are bright red in colour, others yellow, some almost transparent. They can be prepared in a variety of ways, as a vegetable plain and simple, boiled, baked, fried, mashed, whole or sliced – and eaten raw, what better way when they are straight from the garden. Rabbits are no fools. And carrots can be made into sweet puddings of several kinds, baked and boiled, and into a cake. Generally speaking the deeper the red of the carrot the better its flavour. Incidentally, those small round carrots have no core, as the long carrots do when they are old.

Preparation and Cooking

Cut off the foliage and any green part at the root end. Wash and scrape, even old carrots should be scraped and not peeled. Very young carrots need only to be scrubbed. Like most vegetables, carrots are better steamed than boiled. It takes longer to steam but the results are worth it. Garden carrots are rarely left so long that they become hard-cored, but should such a thing happen, then cut them in half and remove the hard core. Old carrots also should be given a

previous blanching by dropping them into a pan with cold
water and brought to the boil and boiled for 5 to 15 minutes,
according to the age of the carrots. Garden fresh tiny carrots, after being washed and their skins rubbed off and
trimmed are best cooked whole, preferably steamed, or
boiled in just enough water to cook them and with a good
pat of butter and a sprinkling of finely chopped parsley,
plus a pinch of sugar and salt. Young carrots should not take
more than 20 minutes to cook uncovered. If in a hurry,
older carrots, after being blanched, can be shredded and
steamed. It is a pleasant way of dealing with them.

Quantities. Allow 110–170 g (4–6 oz) per serving.

Carrots Flemish Style

4 servings

450 g (1 lb) young carrots	salt and pepper
30 g (1 oz) butter or margarine	1 teaspoon sugar
2–3 shallots, thinly sliced	vinegar

Since we are told the Flemings brought carrots to Britain,
we should include a recipe named after them, although there
are several versions of this particular recipe. This is auth-
entic in that it comes from a Belgian.

Wash and scrape the carrots and drop them into boiling
water for 5 minutes, not a minute longer, then drain well.
Heat the butter in a pan, add the carrots, shallots, a pinch
of salt and pepper, sugar and a dash of vinegar. Cook over a
low heat until the carrots are tender; the time will depend
on the carrots but at least 30 minutes, if not a little longer.
Serve hot in their sauce.

Carrots with Fresh Herbs

4 servings

2 tablespoons finely chopped fresh herbs	15 g (½ oz) softened butter
	450 g (1 lb) buttered carrots

Mix the herbs into the butter, which does not require to be absolutely melted. Add the carrots, lightly toss in the herb butter and serve at once. Parsley, chervil, chives and mint go well with carrots.

Creamed Carrots

4 servings

280 ml (½ pt) single cream   *herb butter as in previous recipe*
450 g (1 lb) buttered carrots

Gently scald the cream in a small pan and pour it over the carrots while they are still in the pan. With the pan uncovered keep the mixture gently bubbling, stirring gently from time to time until all the liquid has been absorbed. Prepare a herb butter and add to the carrots immediately before serving, gently shaking the pan to disperse the herb butter. Serve hot as a side dish to meat, or with a mixture of other vegetables.

Carrots Vichy

6 servings

1 kg (2¼ lb) young carrots   1 tablespoon finely chopped
60 g (2 oz) butter   parsley
15 g (½ oz) sugar

Rub the carrots with a damp cloth, cut into thin strips and put into a thick saucepan with the butter, sugar, salt and just enough water to cover; some recipes suggest Vichy water, some none at all. Cover the pan, bring the carrots gently to the boil, lower the heat and cook gently until they are tender and no liquid is left in the pan. Shake the pan from time to time to avoid sticking or scorching, carrots scorch quickly. When the carrots are ready they should be a golden brown colour and soft. Sprinkle with parsley before serving.

Marinated Carrots as an Hors d'Oeuvre

4 servings

1 *cup water*	1 *small stalk celery*
½ *cup dry white wine*	2 *sprigs parsley*
5 *tablespoons salad oil,*	1 *bay leaf*
preferably olive	*a little thyme*
scant tablespoon sugar	450 g (1 *lb*) *young carrots*
1 *teaspoon salt*	*finely chopped parsley*

Bring the first 9 ingredients to a gentle boil and continue boiling gently for about 5 minutes. Wash and scrape the carrots and cut into halves lengthwise. Add to the marinade and continue cooking until the carrots are tender but still quite firm. Leave them in the marinade until cold. Arrange the carrots in a serving dish, drain the marinade and add as a dressing, and sprinkle with chopped parsley.

Baked Carrots

4 servings

450 g (1 *lb*) *carrots*	1 *crushed clove garlic*
melted butter or margarine or	*salt and pepper*
dripping (*see below*)	

Wash and scrape the carrots but keep whole. Put them in a baking pan with enough fat to almost cover. Add the garlic, sprinkle with salt and pepper and bake in a moderate oven (180C, 350F, Mark 4) for about 1 hour, or until they are brown.

Serve with cold roast beef, pot roasted beef, or with roast lamb or mutton.

Carrot Halva

6–8 servings

1 *kg* (2¼ *lb*) *carrots*
2⅓ *l* (4 *pt*) *milk*
pinch saffron (optional)
340 *g* (12 *oz*) *sugar*
1–2 *tablespoons sultanas*
  (optional)

90 *g* (3 *oz*) *butter or margarine*
silver or gold leaf (optional)
blanched slivered almonds or
  cashew nuts to taste
cardamom seeds, crushed

In the Indian subcontinent they use a large translucent carrot for this dish but I have made it in Europe using ordinary but rather large carrots. More important than the type of carrot is their shredding, for the shreds should be kept as long as possible. It is usual to make fairly large batches of carrot halva which will keep in a refrigerator for at least 7 days.

Wash, scrape and shred the carrots. Bring the milk to the boil in a large saucepan, add the carrots and saffron (the saffron should have been soaked for 30 minutes in milk before using). Cook over a low heat until the carrots are a thick mass and soft and all the milk has been absorbed. Stir from time to time, the more often the better. Add sugar, sultanas and butter and stir well, turn the mixture into another and dry pan and bring to the boil, stirring constantly until it begins to solidify and turn a deep red colour. Turn it out on to a dish, spread over the top the silver or gold leaf and sprinkle with chopped nuts and cardamom seeds.

Carrot halva is served both hot and cold, and it reheats easily. The leaf does nothing to the flavour of this typical subcontinent dish but looks rather exotic. It is available in many Indian or Pakistani stores.

❧ Cauliflower and Broccoli

The cauliflower and broccoli are both variants of *Brassica oloracea*, the same family to which the cabbage belongs. They are natives of Asia and northern Europe and have long been cultivated. Both have been much developed and the flower or curd of both has been much improved by careful garden cultivation. Neither cauliflower nor broccoli were well known in England before the days of Charles II, although the cauliflower was introduced into Britain about 1603 from Cyprus, and broccoli came to England earlier from Italy. By the end of the seventeenth century a writer described them as 'a common feature of the poor man's garden'.

When correctly cooked the cauliflower is one of the nicest members of the cabbage family. The long leaves which surround the curd or white portion usually are cut down but this is not necessary when the cauliflower is garden fresh. Large or small cauliflowers are equally good, for size bears no relation to the flavour. What is important is that the curd is solid. However, if the cauliflower has been allowed to become granular, it can still be cooked unless it has progressed so far as to become objectionable.

How to Cook Cauliflower

Cauliflowers may be cooked either whole or in flowerettes and in this lies the main difference between British and Continental cooks in their approach to this vegetable. On the whole, the British cook prefers to deal with it whole. This takes longer to cook and the cauliflower has a stronger flavour. The Continental cook usually breaks the curd into neat flowerettes and plunges them into boiling salted water. It takes far less time to cook in this way and if the sprigs or flowerettes have been neatly divided, when the cauliflower is served it can be shaped back to its original form. Before cooking cauliflowers whole they must be trimmed and the projecting or really hard part of the stalk removed and a cross made in the stump, as for Brussels sprouts. Leave a few of the tender leaves around the curd, they add to the flavour and appearance of the head, and also help to keep the cauliflower intact while cooking. After washing, soak in cold heavily salted water, although many cooks favour washing in lukewarm water, for 15 minutes, then rinse in cold water. The main object is to ensure there are no small insects lurking in that tightly packed curd.

To preserve both the colour and flavour during cooking, take care that the cauliflower is not over-cooked. This can be done in one or two ways; (1) steam flower-side up in a tightly covered pan with very little water, about 1 cm ($\frac{1}{4}$ in), for 20 to 45 minutes, depending on the size and whether cooked whole or in sprigs; (2) boil uncovered in plenty of boiling salted water for 15 to 20 minutes. Many cooks add a slice of lemon to the water to keep the whiteness of the curd; others add a little sugar, while some put a bay leaf into the water to lessen the rather strong smell, also to give it a delicate flavour. Others suggest a bread crust. The green leaves, if they are tender – and usually they are when the cauliflower is garden fresh – can be cooked with the cauliflower, then taken off, chopped and served with a butter, cheese or other sauce, either alone or as a garnish to the cauliflower, making of it all a main dish.

When cooking the cauliflower whole it helps to cook it in a wire strainer and drain carefully. Then, if handled carefully, the cauliflower will come out of the pan intact, unless over-cooked when nothing will stop it breaking up.

It is important when serving hot cauliflower that all serving dishes are hot.

Quantities. 1 large head serves 4 to 6.

BROCCOLI

This is a variety of the cauliflower. The name broccoli comes from the Italian *brocco*, a shoot, the earliest form of this vegetable being loose spikes. Like most vegetables, it has a long and ancient history and was a favourite with the Romans from whom we have one of those, perhaps useless but endearing, anecdotes which makes history live. Drusus, son of the Emperor Tiberius (who keeps appearing in these pages), was chided by his father for eating too much broccoli. Considering the appetites of those Romans one wonders how much broccoli the young man did in fact eat.

Among the varieties of broccoli there is one which is identical in appearance with cauliflower except that it is smaller and is cooked in exactly the same manner as cauliflower. Then there is the Calabrese which has a small green head like a cauliflower and is cooked like one. Then we have sprouting broccoli, purple or white varieties but more often purple which grows quite well and tall with very small heads. The stalks, buds and most of the leaves, especially when fresh from the garden, are edible. Broccoli of this variety should have firm dark leaves with compact bud clusters, or if you like, small heads. They should be cooked in very little water until just tender, drained and served with melted butter. The little heads must remain whole after cooking, don't let them become mushy. I serve sprouting broccoli as a main dish, I feel it has too delicate a flavour to accompany a meat dish.

Cauliflower with Buttered Breadcrumbs

4–6 servings

1 *cauliflower* – 1 *kg* (2¼ *lb*)	1 *hard-boiled egg, chopped*
30 *g* (1 *oz*) *butter*	*salt and pepper*
1 *cup soft white breadcrumbs*	

Prepare and cook the cauliflower whole as directed. Just before it is ready to serve, cook the butter until a golden brown in a small frying-pan, add the breadcrumbs and fry to a golden brown, then add the egg, stirring all the time. Take the cauliflower from the pan, break into large sprigs, arrange on a hot, round dish in its original form, sprinkle with salt, pepper and the breadcrumb mixture. Serve at once as a main dish.

Instead of hard-boiled egg, a few slivered and fried almonds can be used.

Buttered Breadcrumbs

60 g (2 oz) unsalted butter | 170 g (6 oz) soft fresh breadcrumbs

Heat the butter until hot in a frying pan. Add the breadcrumbs and stir until they are brown and all the butter is absorbed. The crumbs can be used immediately or kept for a short while. The above quantity is enough to garnish one large cauliflower or spread over a large pie.

Cauliflower Milanese Fashion

4–6 servings

1 *cauliflower* – 1 *kg* (2¼ *lb*)   *grated Parmesan cheese to taste*
30 *g* (1 *oz*) *butter*   *salt and pepper*

Prepare and cook the cauliflower as directed. Just before it is ready, melt the butter and keep it hot. Take the cauliflower from the pan, drain thoroughly and break into small sprigs. Arrange these in a round, hot dish, sprinkle with cheese, salt and pepper and finally with the melted butter. Serve as a main dish.

Cauliflower Cheese Custard

4–6 servings

1 *cauliflower* – 1 *kg* (2¼ *lb*)   140 *ml* (¼ *pt*) *scalded milk*
bay leaf, lemon slice and sugar   *butter*
  (*optional*)   *breadcrumbs*
3 *eggs*   60 *g* (2 *oz*) *grated cheese*
salt, white pepper and nutmeg

Prepare the cauliflower as directed and cook in boiling salted water, uncovered, for 15 minutes, adding the bay leaf, lemon and sugar. Take from the pan, drain well, chop finely but do not mash. Lightly beat the eggs, add salt, pepper and nutmeg then beat in the milk. Rub a soufflé dish with butter, sprinkle with breadcrumbs, dot the bottom with slivers of butter and sprinkle lightly with cheese. Add a layer of cauliflower, sprinkle this with cheese and continue this way until the cauliflower and cheese are used up, the top layer being of cheese. Pour in the egg and milk mixture. Dot this with slivers of butter and bake in a moderate oven (180C, 350F, Mark 4) for about 45 minutes, or until the custard has set. Unmould to serve, garnished if liked with crisply fried bacon, or with watercress, or a tomato sauce. Can be served either hot or cold as a main dish.

Cauliflower au Gratin

4–6 servings

1 *cauliflower* – 1 *kg* (2¼ *lb*)	*sugar*
450 *g* (1 *lb*) *ripe tomatoes*	*butter or margarine*
1 *medium-sized onion, minced*	*fine breadcrumbs and grated*
salt	*cheese combined*

Wash and cook the cauliflower whole as directed. While it is cooking, blanch and peel the tomatoes and cook in a little water until very soft together with the onion, salt and a little sugar. Rub through a coarse sieve. As soon as the cauliflower is just tender, take from the pan, drain thoroughly and break into large sprigs. Rub a round baking dish with butter and add the cauliflower. Pour the tomato sauce over the top and sprinkle generously with breadcrumbs and cheese, dot with slivers of butter and bake in a moderate oven (180C, 350F, Mark 4) until the top is a golden brown and begins to bubble. Serve hot as a main dish.

Cauliflower Cheese

4 servings

1 *cauliflower* – 1 *kg* (2¼ *lb*)   15 *g* (½ *oz*) *flour*
butter and breadcrumbs   140 *ml* (¼ *pt*) *milk or single*
grated cheese   *cream*
2 *eggs*   *salt and white pepper*

Wash and cook the cauliflower as directed. When just
tender, take from the pan, cool slightly and break into
flowerettes. Rub a shallow baking dish generously with
butter and sprinkle lightly with breadcrumbs. Arrange the
flowerettes in this and sprinkle with grated cheese. Beat the
eggs, add the flour, mix well until the mixture is smooth
then add the milk, salt and pepper. Pour this over the top
of the cauliflower, sprinkle with slivers of butter and bake in
a moderate oven (180C, 350F, Mark 4) until the top is a
golden brown, about 25 minutes. Serve as a main dish.

Cauliflower Fritters

4–6 servings

1 *cauliflower* – 1 *kg* (2¼ *lb*)   *oil for frying*
1 *whole egg and* 1 *egg white*   *salt*
fine breadcrumbs

Prepare the cauliflower as directed. Break into large sprigs,
cutting off most of the stalks (these can be used in a soup).
Cook in boiling salted water for 10 to 15 minutes, or until
just tender. Take from the pan, drain thoroughly and leave
until cold. Beat the whole egg and the egg white in a bowl.
When the cauliflower is cold, break into smaller sprigs, dip
these first into beaten egg then in breadcrumbs and fry in
hot oil until brown. Take from the pan, drain on absorbent
paper and sprinkle generously with salt immediately before
serving. Can be served as a starter to a meal.

Battered Cauliflower Fritters

4–6 servings

1 *cauliflower – 1 kg (2¼ lb)*	1 *whole egg, well beaten*
110 g *(4 oz) flour*	140 ml *(¼ pt) light beer*
salt and pepper	*oil for frying*

Prepare the cauliflower as for cauliflower fritters (qv) to the point of breaking into small sprigs. Put the flour into a bowl, add salt and pepper, not too much, and the egg and mix to a thick paste. Gradually add the beer and continue beating until the batter is thick and creamy. Have ready a large pan with plenty of very hot oil, dip the cauliflower sprigs into the batter then put a few at a time into the hot oil and fry until they are brown all over. Take from the pan with a perforated spoon and drain on absorbent paper. Sprinkle with salt before serving, as hot as possible.

Milk may be used instead of beer but the latter does produce a lighter and more flavoursome batter.

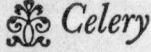 *Celery*

General Instructions

Celery came to England and France somewhere in the sixteenth or seventeenth centuries but later to the United States. However, celery is considered by some to be a native British plant, although it was known to the ancients. Maecenas, a Roman nobleman, we read, used to feed celery to asses which were destined for the table; asses meat is still consumed in Italy but whether celery-fed I doubt. Apart from asses, all kinds of poultry were also fed on celery to improve their flavour. And when Roman bibblers were not wearing garlands of parsley to counteract over-indulgence in wine, they made celery leaf garlands. Maybe these

Romans were not far wrong, since the Chinese also credited celery with medicinal properties and used it as a blood purifier.

Celery stalks, by which is meant the whole plant, are by nature green, but blanching the stalks makes them white, although there is one variety, the kalamazoo, which is naturally white. When eaten raw, only the most tender parts of the celery are used, but the rest can be cooked and made into soups and flavourings for ragoûts. A head of celery is the complete plant, minus its root and the leaves, while the individual ribs are variously called sticks, stalks or ribs.

How to Prepare and Cook Celery

Cut off the root, any bruised or discoloured outer ribs and the green leaves. Wash thoroughly to remove any dirt which may be lodged in the ribs. If the celery is inclined to be stringy, pull off the strings down the length of the stalk. The tender heart of the celery is best served raw, crisped by putting in iced water in the refrigerator. If using large heads which are to be cooked, they are best cut in half lengthwise, unless otherwise directed. If to be simply stewed, put the celery into a pan with boiling salted water and simmer until tender, the time will depend on the tenderness of the celery. Drain it thoroughly. At this stage the celery is ready for further treatment, to be served with butter, cream, or cheese, or a white sauce. Celery also can be stewed in clear stock.

Boiled Celery in a Sauce

4 servings

2 *heads celery*	140 *ml* (¼ *pt*) *milk*
30 *g* (1 *oz*) *butter*	*salt, pepper and sugar*
30 *g* (1 *oz*) *flour*	

Wash and prepare the celery as directed. Trim off all the leaves and cut the ribs into convenient lengths. Put into a

pan, cover with boiling salted water and cook over a
moderate heat until the celery is tender, 20 to 30 minutes.
The liquid should have reduced by half. Drain off the
celery but retain the liquid. In another pan heat the butter,
add the flour and stir to a roux, add the milk and finally the
liquid from the celery. Add the celery, salt, pepper and
sugar and cook for 3 to 4 minutes. Serve hot.

Celery au Gratin

4 servings

2 *heads celery*	*grated cheese*
30 g (1 oz) butter	*slivers butter*
280 ml (½ pt) stock	

Prepare the celery as directed and cut into convenient
lengths. Drop into boiling water and blanch for 15 minutes.
Drain well and put into a baking pan with the butter, add
stock to cover, spread with buttered foil and bake in a hot
oven (220C, 425F, Mark 7) until tender, 30 to 40 minutes.
Take the pan from the oven, sprinkle with grated cheese and
slivers of butter, return to the oven and continue to cook
until the top begins to brown.

Braised Celery

4–6 servings

3–4 *heads celery*	*salt and pepper*
45 g (1½ oz) butter or margarine	280 ml (½ pt) stock
1 *large onion, diced*	280 ml (½ pt) gravy
2 *medium-sized carrots, sliced*	*finely chopped parsley*

Prepare the celery as directed. Blanch in boiling salted
water for 10 minutes. Drain. Heat the butter in an oval
dish, add the onion and carrots, cook gently until they
begin to brown, then add the celery, salt and pepper. Shake
the pan gently, add the stock, cover the pan tightly and

cook slowly for 30 to 40 minutes. Fifteen minutes before serving, add the gravy. Serve hot on a hot serving dish sprinkled with parsley.

If an oval pan is not available to take the celery ribs whole, cut them into sizes to fit whatever pan you have but try to keep the ribs as long as possible. Serve as a main dish or as an accompaniment to a meat dish.

Cheese Stuffed Celery

4 servings

Gorgonzola, Stilton, Roquefort	*pepper to taste*
or Danish Blue cheese	*1–2 celery hearts*
butter or cream cheese	

This is a change from the usual stuffed ribs of celery. Obviously it is not easy to give exact quantities of cheese, butter or cream cheese required, it depends on the size of the celery hearts and how much stuffing is preferred. The quantity of blue cheese should equal that of the butter or, better still, cream cheese, such as Italian *ricotta* which is very dry and has plenty of flavour.

Mix the blue cheese and butter to a thick paste. Add pepper to taste. Wash the celery hearts, trim off the leaves and slice off the root. Carefully pull off all the outer ribs but leave the tightly packed heart and centre ribs intact. Stuff all the outer ribs with the creamed cheese then push as much of the stuffing as you can inside the tightly packed centre ribs. Now return the outer ribs to the heart, as they were originally. Wrap in foil and tie top and bottom – even the middle of the heart is long – so that the ribs are closely packed. Leave in the refrigerator for several hours. Cut into medium-thick slices to serve.

Curled Celery

This is used for garnishing or sometimes as an hors d'oeuvre. Cut the celery into very thin strips down the length of its ribs. Hold one end and with a sharp knife pull down firmly along the length of the strip, curling it as you go. Drop into iced water where the curling process will continue. Drain thoroughly before using.

Celeriac

This close relative of celery is also called celery knob or turnip-rooted celery. It is not a root crop in the botanical sense of the term, however, whereas the ribs of true celery are edible parts, with celeriac it is the swollen base at the stem. Its flavour is like that of celery. The leaves of celeriac are bitter and not fit for eating, being also swollen and short. It is not a beautiful looking vegetable but a very useful winter one. The smaller the knobs the better for, if left too long in the ground, they will become hollow or woody. It must be peeled before cooking as the skin is tough and stringy. It can be grated and served in salads; boiled, or served as a separate vegetable, and is useful as a flavouring in soups and stews.

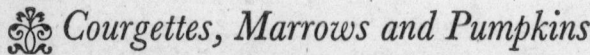 *Courgettes, Marrows and Pumpkins*

General Instructions

These three vegetables all belong to the same family, the *Curcurbitaceae*, which includes the American members of the squash tribe. They are varieties of a single species of uncertain but probably American origin, *curcurbita pepo*, which is a change from the usual Mediterranean via Asia formula. That squash – the name is derived from an American Indian word *asquutasquash* – pumpkins, etc were common foods for centuries for the then inhabitants was borne out by archaeological finds of rinds and seeds in cliff dwellings in the USA dating back to about 2000 BC. All members of this large family, like their relatives cucumbers and melons, are trailing, climbing plants with flowers which are unisex and usually a bright yellow or orange in colour.

COURGETTES

This French marrow variety, like the Italian *zucchini*, has been developed for cutting when young and small, but if left to mature are no different from the British marrow. They are usually green in colour but a bright yellow variety has been developed recently. Courgettes look like baby marrows, have a firm texture and a delicate flavour.

MARROWS

Of all garden vegetables surely the marrow is the most abused. It would seem that its main function is to let it grow to a monstrous size for presentation at harvest festivals or vegetable shows. It deserves better treatment. If kindly dealt with it can be made into an edible and pleasant dish. In Britain it is a late summer vegetable and should be picked while still small for kitchen use, when the flesh, like that of the courgette, is tender and delicately flavoured. Thus picked, they can be cooked whole.

PUMPKINS

As grown in England, pumpkins usually are large, round and yellow and do not arouse in the British either the enthusiasm or the nostalgia they evoke in Americans. To the Americans nothing conjures up the past more than the homely pumpkin with memories of family gatherings. A simple mention of pumpkin pie (there are several varieties), pumpkin soups and, of course, hallowe'en with the leering jack-o'-lantern, brings tears into American eyes, for they are sentimental symbols of America's pumpkin heritage.

All this nostalgia goes back to the days when the English settlers faced the failure of general crops and there would have been starvation had there not been the pumpkins. But the pumpkin itself has a history of some 9,000 years when they were grown in the Mexican highlands. The settlers were impressed by the diversity of pumpkins and squash in general but were grateful to the friendly Indians who taught them how to use this valuable crop. Then it is no wonder that there cannot be a Thanksgiving celebration in the USA without that pumpkin pie. But this, surely, had its origin in England where pumpkins had been cultivated in the fifteenth and sixteenth centuries and 'were eaten by the poorer classes'. They were called pompian and often made into sweet pies but not with pastry crust. A hole was scooped out in the side of the pumpkin, the seeds and filaments dug out and the hollow filled with apples, spicery and honey to sweeten it all. The hole was closed again and the pumpkin baked either in embers or in a brick oven. This is also what those early settler women did, except they filled their pumpkins with milk, spices and honey or maple syrup.

How to Cook Courgettes

Courgettes can be cooked whole, sliced or cut into chunks, peeled or left unpeeled. If picked as they should be, young and small, there is no better way to cook them but whole and stewed gently in butter in a covered pan. When they are tender, after 15 to 20 minutes cooking, they can be served as they are, together with their buttery sauce. Or they can be taken from the pan and the sauce thickened slightly with some double cream. If they are longer than, say 13 cm (5 in), then they are best sliced into rings or slantingly into lengths. Generally speaking courgettes should not be peeled but some people insist that their flavour is too pronounced when cooked in their skins.

Julienne of Courgettes and Carrots

4 servings

225 g (8 oz) courgettes	melted butter
225 g (8 oz) young carrots	salt and pepper

Wipe the courgettes and wash the carrots. Trim the ends of both and cut into 1 cm ($\frac{1}{4}$ in) julienne sticks. Put the carrots in a steamer, cover with the courgettes and cook over boiling salted water until tender. Transfer to a hot serving dish and toss them with hot melted butter and add salt and pepper to taste. Serve hot.

Courgettes au Gratin

4 servings

450 g (1 *lb*) *courgettes*	140 *ml* (¼ *pt*) *double cream*
140 *ml* (¼ *pt*) *water*	30 g (1 *oz*) *grated cheese*
salt and pepper	*fine breadcrumbs*
1 *egg*	*butter*

Wipe the courgettes, trim their ends and cut into slanting thick slices. Put in a shallow pan with the water and salt and cook over a moderate heat until tender. Beat the egg, add the cream and cheese and generously season with pepper. Drain the courgettes and put into a gratin dish. Spread the cream and cheese sauce over the top, sprinkle lightly with fine breadcrumbs, dot with slivers of butter and bake in a moderately hot oven (200C, 400F, Mark 6) for about 15 minutes, or until the top is brown.

Courgettes Niçoise

A pleasant dish from Provençe in the south of France. Ingredients are 'as required'. Stew some tomatoes until they are soft. Rub through a sieve. Add salt and pepper. Wipe some courgettes, cut into thick chunks and cook in the tomato sauce until tender. Sprinkle with finely chopped tarragon before serving, either hot or cold.

Marinated Courgettes

4 servings

450 g (1 *lb*) *courgettes*	½ *onion, finely chopped*
3–4 *tablespoons oil*	*sage and salt*
3–4 *cloves garlic, finely chopped*	560 *ml* (1 *pt*) *vinegar*

Wipe the courgettes and cut into slices lengthwise without peeling. Heat the oil, add the sliced courgettes and cook until tender and just beginning to change colour. Drain on absorbent paper. In the same oil lightly fry the garlic and onion, add sage, a good pinch of salt and finally the vinegar. Stir well and bring to the boil. Arrange the courgettes in a shallow salad dish, pour the marinade over them and leave for at least 24 hours. Serve as an hors d'oeuvre or salad.

Fried Courgette Slices

4 servings

450 g (1 *lb*) courgettes	1 *egg, well beaten*
salt	*fine breadcrumbs*
flour	*oil for frying*

Wipe and scrape the courgettes and slice lengthwise. Sprinkle each lightly with salt, roll in flour, dip into beaten egg and then into breadcrumbs. Have ready a pan with plenty, but not deep, frying oil and fry the courgettes until a golden brown. Serve hot.

Stuffed Courgette Flowers

Stuffed courgette flowers, as well as flowers from similar gourds, is a favourite recipe from Liguria and Provençe. They are extremely good and not difficult to prepare and cook. Courgettes and gourds generally produce a large number of male flowers which are collected as early as possible in the morning, while the dew is still on them, and prepared as soon as possible afterwards as they wilt easily. The flowers do not require washing, coming as they do straight from the garden, and they must be fully open before taking them from the vine. It is important to know the male from the female flower, otherwise there will be a gardening disaster (see p. 107).

The stuffings vary from kitchen to kitchen. The most usual is a mixture of cooked rice with minced cold meat, or grated cheese, a savour of minced onions, maybe a little

garlic, often some pine-nuts, salt and pepper. This mixture
is bound together with beaten egg. The stamens are removed
from the flowers which are then lightly filled with a little
of the mixture, to stuff them too tightly is fatal as they
become soggy. When all the flowers are stuffed, fold over
the ends of the petals to encase the filling and bake on a
baking sheet in a moderate oven (180C, 350F, Mark 4)
until brown, about 20 minutes. They can be served hot or
cold although I think they are better hot. Instead of rice, a
very thick white creamy sauce may be used.

Fried Courgette Flowers

male courgette flowers   *oil for frying*
a light batter

Pick the flowers as early in the morning as possible, or take
them from the vine immediately before cooking. Remove
the stamens, dip into batter and fry in deep hot oil until a
golden colour, only a couple of minutes or so. They should
be eaten hot when crisp. Even flowers which are just slightly
wilted can be fried in this manner. And, if using half opened
or wilted flowers, do not be surprised if they suddenly blow
up like a bubble fish. They subside almost immediately
however.

How to Cook Marrow
Picked when about 23 cm (9 in) long, marrows can be
cooked whole, skin, seeds and insides, and in any of the ways
of cooking courgettes. Large ones must be peeled and have
the centre pith and skin removed.

Stewed Marrow (Large)

4 servings

$1\frac{1}{2}$ kg ($3\frac{1}{4}$ lb) large marrow   *finely chopped parsley and*
salt   *chives*
30 g (1 oz) butter

Peel the marrow, remove the pith and seeds and cut into large pieces. Put into a small quantity of salted water, about 1½ cm (½ in), and cook gently until tender. Do not over-cook or the marrow will become tasteless and mushy. Drain throughly, return to the pan with the butter and cook gently until the butter is melted. Serve on a hot dish and sprinkle with parsley and chives.

Many people seem to think that marrow should always be drowned in a thick white sauce; for my taste nothing could be more unpleasant. However, if a sauce is wanted, take the marrow from the pan and keep hot. Take the pan from the heat add to what remains of the liquid a well beaten egg yolk and the juice of 1 lemon. Stir well, return to the stove and cook gently until the sauce thickens; do not boil or the egg will curdle.

Stewed Baby Marrows

4 servings

1 kg (2¼ lb) baby marrows   30 g (1 oz) butter or margarine
salt

Wash the marrows and, if really small, leave whole, other-wise cut into halves or quarters. Cook as for large marrows.

Baby marrows also can be simply stewed in butter or margarine until tender.

Vegetable Marrow au Gratin

4 servings

1 kg (2¼ lb) marrow   grated cheese
280 ml (½ pt) tomato sauce   buttered (p. 177) or fine
    (p. 238)   breadcrumbs

Stew the marrow whole and unpeeled in a little boiling salted water until just tender and still firm. Cut into slices and arrange them in a large shallow dish, cover with tomato sauce and sprinkle with cheese and breadcrumbs.

Bake in a moderate oven (180C, 350F, Mark 4) until the marrow is brown on top and reheated.

The marrow can be peeled and cut into rings while still raw, put into a baking dish with the tomato sauce, cheese and breadcrumbs, then baked in a hot oven (220C, 425F, Mark 7) until tender. Test with a fork.

How to Cook Pumpkin

I am turning to the Americans for the cooking of this vegetable for they have turned it to a fine art. One pound (450 g) will produce two cups of purée or pulp and will serve two people.

To prepare the pumpkin for purée, wipe and cut it into halves. Do not scoop out seeds and fibres but rub the cut surface with vegetable fat and place on a baking sheet cut side down. Bake in a moderately hot oven (220C, 400F, Mark 6) until tender when pierced with the tines of a fork going right through the skin. Take from the oven, scrape off the fibres and seeds, scoop out the flesh and either mash or press through a ricer.

To boil the pumpkin, wipe it and cut into pieces, remove the seeds and the peel. Cut into large cubes and cook in a small quantity of water until tender, 45 to 55 minutes. When soft, mash and rub through a sieve to make sure all stringy fibres are removed. The pulp can be used for any recipe called for mashed pumpkin.

Pumpkin Pie

4 servings

225 g (8 oz) pastry	60 g (2 oz) brown sugar
450 g (1 lb) cooked mashed	good pinch salt
pumpkin	½ teaspoon each ground ginger,
30 g (1 oz) butter	nutmeg and cinnamon
4 eggs	

Line a 23 cm (9 in) deep pie dish with pastry, puff or short, this is a matter for choice. If the pumpkin pulp is moist, cook over a low heat until it is dry. Blend in the butter. Beat the eggs. Take the pan from the stove, beat the eggs into the pumpkin mixture, return the pan to the stove, add sugar, salt and spices and mix thoroughly. Turn the mixture into the pie dish and bake in a very hot oven (230C, 450F, Mark 8) for 12 minutes, lower the heat and bake for 20 to 25 minutes longer, or until the centre of the filling begins to puff up. Serve warm or cold.

Casserole of Browned Pumpkin

4 servings

butter	*4 cups boiled or baked mashed*
salt, pepper and nutmeg	*pumpkin*
	2 teaspoons sugar

Generously rub an earthenware casserole with butter. Mix the salt, pepper and nutmeg with the pumpkin pulp. Turn into the buttered casserole, smooth down gently and sprinkle with sugar. Brown under the grill or in a very hot oven (230C, 450F, Mark 8). Serve as a vegetable.

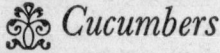 *Cucumbers*

General Instructions

The cucumber was mentioned by the Prophet Isaiah and it has been used in many forms for thousands of years. It came into Europe via Egypt; under the Pharaohs it was a common, even cheap, food and one missed by the Israelites when wandering in the desert. As far as generally known, it was introduced into Britain in more or less its present form towards the end of the sixteenth century but it was mentioned in the fourteenth. In the seventeenth and early eighteenth centuries it was called cowcumber but by 1836 we read that 'no well taught person, except of the old school, now writes cowcumber'. Pliny was of the opinion that cucumbers were apt to cause digestive trouble unless pared, or boiled in oil, vinegar and honey. Maybe it was he who spread the rumour that cucumber causes indigestion. Apicius included several recipes for cucumber in his works.

If you should come across a plain glass tube with parallel sides looking like a glass lamp chimney in an old glass collection, it could well be an old English cucumber glass. It seems that George Stephenson, of steam locomotive fame, was fond of cucumbers and grew them but was distressed because his cucumbers persisted in growing in the oddest of shapes. So he invented and had made glass straight-jackets into which he put his stubborn cucumbers. As the cucumbers grew they were forced to grow straight. These tubes were then adopted by other gardeners, so there must at one time have been a lot of them around. Today the cucumber has learned its lesson for horticulturists give us straight well-behaved cucumbers.

How to Prepare and Cook Cucumbers

Cucumbers belong to the same family as the gourd and are a useful vegetable although some people find them indigestible, but there are various treatments to overcome this defect. Some suggest they should be sliced and salted as for aubergines (p. 144) and their liquid drawn off; others feel that peeling and discarding the seeds is enough, while others declare that peeling cucumbers is to ask for indigestion.

In Britain they are usually served raw in salads and sandwiches, or in pickles and relishes. But they can be cooked, not only in the same ways in which courgettes and marrows are cooked, but also with recipes of their own. They cook well and easily and very young cucumbers are best left with their skins on. For boiling, on the whole choose medium to large cucumbers and if the skin looks tough they are best peeled and the seeds discarded, especially if these are large for they are also tough and no amount of cooking

F.F.G.—9

will soften them. 10 to 15 minutes should be long enough for boiling. Since the cucumber is a watery vegetable, it must never be over-cooked and it must also be well seasoned since by itself it has not a great deal of flavour. Other ways of cooking cucumbers will be found in the following recipes.

Scalloped Cucumbers

If you want to give a professional or decorative touch to your cucumbers this is done by drawing the tines of a fork down the length of the cucumber. Strips of loose skin can then be removed and the resulting slices will have a decorative edge.

Boiled Cucumbers with a Sauce

4–6 servings

2 *large cucumbers*	*single cream*
salt	*white pepper*
1 *teaspoon sugar*	*chervil or tarragon, finely*
280 *ml* ($\frac{1}{2}$ *pt*) *Béchamel sauce*	*chopped*

Prepare the cucumbers as directed and cook either in boiling salted water or stock, add the sugar and cook until tender; cooking time will depend on the size and number of pieces. While it is cooking, make the sauce, diluting it with a little single cream. Drain the cucumbers, add to the sauce, add salt and pepper, gently stir to coat the cucumber pieces and serve sprinkled with chervil.

Instead of a white sauce, melt about 45 g ($1\frac{1}{2}$ oz) of butter, stir into it some finely chopped tarragon or chervil and, when the butter has browned, pour it over the cooked and drained cucumbers. Serve as an accompaniment to meat or fish.

Sautéed Cucumbers

large cucumbers as required	*salt and sugar*
butter or other fat for cooking	*finely chopped parsley*

Prepare the cucumbers as directed for boiling. Halve and cut into 3 cm (1 in) lengths. Put these into boiling salted water to cover and cook for 10 minutes, or until just tender. Take from the pan and thoroughly drain. Heat just enough butter to cover the bottom of a frying-pan, sprinkle the cucumbers lightly with salt and sugar and sauté them in the hot fat until they turn a golden colour. Take from the pan, sprinkle with parsley and serve.

Cucumber Relish

3–4 *cucumbers*
juice 1 *lemon*
3 *tablespoons olive oil*
2 *tablespoons wine vinegar*

½ *teaspoon each salt and mild*
paprika pepper
1 *tablespoon French mustard*

Prepare the cucumbers as directed for boiling and cut into evenly shaped cubes. Put into a pan with salted water and lemon juice to cover and cook for 4 minutes. Drain well, drop into cold water and drain once again. Return to the pan, add the oil and vinegar, stir gently and cook gently for 10 minutes. Add the salt, paprika and mustard, stir gently again then leave the cucumbers in the mixture until cool, then chill.

Serve with fish or meat.

Cucumbers au Gratin

4–6 servings

4–6 *medium-sized cucumbers*
560 *ml* (1 *pt*) *Béchamel sauce*

110 *g* (4 *oz*) *grated cheese*

Peel the cucumbers and cut into halves or, if preferred, into thick strips. Cook in a little boiling salted water until tender. Drain thoroughly and put into a shallow baking dish, cover with sauce, sprinkle with cheese and bake in a hot oven (220C, 425F, Mark 7) until the top is brown, or put the dish under a hot grill.

Cucumber Mousse

6 servings

2 *good-sized cucumbers*
1 *tablespoon vinegar or lemon juice*
1 *teaspoon Worcestershire Sauce (optional)*
salt and pepper to taste
½ *cup mayonnaise*
15 g (½ oz) *gelatine*

½ *cup double cream, stiffly whipped*
green vegetable colouring

Dressing:
1 *small cucumber*
salad dressing (p. 248)
watercress or parsley

Peel and cut the cucumbers in half and discard seeds. Cut into lengths. Drop into boiling acidulated water and blanch for 5 minutes. Drain and put under cold running water. Rub through a vegetable mill. Mix the purée with Worcestershire Sauce, salt, pepper (preferably white pepper) and the mayonnaise. Soften the gelatine in 1 tablespoon of water and dissolve over hot water. Add this to the cucumber purée then fold in the cream. Blend well and add 1 to 2 drops of green vegetable colouring and turn into a chilled, rinsed round mould. Chill until firm. In the meantime score the peel of the remaining cucumber and slice thinly. Marinate the slices in a salad dressing. When ready to serve, unmould the mousse and garnish the top in an overlapping design with most of the cucumber slices. At regular intervals push one slice of cucumber into the sides of the mousse so that only one side of the slice is visible, spaced for example for the portions to be served. This mousse is most effective when served on a dark green plate and garnished with watercress.

🏵 Leeks

General Instructions

Everyone, in Britain at least, knows that the leek is the national emblem of Wales although not everyone, even the Welsh, really know why. The usual story or legend is that St David ordered the Welsh to wear it in their caps after a particular victory. St David was also said to have been the uncle of King Arthur who, it was rumoured, consumed vast quantities of leeks and lived happily for 146 years, whether because he ate so many leeks is not revealed. However, there is yet another Welsh story. When Cadwallader, the Welsh leader and king, was about to meet the King of Northumbria in battle, he ordered his men to wear a leek in their helmets so that they could distinguish each other from the enemy. The result of the battle was a victory for the Welsh and thus leeks became their national emblem.

But, before the Welsh were honouring the leek, it was sacred to Latona, the mother of Apollo, and it was one of the plants worshipped by the Egyptians. The ancients, it is said, vied with each other as to who could produce the largest leeks to give to the priestess, who liked them raw. The Greeks also credited the leek with being a great cure-all; but the Egyptians dreaded it as a powerful divinity, although they included it in the flesh-pots they gave to the Israelites when working on the great Pyramid and who later bewailed its loss as they wandered through the desert. And, as a bit of curious information, I have read that there is a tradition that its seeds will amalgamate in germination if as many of them which can be taken up with three fingers are placed in a piece of linen, covered with manure and watered with care, then they will form themselves into a single plant and produce in due season a monstrous leek.

Leeks are supposed to have reached Britain from Asia, via the Mediterranean, as did so many of our most popular vegetables. They are not often served as a main dish, although they are certainly good enough for such treatment. The French call them 'the asparagus of the poor' and they lend themselves to some asparagus recipes. The leek is actually a first cousin to the onion and Nero, famed more for his cruelties than his eating habits, is depicted to have been a connoisseur of leek soup, indeed, Vichyssoise is directly descended from the Roman *porrophagus*, or leek soup, for *porrum* was the leek of ancient Rome, as the *porro*, or leek, in Italy today, and the *poireau* of France.

How to Prepare and Cook Leeks

The leaves of the leek are flat, unlike the rest of their onion relatives, and this is one of the reasons why it is essential to thoroughly wash them, as sand and grit have a tendency to lurk between the leaves. To clean a leek so that it remains intact, first cut off any coarse leaves, these can be used to flavour a soup stock, slice off the root without disturbing the base, cut the leek lengthwise through the centre to about 4 cm (1½ in) from the base, turn the leek and cut through again in a similar manner, thereby quartering the leek without actually cutting it through. Now flush cold running water through the leek and all the grit and dirt will be washed away.

If the leeks are small, after washing tie them in small bundles with thread and cook in boiling salted water for about 25 minutes, depending on the size of the leeks. If the leeks are large, they can be cooked whole without tying and they will of course take longer to become tender, 30 to 45 minutes. Drain well and serve on a hot dish with any of the following sauces: butter, parsley butter, maître d'hôtel, Béchamel or white sauce, Hollandaise, etc, or as in the following recipes.

Leeks with a Cream Sauce

4 servings

1 kg (2¼ lb) leeks
60 g (2 oz) butter or margarine
1 tablespoon flour

560 ml (1 pt) warmed water or
  milk
salt and pepper
4 tablespoons cream

Prepare the leeks as directed. Cut into 2 or 3 pieces according to their length and cook in boiling salted water until tender. Heat the butter, add the flour, stir well then gradually add the warmed water or milk, stirring gently all the time. Add salt and pepper. Cook the sauce for a good 5 minutes then take the pan from the heat and whisk in the cream. Drain the leeks thoroughly from their liquid, arrange on a hot serving dish and garnish with the sauce.

Leeks in a Tomato Sauce

4 servings

1 kg (2¼ lb) leeks
30 g (1 oz) butter or margarine
30 g (1 oz) fat bacon, diced
1 small onion, sliced

225 g (8 oz) tomatoes, peeled
  and chopped
chopped parsley to taste

Prepare and cook the leeks as directed but only for 15 minutes. Drain off the leeks but reserve their liquid. In another pan heat the butter, add the bacon and onion and fry until the onion begins to change colour. Add the tomatoes and cook until soft, then add the parsley and leeks and continue cooking in this sauce for 5 minutes. Add 1 cup of the leek liquid and continue to cook the leeks until they are quite tender. Add, if required, a little of the leek liquid from time to time but not too much or you will have a soup and not leeks in a sauce.

Leeks au Gratin

4 servings

1 *kg* (2¼ *lb*) *leeks*	*salt and pepper*
butter or margarine	*grated cheese*
110 *g* (4 *oz*) *white sauce*	

Prepare the leeks as directed and cook whole until tender. Take from the pan, drain thoroughly and cut them into short lengths. Heat a little butter in a shallow casserole. Add the leeks and arrange them in one layer on the bottom. Cover with the sauce and sprinkle with salt, pepper and generously with cheese (if preferred, this can be cut into thin slices instead of being grated) and bake in a moderate oven (180C, 350F, Mark 4) until the top browns or, if using sliced cheese, put the dish under the grill and cook until the cheese melts. Serve as a main dish.

Leeks with Bacon

4 servings

1 *kg* (2¼ *lb*) *leeks*	*grated cheese*
streaky bacon	*salt and pepper*
butter	

Prepare and cook the leeks as directed. Drain thoroughly. Wrap around each leek 1 or 2 rashers of bacon. Rub a long shallow pan generously with butter, add the leeks, sprinkle with cheese, salt and pepper and slivers of butter and bake in a moderate over (180C, 350F, Mark 4) until the bacon is crisp. Serve hot as a main dish.

Braised Leeks

4 servings

1 *kg (2¼ lb) leeks*	*salt and pepper*
celery, carrot and onion	*2 cloves*
280 ml (½ pt) stock, meat or	*parsley*
vegetable	*bay leaves*

Prepare the leeks as directed. Dice the remaining vegetables, how much to use is a matter of preference. In a large pan arrange a layer of mixed diced vegetables, cover with the leeks, add the stock, salt, pepper, cloves and herbs and cook until tender, about 30 minutes depending on the size of the leeks.

The leeks can be served as they come from the pan, or you can rub a gratin dish lightly with butter or other fat, arrange the vegetables in this and cover them with a mixture of 2 whole eggs beaten into a scant 280 ml (½ pt) of milk and bake in a moderate oven (180C, 350F, Mark 4) until the custard thickens.

Serve as a main dish.

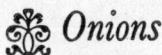 *Onions*

General Instructions

Onions are important members of the lily family and were worshipped by the ancient Egyptians. Perhaps onions originated in the Mediterranean but some authorities are convinced the Hindu Kush is their home. In any case, they are older than recorded history. The Babylonians taught the Egyptians that the onion is a symbol of perfection because the onion layers form a circle and one can travel the line round, throughout the circle, so the onion was given full honours by the Ancients and reserved for immortals. A bunch of onions was placed in the hand of a mummy to help the soul on the stage to eternity. And by the Christian era the mystique surrounding the onion was maintained, it had become so sacred that priests forbade the people to eat it. Horace and Pliny were among those who paid written tribute to the onion. Also, said Pliny, the Romans believed onions cured the sting of serpents and they gave onion and barley water poultices to those who had watery eyes, because, they claimed, onions clear the sight by the tears they draw. Onion juice was also given to those who suddenly became speechless.

However, some claim an even earlier history for the onion, relating that when Satan stepped out of the Garden of Eden after the fall of man an onion sprang from where he placed his right foot, and garlic from the spot touched by his left foot. Onions and garlic (also radishes) were eaten in vast quantities by the labourers who built the pyramids and among the grumbles of the Israelites as they roamed the desert with Moses was 'we remember the fish we did eat in Egypt freely ... the leeks and the onions and garlic ...' Alexander the Great discovered the onion in Egypt and later had it cultivated in Greece to give as food to his troops, believing it excited martial ardour. Whoever wishes to preserve his health, ran an ancient law, should eat before breakfast every morning young onions and honey.

Great would be the loss to the culinary world if the onion were to be removed. After salt, it is one of the greatest seasonings. And it has inspired men to poetise. Sydney Smith, the lovable cleric, wrote in his rhymed *Receipt for a Salad*:

> Let onion's atoms lurk within the bowl,
> And, half suspected, animate the whole.

And Dean Swift had this to say:

> This is every cook's opinion
> No savoury dish without an onion
> But lest your kissing should be spoil'd
> Your onions must be thoroughly boiled...

There are several varieties of onion, the warmer the climate the larger and milder it is. Cold, stern climates produce stern and strongly-flavoured onions. Where onions grow all the year their quality tends to be poor. Colours, which vary through white, yellow to a purple red, also are an indication of their taste and quality. White onions are usually milder than red or yellow and are the best for making creamed soups or sauces.

Onions Without Tears

Well, this is a problem. I have tried all the usual tricks, peeling onions under a spray of cold water from the tap; holding a crust of bread between my teeth; I have a fork-like gadget with which I am supposed to hold the onion it seems yards away from my eyes and deal with it, and my granddaughter appears to achieve success by kneeling on the ground in front of the table with the onion above her when she peels and cuts without any tears. She has something, for the tearing, jerking vapours do rise, so she puts herself below the onion vapours. But then kneeling when one is no longer young is almost as painful as tears. Wearing glasses helps. But getting one's husband to deal with onions is the best method I have come up with yet. There are several gadgets on the market designed to keep onions covered during chopping and some are very good indeed. One method of chopping is to slice the peeled onion to almost the root in thin slices and then slice again at right angles. Finally slice horizontally when the onion theoretically will fall away into small dice and you will not weep.

Quantities. Allow 110–170 g (4–6 oz) per serving.

To Boil Onions

Choose medium-sized or even smallish onions for boiling whole. Large ones are better thickly sliced. Cut off a little from the top and bottom of the onion, remove the outer brown skin and peel off the outer layer, sometimes one or two other layers come off as well. Make a criss-cross cut in the top of each onion. This prevents the centres coming

out as the moisture inside the onion swells while cooking.
Put into cold water, bring to the boil and boil the onions
for 10 minutes: this will blanch them. Take from the pan,
put fresh cold salted water in the pan, return the onions
and cook until tender, this will take between 30 minutes and
an hour, depending on the size of the onions. But take care
the onions are not over-cooked or they will darken; equally,
they will darken if too few onions are put into the pan. A
dash of vinegar or a little lemon juice in the water will help
to keep the onions light. New onions can be cooked directly
in boiling water, however, it is better for old onions, like
potatoes, to be started in cold water and soften slowly. When
cooking onions together with other vegetables, remember
they take longer to cook than do most vegetables.

To Fry Onions

Fried onions, to remain crisp, must always be fried in deep
fat and there should never be too many in the pan at one
time.

Stewed Onions

onions	*capers*
butter	*salt and pepper*
stock	

Peel and cut the onions into thick slices. Blanch for 5
minutes only in boiling water. Drain thoroughly. Return
the onions to the pan with some butter, not too much, a
little stock and a few capers. Cook the onions over a low
heat until very tender. Add salt and pepper and serve hot.

Baked or Braised Onions

No 1

Trim off the root end only of several large onions, preferably
all of the same size, wipe but do not peel them. Put a little
butter in a baking dish, add the onions and bake in a
moderate oven (180C, 350F, Mark 4) until tender, about

1 hour. Take the onions from the oven, peel and return to the pan, topping each with a little butter and seasoning. They will be ready to serve in a few minutes and be of excellent flavour from having been baked in their jackets. In Italy they bake large onions in their skins in hot embers until the onions are almost black and oozy.

No 2
Wrap the unpeeled onions in foil, each separately, and place on the baking shelf. Bake in a moderate oven (180C, 350F, Mark 4) until they are soft when squeezed, 45 to 60 minutes.

No 3
Peel the onions and put in a baking pan with a little fat and bake in a moderate oven (180C, 350F, Mark 4) until tender. They can also be baked round a joint of meat, like baked potatoes.

Baked Stuffed Onions

4–6 servings

4–6 *even-sized large onions*	*finely chopped parsley*
stuffing (*see below*)	*sauce* (*see below*)
margarine or butter	

Peel the onions as directed. Put into a pan of cold water, bring to the boil and boil for 30 minutes. Drain and pour cold water over them. Scoop out the centres and fill the cavities with stuffing. Rub a shallow baking dish with margarine, add the onions and top each with a sliver of margarine. Bake in a fairly hot oven (200C, 400F, Mark 6) about 1 hour, or until tender but still firm. Sprinkle the onions with parsley.

Stuffings
These are very much a question of what is available, with the quantity being to taste and dependent on the size of the onions.

1. Chop the scooped-out onion and mix with finely chopped, lightly fried mushrooms, a few soft breadcrumbs, enough stock or brown gravy to moisten it all, salt and cayenne pepper to taste.
2. Mix the scooped-out onion with soft breadcrumbs, add chopped or minced left-over meat, chicken, ham, tongue, etc and bind together with a sauce, stock or gravy.
3. Mix soft breadcrumbs, grated cheese, dry mustard and bind with a white sauce (the scooped-out onions can go into a sauce).
4. Finely diced fried bacon, breadcrumbs and finely chopped sage.

If not using cheese in the stuffing, the onions can be sprinkled with grated cheese and put under the grill to brown. Serve plain or with a sauce: almost any savoury sauce can be used in this recipe.

Fried Onion Rings

onions	*oil for deep frying*
milk	*salt*
flour	

No 1
Choose large firm onions, preferably Spanish. Peel and cut them into thick slices ½ cm (¼ in) thick. Soak barely covered in milk for 30 minutes then drain, dry and separate the rings. Roll in flour, brush off excess and fry a few at a time in deep, very hot oil until they are a golden brown. Take the rings from the oil with a perforated spoon as they brown, drain on absorbent paper, sprinkle with salt and keep warm in the oven until all the rings are fried. Serve at once.

No 2
Cut the onions into rings, dip them first in flour then in beaten egg white and fry in deep hot fat. Drain as above.

No 3

Cut the onions into rings, drop first into beaten egg then breadcrumbs and fry in deep fat.

Onion Sauce (French)

6 servings

450 g (1 *lb*) *mild onions*
30 g (1 *oz*) *butter*
70 ml (⅛ *pt*) *dry white wine*
70 ml (⅛ *pt*) *clear light stock*

280 ml (½ *pt*) *white sauce*
70 ml (⅛ *pt*) *cream*
salt and pepper

Peel the onions as directed and coarsely chop. Drop into boiling water and boil for 10 minutes. Drain. Melt the butter in a saucepan, add the onions, stir, add the wine and stock and cook gently for 20 minutes. Rub through a vegetable mill. Return to the pan, add the white sauce, stir thoroughly until mixed, lower the heat, add the cream, salt and pepper, stir well until the sauce is hot.

Serve with poached eggs, chicken and other white meats, lamb or mutton.

Onion and Apple Casserole

4 servings

450 g (1 *lb*) *large mild onions*
450 g (1 *lb*) *tart apples*
butter or margarine
salt and pepper

sugar and cinnamon
2–3 *tablespoons double cream*
   (optional)

Peel the onions as directed, slice thinly and cook in boiling water to cover for 10 minutes. Drain but reserve the liquid. Peel, core and thinly slice the apples. Rub a baking dish with butter. Arrange a layer of onions on the bottom, sprinkle with salt and pepper, spread with a layer of apples, sprinkle with sugar and cinnamon and slivers of butter. Repeat these layers, making onions the top layer. Add enough of the reserved liquid to moisten, then the cream.

Bake in a moderate oven (180C, 350F, Mark 4) for 40 to 45 minutes, or until the mixture is soft.

Serve with roast or boiled pork or cutlets. Although the quantity of sugar is to taste, the dish is meant to be spicy and sweet.

The above mixture, omitting moistening with the onion liquid, makes an admirable filling for a double crust Onion and Apple Pie. Line a flan dish with short-crust pastry, arrange the onions and apples on top as above, cover with pastry and press hard all round the sides to ensure the filling is intact. Bake in a fairly hot oven (200C, 400F, Mark 6) for 40 to 45 minutes.

Serve hot, warm or take cold on a picnic.

Parsnips

There is considerable evidence that the cultivated parsnip was known both to the Greeks and the Romans and that the latter were said to have served them with a sauce, the basis of which was mead or honey wine. The Emperor Tiberius liked them so much that he imported them from France and Germany where the climate allowed them to grow to perfection. They were, before the potato was introduced into Britain in 1563, always roasted along with the meat and, indeed, often still are. But they have had a chequered career and today it seems there are no half measures where taste is concerned. The French we are told despise them and, says one writer, 'on the whole they are right', adding rather condescendingly 'but if young and carefully cooked, they can be pleasing enough for a change.' However, another writer more kindly says, 'parsnips, which so many people never touch until the correctness of eating salt cod on Good Friday reminds them of their existence, are most delicious.' While an early cookbook warns us: 'Parsnips eaten too old and in great quantities, cause delirium and insanity, on which account they have been called fool's parsnips', and, as a footnote, Sir Kenelm Digby wrote: 'Parsnips cut into little pieces is the best food for tame Rabets, and makes them sweet'.

How to Cook Parsnips

Obviously the best parsnips are those young and fresh from the garden. They should be washed, brushed or scraped, not peeled, the stem end and tips cut off and the parsnips put into cold, acidulated water and left for about 30 minutes. If your parsnips have brown marks on the shoulder of the root, this indicates canker, a common disease of the parsnip. Simply cut this away. If the parsnips are large, then thinly peel with a potato peeler, cut into halves or large chunks.

Quantities. Allow 170–200 g (6–8 oz) per serving.

Boiled Parsnips

6 servings

1 kg (2¼ lb) parsnips   salt and pepper to taste

Wash and prepare the parsnips as directed. If small and young, keep them whole; otherwise cut into halves or chunks. Put into a pan with cold, salted water, bring to the boil and boil gently, i.e., with the water just bubbling, until tender. Test with a skewer or fork after about 30 minutes. If the skewer pierces the parsnips easily, they are ready; if not, continue cooking until they are. Young parsnips usually take between 40 and 45 minutes, but I have known really large, old fellows take up to 90 minutes. If they are large and ancient, it is better to cook them in a pressure cooker. In fact, parsnips cook well in a pressure cooker whatever their age or size.

Buttered Parsnips

6 servings

1 *kg* (2¼ *lb*) *parsnips*   salt and pepper to taste
melted butter

Prepare and cook the parsnips as for Boiled Parsnips. When tender, take from the heat, drain and either slice or cut into cubes. If they have any hard core, this should be removed. Return the parsnips to the pan for 2 to 3 minutes to dry off their moisture and reheat. Serve in a hot dish with the melted butter poured over the top and sprinkled with salt and pepper.

Puréed Parsnips

6 servings

1 *kg* (2¼ *lb*) *parsnips*   salt and white pepper to taste
85 *g* (3 *oz*) *butter*

Prepare and cook the parsnips as directed for Boiled Parsnips. When very tender, drain thoroughly, put into a warmed bowl and crush the parsnips with a fork or potato masher, or rub through a coarse sieve. Melt the butter in a saucepan, add the parsnips and cook gently for a few minutes, add salt and white pepper, mix well and continue to cook gently until the purée is hot.

Serve hot, garnished with melted or lemon butter, cream sauce or a Béchamel sauce.

Roast Parsnips

4–6 servings

Prepare the parsnips as directed and cut into halves or quarters, depending on their size. Have ready a baking pan with hot fat, add the parsnips, roll them in the fat, then bake in a moderate oven (180C, 350F, Mark 4) until tender for 30 to 45 minutes. Turn once or twice to ensure even browning all over.

Because of the sugar contained in parsnips, they will caramelize on the outside as they roast which does give them a delicious flavour. Parsnips also can be roasted with meat, in particular pork.

Fried Parsnips

Prepare and boil the parsnips as directed. When tender, take from the pan and thoroughly drain, then pat gently dry. Cut into slices, sprinkle with seasoning, roll lightly in flour and fry in deep, hot oil or fat.

Sautéed Parsnips

Prepare and boil the parsnips as directed then take from the pan to drain and dry as directed in Fried Parsnips. Have ready just enough butter or other fat in a wide shallow pan, add the parsnips and cook gently but quickly until they are slightly discoloured, tossing them once or twice. Drain off any excess fat, sprinkle with salt, white pepper and finely chopped parsley, stir lightly and serve at once, as hot as possible.

 *Peas*

General Instructions

Like many of our everyday foods, peas have a long history. Relics have been found in dwellings of the Bronze Age, in a tomb at Thebes, and among the ruins of ancient Troy. They were extolled both in Greece and Rome. The oldest use of peas was in the dried form and it was not until the Middle Ages that people began to use green peas, cooking the pods and then eating the peas from the pods. In the days of Elizabeth I they were expensive, many being imported from

Holland and considered 'fit dainties for ladies, they come so far and cost so dear'.

The shucking of peas before being cooked marked a great step in the evolution of pea eating, a method of cooking which was taken up by the French Court during the reign of Louis IX. Madame Maintenant wrote in 1696 'that the subject of peas (i.e., fresh and green out of the pod) continues to absorb all others . . . and some ladies, having supped at the Royal Table, will go home and have a dish of peas . . . it is both a fashion and a madness'. The French liked and still prefer the small round pea, while the English developed a larger, smooth and unwrinkled variety. When the British colonists settled in the United States they took their peas with them and already in 1629 the Rev. Francis Higginson wrote: 'There is in Massachussetts a store of green peas as good as I ever ate in England . . .'.

Today peas are one of the favourite vegetables almost everywhere and horticulturists are constantly improving on existing varieties. It is difficult to say exactly how many peas will result from shucking a pound of them, but it should be around 1 good cup. At any rate, when cooking peas, allow at least 225 g (½ lb) unshelled and 110 g (4 oz) shelled per person.

If possible, pick and shuck peas just before cooking them; however, if they must be shucked in advance, wrap them in a slightly damp cloth and leave until required. Before cooking, pour cold running water over the peas. Separate the small peas from the larger ones and put the former into the pan after the larger ones have been cooking for a while.

British housewives throw away the pods; this is a pity for when they are young and tender they can be cooked and made into a purée or soup. They can be boiled in salted water until soft then rubbed through a sieve or whirled in a liquidiser. The purée can then be made with the addition of some stock into a very pleasant soup.

To Cook Young Fresh Garden Peas

Put the freshly shucked peas into a pan with very little
boiling, lightly salted water and cook until tender, about
10 minutes. They should not have any additives, not even the
cherished mint, nor sugar; the flavour, especially those of
the first sowing, is too delicate to take extra flavourings.
When the peas are tender, strain well, put into a dish, add
slivers of butter, a little salt and pepper and serve at once.

Older peas can be cooked in the same manner but both
mint and sugar may be added.

Do not discard the liquid in which peas are cooked but
serve it with the peas, for it should be very little. However,
if you have used too much water, drain the peas and put the
liquid aside to flavour a soup or stock.

Peas Bonne Femme

4 servings

30 g (1 oz) butter or margarine
450 g (1 lb) shucked peas
heart 1 small lettuce, shredded
4–5 small spring onions,
  trimmed and sliced

1 teaspoon sugar
salt and pepper
15 g (½ oz) butter
1 teaspoon flour

Heat the first quantity of butter in a pan, add the peas,
lettuce, spring onions, sugar, salt and pepper (preferably
black pepper, freshly ground) and just enough boiling water
(even better, stock) to cover. Cook gently over a low heat
until the peas are tender. Soften the second quantity of
butter and knead with the flour, stirring all the time, until
the butter has blended in. Take the peas from the stove and
add the kneaded butter bit by bit. Cook for a few minutes
longer, test for seasoning and serve the peas as a main dish.

Instead of kneaded butter and flour, 1 to 2 tablespoons of
cream may be used.

Green Peas with Cream

4 servings

450 g (1 *lb*) *shucked peas*
140 ml (¼ *pt*) *stock*
mixed chopped parsley and mint
*   to taste*
½ *teaspoon sugar*

140 ml (¼ *pt*) *single cream or*
*   top-of-milk*
2 *egg yolks, well beaten*
salt and nutmeg to taste
fried bread sippets

This dish of peas is meant to be served as a main dish not as an accompaniment.

Prepare and cook the peas as directed until they are *almost* tender. Drain and transfer to the top of a double boiler. Add the stock, herbs and sugar and cook over boiling water until the peas are quite tender. Mix the cream with the eggs and pour this mixture into the peas, stirring gently all the while but take care the mixture does not come to the boil or the eggs will curdle. Add salt, if required, and a good grating of nutmeg. Serve on a hot dish with the fried bread sippets separately.

Purée of Peas

4 servings

450 g (1 *lb*) *shucked peas*
a little chopped onion
4–5 *lettuce leaves, shredded*

salt and sugar
1–2 *tablespoons single cream*
few slivers butter

A method of cooking older peas which makes them more digestible than serving them whole.

Prepare the peas as directed and cook in a little water until tender, with the onion and lettuce leaves. Strain and rub through a sieve. Return the purée to the pan and continue to cook until it dries, stirring constantly. Add salt and a little sugar to bring out the flavour. Just before serving, add cream and butter, stir well together and serve hot.

Green Peas with Carrots

4 servings

225 g (8 oz) baby carrots   salt and sugar to taste
225 g (8 oz) shucked peas   1–2 tablespoons cream
30 g (1 oz) butter or margarine   (optional)

Wash, dice and cook the carrots as directed. Cook the peas
as directed. When both are tender drain thoroughly. Put the
butter with the vegetables, salt and sugar into a separate
pan and continue to cook until the butter has melted,
stirring all the time to coat the vegetables. At the last
moment add the cream.

Peas Cooked in Their Pods

4–5 servings

1 kg (2¼ lb) peas, unshucked   some fresh mixed herbs
1 small onion, coarsely chopped

For this recipe, which comes from Italy, the peas must be
picked young and the pods very tender. Wash well and
remove any strings in the same manner as for string beans.
Put into a pan with enough boiling salted water to cover,
add the onion and herbs and cook until tender. Drain and
serve hot.

Often the Italians, after draining the peas, put them into
another pan together with a little melted butter and simmer
them for about 10 minutes then sprinkle grated Parmesan
cheese over them.

❧ Potatoes

General Instructions

Potato cultivation in South America goes back at least to the beginning of the Christian era, if not earlier. Pottery found in graves of that date confirm this view. Spaniards returning from the South Americas brought the potato back with them and it was described as 'this ground nut which, when boiled, became as soft as a cooked chestnut but has no thicker skin than a truffle'. The word potato is derived from the Spanish *patata* which is also the Italian name and is a variant of a South American word *batata*.

About 1565 Sir John Hawkins introduced the potato into Ireland, and twenty years later Sir Walter Raleigh brought it into England. Although some say it was Thomas Herriot who brought it from Virginia, while the Germans cheerfully attribute the honour to Sir Francis Drake and have erected a statue to him at Offenburg. However, whatever the story, it is obvious that potatoes used as a vegetable got off to a slow start in Britain, for it was not until the middle of the eighteenth century that they became popular. Gilbert White writing from Selbourne at the end of the century said potatoes 'are much esteemed here now by the poor'. But elsewhere on the Continent potatoes were being grown freely and considered by many (naturally) as an aphrodisiac, also a cure for rheumatism. In Scotland right up to the middle of the eighteenth century Scottish preachers condemned the innocent potato as not a fit food for Christians since there was no mention of them in the Bible.

Today the potato is one of the world's main crops despite the fear that they are fattening, a fear that has been with potato eaters certainly since 1655 when one Dr Muffet wrote sternly, 'Potatoes (*patade*) engender much flesh'. But do they? Anything is fattening if you eat too much of it. It is one of our finest vegetables and goes with almost everything, as well as producing some fine main dishes. One medium-sized boiled potato has the same number of calories, 76, as one medium-sized apple. No one seems to accuse apples as being fattening.

How to Prepare Old Potatoes

Wash well, scrub if very dirty. For the greatest retention of vitamin content, says the Potato Marketing Board, always cook them in their skins and serve in their jackets when possible. However, if they must be skinned, the skins come off easily after boiling. Remove the eyes and any bruised parts, although this, hopefully, does not often appear with one's own garden potatoes. Do not leave them too long in water. If using a mechanical peeler, take them out as soon as they are peeled and put into the pan to cook. However, if potatoes must be prepared in advance, keep them covered in cold water to prevent discolouration Unless preparing potatoes for chips, do not cut them until about to be cooked or they will lose much of their vitamin content. Always remember the old adage, 'a potato quickly boiled is quickly spoiled'. To prevent discolouration in old potatoes, add 1 or 2 tablespoons of lemon juice or vinegar 10 minutes before draining. At the same time, i.e., 10 minutes before draining, salt should be added, not earlier. It is interesting too that the Potato Marketing Board recommends using margarine for all mashed potato mixtures.

Quantities: allow 225 g (8 oz) per serving.

Potatoes Boiled (Old)

4–6 servings

1 *kg* (2¼ *lb*) *old potatoes*   2 *teaspoons salt*

If possible choose potatoes of uniform size; if not possible, after scrubbing and maybe peeling, cut the larger potatoes to the same size as the smaller; this is important as then all the potatoes will cook in the same time.

Put the potatoes into a pan, add just enough cold or

boiling water to cover. There is a large school of thought which insists on using boiling water from the start, but the texture of old potatoes seems to improve when started in cold water. Also, to prevent discolouration, add one or two tablespoons of lemon juice or vinegar to the water about 10 minutes before they are ready. Cover the pan, bring the water to the boil, lower the heat and simmer until the potatoes are tender. After 10 minutes add salt and after 20 minutes test with a fork. If not ready, continue cooking but do not let them over-cook or they will turn into a mush. Drain well, return to the dry pan and dry by shaking them well over the heat. Serve at once. If cooked in their skins, they can be peeled or left as they are. Or the drained potatoes can be returned to the pan, topped with a few slivers of butter, the pan covered but with the lid tilted to let out the steam as the potatoes continue to dry and become coated with the butter.

Basic Method for Cooking New Potatoes

Wash the potatoes, rub them with a rough towel to rid them of loose skins. But if you feel strongly about skins, and some people do, then scrub or lightly scrape them after washing. Cook the potatoes in boiling water; after 10 minutes add 1 teaspoon of salt to each pound of potatoes. They should cook in 15 to 20 minutes: take care not to over-cook. When ready, take from the heat, drain and return the potatoes to the dry pan. Add butter to taste and swirl the potatoes round and round until the butter melts over the lowest possible heat and the potatoes are well coated. Turn into a heated vegetable dish; they are ready to serve but you can sprinkle them lightly with finely chopped parsley, savory, mint or chives, even watercress.

It will be noticed that I do not suggest adding a sprig of mint to the pan when cooking new potatoes. There are two reasons for this: I think the mint discolours the potatoes but even more important is that mint is too strong a flavour for really new garden potatoes. Continental cooks are astonished at our general use of mint, in particular using it in new potatoes. New potatoes should be served in as simple a form as possible.

New potatoes can be sautéed, either whole or cut into halves or slices. Because of their waxy texture, new potatoes are good for potato chips and salads.

How to Steam Potatoes

It is a safe maxim to state that potatoes are always better steamed than boiled as they lose less of their intrinsic value with slow cooking. Certainly they take on a different flavour. They may be steamed in their jackets or peeled. Place the potatoes in a steamer, sprinkle with salt and steam over boiling water for 40 minutes to 1 hour. When tender, dry over a direct heat for a minute or so then serve immediately, as for boiled potatoes.

How to Bake Potatoes in their Jackets

This is a favourite British method of cooking potatoes, one not much appreciated on the Continent in general, which seems strange. Select large, floury, even-sized potatoes. Wash and scrub them, dry well and prick all over with a fork to allow the steam to escape and produce a light and fluffy potato, but do not dig the fork into the flesh. If the potatoes are not punctured in this way they often explode in the oven as they bake. However, some cooks strongly disagree with puncturing, declaring it makes not a whit of difference. If a soft skin is liked, rub the potatoes with oil or butter before putting them into the oven.

The potatoes can be baked on a baking sheet which has first been sprinkled with a layer of coarse salt. The salt actually assists in the cooking as it contains a certain amount of moisture. The object of the salt is to prevent a hard skin forming on the bottom of the potatoes. Or the potatoes can simply be baked on the rungs of the baking shelf. Bake in a very hot oven (230C, 450F, Mark 8) for 45 to 60 minutes, or until they feel soft when pinched with the fingers. When ready, prick deeply with a fork and leave in the oven for a minute or so to let the steam escape. This makes for a mealy potato.

Baked potatoes can be served in a number of ways. Bring them to the table as they are for margarine, salt and pepper to be added as desired. Cut a slit in the potato and sprinkle this with salt, pepper, grated nutmeg and push in a sliver of margarine. Or cut a deep cross on the top of each, hold it with a cloth and squeeze it gently until the flesh comes through the opening and put a pat of margarine on the top.

Stuffed Baked Jacket Potatoes

baked jacket potatoes (p. 219)   *salt and pepper*
finely chopped chives or parsley   *grated cheese*

Bake potatoes as directed. Cut off a slice from the top of each potato. Scoop out the inside but be careful not to break the skin; also, leave enough of the potato to form a shell. Mix the scooped-out potato with chives or parsley, add seasoning and mash until smooth; a little margarine can also be added. Replace the mashed potato into the shells, sprinkle with grated cheese and reheat, either in the oven or under the grill.

Prepared in this manner the potatoes can be served either with meat or as a main dish.

Roast Potatoes No 1

Select medium-sized potatoes, peel and either cut into halves or leave whole. Place in the roasting pan with the meat and plenty of very hot dripping for about 1½ hours before the meat is to be served. Turn and baste once or twice when cooking. The oven should be fairly hot (200C, 400F, Mark 6). Serve with the joint or in a hot dish. To speed up roasting, the potatoes can be parboiled for 15 minutes, drained and dried before roasting, thus reducing the roasting time by half.

Roast Potatoes No 2

Put the prepared potatoes into a roasting pan on top of the stove with enough hot fat, preferably dripping, to cover. Cook them until the fat has been reheated then transfer to a very hot oven (230C, 450F, Mark 8) and continue cooking until the potatoes are brown and crisp. Serve with roast meats.

Mashed Potatoes

4 servings

1 *kg* (2¼ *lb*) *potatoes*
about 280 *ml* (½ *pt*) *milk*

30 *g* (1 *oz*) *margarine, cut into*
   small pieces
salt and pepper

If using large potatoes, these must first be cut into halves or even quarters. Prepare as for boiled or steamed potatoes but make quite certain they are dry before mashing. This is important for if the potatoes are floury they are more easily mashed with a fork, potato masher or ricer. Scald the milk; an exact quantity cannot be given as some potatoes absorb more milk than others. Gradually add the hot milk to the potatoes, mixing well but not beating them; then add the margarine and beat until they are smooth and creamy. Add salt and pepper then beat the potatoes over a low heat until they are white and almost fluffy.

Some cooks add a little baking powder to mashed potatoes to ensure lightness and fluffiness. A generous pinch of freshly grated nutmeg added at the same time as the seasoning also is a good addition.

Golden Mountain Potatoes

4–6 servings

450 *g* (1 *lb*) *hot mashed potatoes*
salt, pepper and nutmeg
30 *g* (1 *oz*) *margarine*
110 *g* (4 *oz*) *cheese, diced*

3 *whole eggs, well beaten*
oil and crushed garlic
grated cheese to taste

To the potatoes add salt, pepper, nutmeg, margarine and the diced cheese, then the eggs, beating well all the time. Rub a shallow baking dish with oil and garlic, add the potatoes in uneven heaps, letting each heap fall into the shape of a 'mountain'. Sprinkle the 'summits' generously with grated cheese and bake in a hot oven (220C, 425F, Mark 7) until the cheese melts, slides down the sides and the tops begin to brown.

Serve with meat, fish, grilled tomatoes, or with chops, steaks, etc, or as a main dish.

Sauté Potatoes

Any kind of potato, raw or cooked, warm or cold, slightly under-cooked, and firm potatoes can be sautéed. If potatoes are over-cooked, they will break up in the pan with the extra cooking.

Peel the potatoes and cut into $\frac{1}{2}$ cm ($\frac{1}{4}$ in) thick slices which may be cut into half again if preferred. Heat just enough fat or oil to cover the bottom of a thick frying-pan. When the fat is just smoking, add the potatoes, sprinkle with salt and pepper and sauté, turning them with a spatula once or twice to cook evenly. As they begin to cook, they will brown round the edges. When they are all thus browned, toss lightly and cook until a light brown on both sides. Handle with care, otherwise the potatoes will break into small pieces, not affecting the flavour but their appearance.

Serve with grilled and fried meats, cutlets and gammon rashers. Very large, cold boiled potatoes may be thickly sliced, dipped into beaten egg and fine breadcrumbs, then sautéed as above.

Potato Chips (Saratoga Chips in the USA)

Choose large, preferably waxy potatoes for chips. Wash and peel and slice the potatoes lengthwise into slices about $1\frac{1}{2}$ cm ($\frac{1}{2}$ in) thick then slice again the other way. (Or use a chip cutting device.) Drop into iced water and leave for 30 to 40 minutes. Drain and dry thoroughly in a towel. Have ready a deep pan of boiling hot oil or fat. Fry the chips a few at a time until brown and tender. Drain on absorbent paper and sprinkle with salt.

If using a wire frying basket, put a few chips at a time into this and immerse it in the boiling fat and fry the chips until they just begin to brown at the edges. Lift the chips out of the fat, reheat the oil and return the chips to the pan to continue frying until a golden brown and tender. Drain on absorbent paper and sprinkle with salt.

Potato Crisps or Game Chips

Choose small, even-sized potatoes; wash, peel and slice in wafer-thin slices, or use a mandolin. Drop into iced water and leave for 30 to 60 minutes. Drain and dry thoroughly then continue as for chips.

A mandolin, which today we think as being a French utensil, was well known in Mrs Beeton's day and earlier but it was called a cucumber slicer.

Match or Julienne Potatoes

Choose old and waxy potatoes; wash, peel and cut into thin match-like sticks. Soak in iced water for 30 to 60 minutes, drain and dry thoroughly. Then continue as for chips, stirring them from time to time. They will not take more than a minute or so to fry.

Straw Potatoes

Peel and coarsely shred the potatoes. Leave in iced water for 30 to 60 minutes, remove with a perforated spoon and carefully dry. This is an important procedure, otherwise the potatoes will stick together while cooking. Fry for a minute or so in a deep pan with very hot oil and drain quickly on absorbent paper.

Straw potatoes can be served hot or cold and will keep crisp for at least a couple of days. They can be reheated in a hot oven.

Scalloped Potatoes

4 servings

450 g (1 *lb*) *floury potatoes*	*flour*
salt, pepper and nutmeg	15 g (½ *oz*) *butter*
1 *small onion, minced*	420 ml (¾ *pt*) *scalded milk*

Wash and peel the potatoes and slice thinly. Place a layer at the bottom of a baking dish. Sprinkle with salt, pepper, nutmeg, onion and flour. Repeat these layers until the dish is almost full, finishing with a top layer of potatoes. Sprinkle this layer lightly with salt, pepper and nutmeg and dot with slivers of butter. Add the milk, which must not come above the potatoes. Cover and cook in a moderate oven (180C, 350F, Mark 4) for 30 minutes, then uncover and continue cooking for 20 to 30 minutes longer.

There are variations such as: use cooked potatoes instead of raw, cooking time will be less; or add grated cheese, or flaked fish, or finely chopped fresh herbs, or fried mushrooms, or diced bacon between each layer of potatoes. Finally, the top may be sprinkled with fine breadcrumbs then dotted with butter.

Brown Potato Hash

cold boiled and peeled potatoes as required	*finely chopped herbs*
	dripping
salt, pepper and cayenne pepper	

Dice the potatoes and mix with plenty of salt and pepper, a good pinch of cayenne pepper and some finely chopped herbs. Heat just enough dripping in a thick frying-pan that, when melted, will cover the bottom of the pan, and spread with the potatoes. Press down and fry until the bottom is brown. Turn and brown the top side, or put under a hot grill. Serve turned out on to a hot dish with a tomato sauce and diced, crisply fried bacon.

Potato Croquettes

4 servings

450 g (1 lb) potatoes
45 g (1½ oz) margarine
salt and pepper
nutmeg
1 egg yolk

2 tablespoons grated cheese
1 whole egg, well beaten
fine breadcrumbs
fat or oil for deep frying

Wash and peel the potatoes, cut into halves and cook in boiling salted water until soft. Drain well, return to the pan and cook over a moderate heat until they are dry. Crush with a potato masher, add the margarine and beat until the mixture is smooth. Take the purée from the stove, add salt, pepper, nutmeg and egg yolk, beat well then beat in the cheese. Leave to cool then break off pieces about the size of an egg and shape into croquettes. Dip first into beaten egg then into breadcrumbs and fry in deep, boiling fat until a golden brown. Take from the pan, drain on absorbent paper and serve garnished with coarsely chopped parsley.

Potato, Onion and Cheese Casserole

4 servings

280 ml (½ pt) milk
1 dessertspoon flour
salt to taste
225 g (8 oz) onion, chopped
1–2 cloves garlic
good pinch cayenne pepper

450 g (1 lb) potatoes
110 g (4 oz) sharp cheese, grated
butter or margarine
fine breadcrumbs

Combine the first six ingredients and purée in a liquidiser. Wash, peel and grate the potatoes, do not soak them in water as their starch is needed for this recipe. Mix into the purée and add the cheese. Rub a 23 cm (9 in) baking dish generously with butter or other fat, add the potato mixture, sprinkle the top with fine breadcrumbs and bake in a moderate oven (180C, 350F, Mark 4) for 1 to 1¼ hours, or until the top is brown.

Can be served as a main dish or with cold meats.

 *Spinach*

General Instructions

Who would have guessed that Popeye's favourite vegetable has a history which can be traced to ancient origins in Persia, also that it has remained a favourite (well, not always perhaps) since the days of King Nebuchadnezzar of Babylon down to the present day? It was brought to Spain by the Arabs and the Spaniards promptly called it a 'prince of vegetables'. Later it spread through Europe, carried, it is said, by the Dutch who dubbed it 'the Spanish vegetable'. Included in *The Forme of Cury*, a cookbook published on the authority of Richard II's highly qualified chief cook, were recipes for 'spinaches'. Much later James Boswell talked of spinach which he called 'green grass'. For years it has basked in a favourable light as possessing iron-giving, body-building qualities, etc, and children were enjoined to eat it; it even made one's hair curl, so they said, and no doubt Popeye the Sailor helped to promote spinach consumption. Then suddenly out of the blue came a nutritional expert to tell us that spinach had none of these body-building, hair-curling properties at all, on the contrary, it was positively harmful. No doubt many children who cared little for body-building or curly hair cheered and sent him presents, but indignant doctors and other experts who had been telling us we should eat spinach emphatically denied all this as arrant nonsense. And, as it has been eaten throughout the centuries without, as far as one can tell, doing us any harm, even if it did not make the hair curl, we shall continue no doubt to eat it.

It is a useful vegetable and figures largely in classical cooking. It can never be over-cooked for, short of actually cooking it to death, the longer it is cooked the better. And, curiously, like the tomato it loses none of its vitamins when preserved, i.e., tinned or frozen.

Quantities, allow 225 g (8 oz) per serving.

How to Prepare and Cook Spinach

As spinach grows close to the ground, it requires considerable washing to remove all its grit. Pick it over carefully and cut off the roots. Drop the leaves and stems into a bowl of warm water and push it around and about several times and leave in the bowl for some minutes. Lift it out of the bowl with your hands, this is important, otherwise if you pour it out together with the water you are merely putting the grit which has fallen to the bottom back into the spinach. Repeat this performance once more then drop the spinach into a bowl of cold water. Lift it up from the bowl and drop it straight into the pan without adding any liquid, there is enough on the leaves. Cook until tender, it drops firmly to the bottom of the pan when tender and reduces itself in the most alarming way. Add salt, pepper and nutmeg. Take from the pan and drain well, for watery spinach is an abomination.

Serve garnished with chopped hard-boiled eggs, triangles of flaky pastry, or sippets of fried bread.

There are some people who object to the dark colour of cooked spinach. To retain its colour, when the spinach is tender, after draining, squeeze it dry and put under cold running water, or immerse it in the colander in a bowl of water. This stops it cooking and keeps its colour. It must then be returned to the pan and reheated in butter.

Hot Spinach Mousse

4 servings

butter
450 g (1 lb) boiled spinach
2 eggs, well beaten

140 ml (¼ pt) double cream
salt, pepper and nutmeg

Rub a ring mould generously with butter. Be sure that the
spinach is well-drained before you start work on it. Rub
through a vegetable mill. Mix with the eggs, fold in the
cream, add salt, pepper and nutmeg (also, if liked a good
pinch of sugar). Pour the mixture into the mould, put this
into a pan of hot water and bake in a moderate oven (180C,
350F, Mark 4) for about 30 minutes, or until firm. Take
from the oven and leave for a minute or so to set. Turn out
carefully on to a hot, round platter and fill the centre with
creamed white fish, prawns, chicken or mushrooms.

Baked Spinach with Eggs (Eggs Florentine)

4 servings

1 kg (2¼ lb) spinach
30 g (1 oz) butter
3–4 anchovy fillets, chopped
salt, pepper and nutmeg

4 eggs
grated cheese
fried bread triangles

Prepare the spinach as directed. Heat the butter, add the
anchovies then the spinach. Cook until it has been reduced
by half, then sprinkle with salt, pepper and nutmeg. Continue cooking until the spinach is very soft. Take from the
pan and drain well, this is important otherwise the dish will
be soggy. Chop finely and spread on the bottom of a shallow
baking dish. With the back of a wooden spoon make four wells
in each corner of the spinach and break an egg into each
well. Sprinkle with cheese; the quantity is to taste but do
not drown the flavour of the spinach. Bake in a hot oven
(220C, 425F, Mark 7) until the eggs are set, about 5
minutes.

Serve with fried bread.

Panna - Spinach Pâté

4–6 servings

450 g (1 *lb*) *spinach*
1 *small onion, chopped*
small piece tarragon
2–3 *sprigs parsley, chopped*
salt, pepper and nutmeg

4 *sardines*
4–6 *anchovy fillets, chopped*
2 *hard-boiled eggs, chopped*
30 g (1 *oz*) *butter, softened*

I came across this recipe many years ago and have never been sure of its origin. Whether it is related to the Irish panah, which is a sardine and anchovy butter flavoured with cayenne pepper, I do not know. Panna makes an interesting and original first course and should be served in the same manner as chicken liver pâté.

Prepare and cook the spinach as directed, together with the onion, tarragon, parsley, salt, pepper and nutmeg. When tender, squeeze absolutely dry. While the spinach is cooking, fillet the sardines and mix together with the anchovies, hard-boiled eggs and butter. Pound to a thick paste and rub this through a fine sieve. This is very important, otherwise the mixture is not smooth enough and the eggs appear as little yellow and white specks, thus spoiling the appearance of the panna. Turn into a round dish, smooth flat and put into the refrigerator to chill. Turn out to serve, cut in the same manner as pâté, with hot very crisp toast.

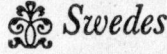 *Swedes*

General Instructions

Swedes, called rutabaga in the United States, also more commonly 'yellow turnips', are today somewhat neglected although I remember as a child in the country they were an everyday vegetable. They were first introduced in Britain towards the end of the seventeenth century and, as its name implies, came from Sweden. It was also known as the Swedish and even Lapland turnip.

How to Cook Swedes

Wash the swedes before peeling. Peel rather thickly to remove the thick outer skin and keep the swedes covered in cold water as soon as peeled but cook them as quickly as possible after peeling. If they are to be cooked and mashed, cut into large pieces; if for scalloping or frying, either into round discs or dice. They should be covered in plenty of boiling salted water; very young swedes will cook in some 30 minutes, older ones will take considerably longer, up to 60 minutes. They can be cooked in a pressure cooker in a matter of minutes.

Quantities, allow 170–225 g (6–8 oz) per person.

Mashed Swedes

4 servings

1 kg (2¼ lb) swedes	nutmeg
salt and pepper	butter or margarine

Prepare the swedes as directed and cut into cubes for mashing. Cook covered in boiling salted water until very tender. Drain well, mash with a little salt, plenty of pepper and a good grating of nutmeg, add about 30 g (1 oz) of butter and serve hot.

For a richer dish, beat in double cream, about 140 ml (¼ pt) should be ample for this dish.

Swedes Cooked in Dripping

4 servings

1 kg (2¼ lb) swedes	diced bacon to taste
dripping	

Prepare the swedes as directed and cut into dice. Heat enough dripping to cover the bottom of a large, thick saucepan. Heat the dripping until very hot, add the diced swede and bacon, stir well, cover the pan and cook over a moderate heat. Stir from time to time and re-cover the pan quickly. When the swedes are tender they will be slightly sugary and a deep golden colour.

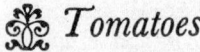 *Tomatoes*

General Instructions

As the tomato plant is a member of the deadly nightshade family, it is perhaps not surprising that at one time it alarmed people and they stayed away from it as from a beautiful but dangerous woman. Its exact origin is in doubt, some experts say it began in India, others in Africa or China. But it was certainly cultivated in Peru where the Spaniards, searching for gold, instead came across what they called 'the golden apple. The Peruvians had been cultivating it assiduously and it was a frequent motif found on their pottery. Its present name is of Mexican origin, *tomatl*.

Certainly it was the Spaniards who brought the tomato to Europe, rather more as a decoration than as food. Then in Italy they became *pomi de mori*, apples from the Moors, and later *pomodori*, or golden apples. The French called them *pommes d'amour*, maybe because red is the colour of love but more prosaically it was their corruption of the Italian *pomi de mori*. But the French did start cooking it, which showed courage, for it was said that only a potential suicide or hapless lover would toy with a tomato.

Today it enjoys no such reputation and tomatoes are grown and sold throughout the world, in tropical and temperate countries. In the USA alone recipes for cooking them are 'as sands on the seashore' and the fruit appears in every kind of salad. But this applies equally to Italy, Greece and Portugal.

Tomatoes vary tremendously and some of those large, untidy looking and almost indecently shaped Mediterranean tomatoes have an incomparable flavour. For eating raw, the English swear by the round, sweet English tomato, and it does take a lot of beating. But it is important to use the right tomato for the right dish.

Among the lesser known varieties of the tomato is the yellow, with an extra sweetness and delicacy. The pear or bell tomato, named for its shape, keeps well and is used in Italy for sauces and canning, also for sun-drying and preserving in oil. There is the sugar or grape tomato, prolific and ornamental and very sweet. It can be used in salads; also with sugar and cream, try it one day and see. The Tiny Tim is a dwarf tomato grown in pots and the fruits are good in salads, soups and savoury dishes. In New Zealand there is the tree tomato. The tree, of a fair height, has tomatoes hanging down in clusters, the fruits eaten principally as a dessert but also to make jams.

How to Cook Tomatoes

Select firm but ripe tomatoes for most cooking, also for salads. To skin and blanch tomatoes, drop them into boiling water for 2 to 3 minutes then into cold. The skin can be easily peeled either with the fingers or with a silver knife. In many recipes the seeds also need to be taken out as these are considered indigestible. To do this, flick them out with the handle of a small spoon. When cooking tomatoes sugar should be added, but with discretion, for a little sweetness mitigates the acidity of the cooked fruit.

Stewed Tomatoes

4 servings

450 g (1 *lb*) *ripe tomatoes*	*some chopped herbs to taste*
15 g (½ *oz*) *butter or margarine*	*salt and pepper*
1 *small onion, minced*	1 *teaspoon sugar*

Blanch and peel the tomatoes, discard the seeds and cut the flesh into quarters or thick slices. Heat the butter, add the onion, cook this gently until it begins to change colour, then add the tomatoes, herbs, seasonings and sugar. Cover and cook gently until the tomatoes are soft, stirring from time to time with a wooden spoon.

Serve with fried bacon, or as a sauce over pasta, or with fried eggs, or as a side dish with fish, poultry or meat.

Green tomatoes can be cooked in the same manner but a little more sugar should be added. Some French cooks add a slice of lemon to the tomatoes when stewing them which is removed before serving.

Tomato Rarebit

4 servings

450 g (1 *lb*) *ripe tomatoes*
30 g (1 *oz*) *butter or margarine*
salt and pepper
1 *teaspoon sugar*

85 g (3 *oz*) *cheese, coarsely grated*
1 *teaspoon dry mustard*
4 *large slices toast*

Blanch and peel the tomatoes and discard the seeds. Mash the flesh with a fork. Heat the butter, add the tomatoes, salt, pepper and sugar and simmer until the tomatoes are soft and dry. Add the cheese, continue to cook gently, add the mustard, mix well and spread on hot toast to serve.

Baked Tomatoes au Gratin No 1

4 servings

450 g (1 *lb*) *ripe firm tomatoes*
salt and pepper
1 *small onion, minced*

85 g (3 *oz*) *cheese, coarsely grated*
30 g (1 *oz*) *fine breadcrumbs*
30 g (1 *oz*) *butter or margarine*

Blanch and peel the tomatoes. Cut into halves and discard the seeds. Sprinkle with salt and pepper. Arrange in a well greased baking dish, sprinkle with onion. Mix the cheese with the breadcrumbs and sprinkle over the tomatoes. Melt the butter, spoon it over the breadcrumbs and cheese mixture and bake in a hot oven (220C, 425F, Mark 7) until the tomatoes are soft, 15 minutes or so.

Baked Tomatoes au Gratin No· 2

Prepare the tomatoes as above but instead of halving them, cut into thick slices and spread them on a well greased baking dish. Sprinkle generously with finely ground black pepper, salt, sugar, some finely chopped green herbs, crushed garlic (if liked) and slivers of butter. Bake in a moderate oven (180C, 350F, Mark 4) for about 15 minutes, or until tender.

Tomatoes Riviera

6 servings

6 *firm large tomatoes*
olive oil
15 *g* (½ *oz*) *butter or margarine*
1 *shallot, minced*
1 *teaspoon flour*
140 *ml* (¼ *pt*) *warmed stock or*
  water

110 *g* (4 *oz*) *mushrooms,*
  minced
1 *tablespoon finely chopped*
  parsley
1–2 *cloves garlic, crushed*
salt and pepper
fine breadcrumbs

Blanch and peel the tomatoes. Scoop out a small hole in the stalk end of each. Rub a medium-sized gratin dish lightly with oil, add the tomatoes, stalk end uppermost. Heat the butter in a small pan, add the shallot, stir well and cook gently until it begins to change colour. Add the flour, stir well, then add the liquid, stirring all the time. Add the remaining ingredients (except breadcrumbs) and simmer for a few minutes. Pour this sauce into the scooped-out centres of the tomatoes and let it spill over the sides. Sprinkle lightly with breadcrumbs – too many will form a thick, soggy crust which is not desirable, and bake for 10 to 25 minutes in a hot oven (220C, 425F, Mark 7). Serve hot as a main dish.

In this recipe it really is important to peel the tomatoes before stuffing and baking, the flavour of the sauce penetrates them so much better and naturally the dish is enhanced. Failing a shallot, use 1–2 spring onions.

Stuffed Tomatoes

6 servings

6 *large firm tomatoes of uniform size*
30 g (1 oz) *butter or margarine*
1 *tablespoon olive oil*

1 *large onion, chopped*
110 g (4 oz) *mushrooms, sliced*
salt, pepper, nutmeg and sugar
breadcrumbs

Slice off the flower end of the tomatoes, scoop out the centres, sprinkle the insides with salt and leave for 30 minutes. Discard the seeds and mash the rest of the tomato pulp. Heat the butter and oil together, lightly fry the onion and mushrooms, add the tomato pulp, salt, pepper, nutmeg and sugar. Drain off the salty liquid from the tomatoes, fill each with filling and sprinkle generously with breadcrumbs. Bake in a moderate oven (180C, 350F, Mark 4) for 30 minutes, or until the tomatoes are soft but not squashed.

The mushrooms for this recipe must be washed but whether they are peeled or not is a matter for preference. Chopped garlic also may be added to the filling.

Whole Grilled Tomatoes

firm ripe tomatoes as required
salt, pepper and sugar

crushed garlic (optional)
oil and butter

The tomatoes should all be of equal size. Pull off the stalk from each and cut a thin slice off the bottom. Sprinkle with salt, pepper, sugar and garlic, if using. Rub the grill with oil, add the tomatoes, top each with a good sliver of butter and grill gently under a low heat until the tomatoes are brown and soft but not mushed.

Serve very hot with meat, poultry, bacon, or eggs, etc. or as a main dish.

Tomato halves or thick slices may be grilled in the same manner.

Tomatoes Provençe Style

6 servings

1 *cup soft white breadcrumbs*	6 *large firm tomatoes*
1–2 *cloves garlic, crushed*	*salt, pepper and sugar*
1 *tablespoon finely chopped parsley*	*olive oil*

Combine the breadcrumbs, garlic and parsley. Cut the tomatoes into halves, horizontally. Squeeze them gently to remove their seeds and excess liquid. If they are as firm as they should be this squeezing will do them no harm and they will spring back into shape. Arrange the halves in a shallow baking dish, cover each with some of the breadcrumb mixture, add salt, pepper and sugar and sprinkle the top with oil. Put under the grill or bake in a hot oven (220C, 425F, Mark 7) until the tomatoes are soft and the tops are browned.

If baking, pour a little oil on the bottom of the dish to prevent drying out. Serve as a main dish.

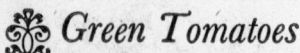 Green Tomatoes

General Instructions

Apart from being used to make a chutney, green tomatoes are excellent cooked in several ways. The Italians always use green tomatoes for salads.

Baked Green Tomatoes

4–6 servings

450 g (1 *lb*) green tomatoes
a few thin rashers bacon
grated cheese
salt, pepper and sugar

butter or margarine
stock
fine breadcrumbs

Cook the tomatoes in water to cover until fairly soft but not a mush. Drain and, as soon as sufficiently cool, peel. Slice the flesh. Line a small gratin dish with bacon, spread with the tomatoes and sprinkle with cheese, salt, pepper, sugar and slivers of butter. Add sufficient stock to moisten but not cover, sprinkle fairly generously with breadcrumbs and bake in a hot oven (220C, 425F, Mark 7) until the top is well browned.

Tomato Juice

450 g (1 *lb*) ripe tomatoes
1–2 ribs celery
a little chopped green pepper
   (optional)
½ bay leaf

1 tablespoon minced onion
salt and pepper
1 teaspoon Worcestershire Sauce
½ teaspoon horseradish, freshly
   grated

Coarsely chop the tomatoes and celery, add the green pepper, bay leaf and onion and cook for about 20 minutes until the tomatoes are soft. Rub through a vegetable mill. Add salt, pepper, Worcestershire Sauce and horseradish and stir well. Chill and shake well before using. This quantity will make 3 cups of juice.

Tomato Juice Sorbet

1 *recipe tomato juice* (above)

After straining the tomato juice, pour into a freezing tray and freeze to a mush, stirring once during freezing time. Just before serving, break up the sorbet with a fork and serve in a small glass as a starter to a meal.

Tomato Sauce

makes about 560 ml (1 pt)

450 g (1 *lb*) *tomatoes, very ripe* 2 *teaspoons sugar*
30 g (1 *oz*) *butter or margarine* *salt and pepper to taste*
1 *strip streaky bacon, chopped* 1 *bay leaf*
1 *each small onion and carrot,* 30 g (1 *oz*) *flour (optional)*
   chopped *milk (optional)*
280 ml (½ *pt*) *water or stock*

For this sauce it is essential that the tomatoes are both very ripe and juicy. The quantity of sauce produced depends on the juiciness of the tomatoes.

Blanch, peel and coarsely chop the tomatoes. Heat the butter in a saucepan, add the bacon and fry this until the fat starts to run, then add the onion and fry until it changes colour. Add the carrot and tomatoes, stir and cook over a moderate heat for 5 minutes, add the stock, sugar, salt, pepper and bay leaf. Bring gently to the boil, lower the heat and simmer for 30 minutes, stirring from time to time.

At this point the sauce is ready for serving. However, if a smooth sauce is preferred – and for some dishes and tastes this is so – rub it through a sieve and return the pulp to the pan. Combine the flour with enough milk or water to make a paste and stir this into the sauce and continue cooking until the sauce has thickened, at least 5 minutes, and serve hot.

This sauce can be served with any kind of baked or boiled fish, with boiled meats of all kinds, as well as with cauliflower, rissoles, fish cake and other similar cakes, and poached eggs.

✿ *Turnips and Kohlrabi*

General Instructions

Turnips have been in wide cultivation for centuries and grow wild in the area between the Baltic and the Caucasus. In 42 AD a writer noted that it was a vegetable eaten by man and beast, and Pliny mentioned that there were five different types of turnips, also remarking on a root which weighed 17 kg (40 lb). If this seems a monster, what can one say to the record-sized turnip produced in California in 1850 which weighed 45 kg (100 lb)? Surely inedible.

Both the ancient Greeks and Romans had turnips (what did they not have?) which they cooked rather plainly with spices, in particular cumin. And there is a story that the King of Bithynia, when on a campaign against the Scythians and far from the sea, expressed a desire for a dish of aphy, a small fish of which he was particularly fond. His cook, not having a supply of aphy but obviously a resourceful fellow, cut a large turnip into the exact shape of the small fish, fried it in oil and sprinkled it with crushed poppy seeds. The king, so we are told, was not only deceived but praised the 'fish' to his guests.

In Britain we did not have turnips quite so early, it seems not until the fifteenth century when they were grown in monastery gardens. There does not seem to be any early records of their being grown in kitchen gardens, not even royal ones. The second Viscount Townshend at the beginning of the eighteenth century, however, grew them so extensively in his kitchen garden in Raynham, Norfolk, that he earned for himself the nickname 'Turnip Townshend'.

Today Pliny would notice there are numerous varieties of turnip, all belonging to one or other of the two main turnip families, the round and the long-rooted, the former being sweeter than the latter. Turnips undoubtedly are at their best when young and in many parts of the Mediterranean they are sliced and eaten raw, or grated, and put into salads as part of the first course.

Turnips can be plainly boiled, puréed, baked au gratin, made into croquettes, used in stews and similar casserole dishes. They are deserving of good treatment and positively no vegetable requires more thorough draining than the watery turnip. Butter, says one vegetable expert, is an essential ingredient in the cooking of turnips or, as they call them across the border in Scotland, neeps, for it softens the rather coarse flavour to which some people object. And remember when combining turnips with other vegetables they should be in a minority as their flavour can be overpowering. Frequently turnips are served with fatty meats such as mutton, duck and goose as they have a capacity to absorb fat in the stomach and assist the digestion.

Young turnip tops can be stewed as spinach and indeed used in many of the ways of cooking and serving spinach.

Quantities. Allow 170–225 g (6–8 oz) per portion. For turnip tops, allow 225 g (8 oz) per portion.

To Cook Turnips

Peel the turnips thickly as they possess two layers of skin. As soon as peeled, drop into cold water to avoid discolouration. Young turnips, obviously the best, may be cooked whole; older ones should be cubed, sliced or diced, depending on the use to which they are being put. Put into boiling, salted water, cover the pan and cook until tender. Overcooking must be avoided, otherwise the turnips will become watery and unpleasant. Drain thoroughly. Serve whole if really small with melted butter and finely chopped parsley, but if the turnips are perhaps a shade too large and have been cut, serve them either with melted butter and parsley or with an egg or white sauce. Generally turnips can be cooked in the same manner as carrots. Swede and turnip recipes are interchangeable.

Cooking time depends entirely on the age, size and freshness of the turnips. Approximate timings are 15 to 20 minutes.

Turnip Tops

Except for those with gardens, turnip tops seem almost to
be a thing of the past but they make an excellent dish if
cooked and prepared with care. First remove the stalks and
discard any bruised leaves. Wash in heavily salted water.
Drain well, tie into little bundles and cook covered in a pan
of heavily salted water until tender. Drain thoroughly in a
colander, remove the strings and serve the tops with melted
butter.

They can also be finely chopped and put into a pan with
melted butter. When tender, pile on to a hot dish and serve
with a bowl of fried bread sippets separately. Or make a bed
of them and top with poached or steamed eggs. A good
grating of nutmeg also can be added with the seasoning.

Glazed Turnips

4 servings

1 *kg* (2¼ *lb*) *young turnips*	280 *ml* (½ *pt*) *stock*
30 *g* (1 *oz*) *butter or margarine*	*salt and pepper*
fine sugar	

Prepare and peel the turnips and trim until all are of the
same shape and about the size of a golf ball. Blanch the
turnips for 5 minutes in boiling salted water. Drain
thoroughly. Heat the butter in a shallow pan, add the
turnips, stir well, sprinkle lightly with sugar and cook over
a moderate heat, stirring frequently to prevent burning.
When they have browned, add the stock, salt and pepper,
cover the pan and cook slowly until the turnips are tender
but still retain their shape.

Serve with roasts, pork chops, etc.

F.F.G.—II

Turnips au Gratin

4–6 servings

1 kg (2¼ lb) turnips	60 g (2 oz) grated sharp cheese
salt	320 ml (¾ pt) white sauce
butter	

Prepare, cook and drain the turnips as directed. Cut into regular, fairly thin slices. Rub a baking dish with butter, add the sliced turnips in layers. Mix about two-thirds of the cheese with the white sauce. Pour this mixture over the turnips, sprinkle with the remaining cheese, dot with slivers of butter and bake in a moderate oven (180C, 350F, Mark 4) for about 10 minutes, or until the top is just brown. Serve as a main dish, possibly with potato chips or crisps.

KOHLRABI

General Instructions

The origin of this vegetable is obscure although it has long been a favourite in the Far East. It is a hybrid of the *Brassica* family with a swollen stem which looks rather like a turnip. Indeed, it has aptly been described as 'a turnip-rooted cabbage'. The flavour of the swollen stem or globe is similar to that of a turnip but more delicate and slightly nutty. Botanically it is closely related to the cabbage. The date of its introduction into Britain seems unknown but the famous herbalist Gerard mentions it in 1597, and so does Abercombie later in his *Gardeners' Dictionary* in 1786. However, it does not seem to have appealed to British taste. The part of the plant which is most appreciated is the globe or swollen stem, which is not the root as one might think. It can grow to about the size of a large orange but it is better taken from the ground before this size is reached. There are two main varieties, the green and purple.

How to Cook Kohlrabi

1. First the tops or leaves, which can be cooked in any of the ways in which spinach is cooked. Wash the leaves thoroughly, drain well and cook in a little salted water until tender. Take from the heat, drain thoroughly, return to the pan with a knob of butter, sprinkle lightly with salt, pepper and nutmeg and serve hot.

2. The young globes. If the globes are not more than 8 cm (3 in) in diameter, do not peel them for they will lose their delicate flavour; steam over boiling water until tender. They are ready to be served at this stage with perhaps a dressing of melted butter. Or they can be peeled, cut into strips and marinated in a salad dressing until cool, then chilled and served as a salad with cold meats.

3. Large kohlrabi globes require peeling. Insert a sharp knife under the tough fibre at the base of the stem and strip off the skin. Cut the globe into slices, cubes or quarters and cook in boiling salted water until tender, 25 to 30 minutes. Drain well, return to the pan with a knob of butter, some finely chopped parsley and/or chives, a little lemon juice and sprinkle lightly with salt, pepper and nutmeg.

Kohlrabi in Yogurt

4 servings

1 *kg* (2¼ *lb*) *kohlrabi*	1 *teaspoon flour*
30 *g* (1 *oz*) *butter or margarine*	*salt and pepper*
a little minced onion	½ *cup yogurt*

Prepare and slice the kohlrabi as for large globes and cook in boiling salted water until tender. Drain thoroughly. Heat the butter, add the onion and cook for a minute or so then add the flour, stirring all the time, then add salt and pepper and stir again. Take the pan from the heat, stir in the yogurt, return to the heat and cook gently until just reheated then pour this sauce over the drained kohlrabi.

Kohlrabi au Gratin

Follow the recipe above then turn into a well-buttered baking dish and top with buttered or fine breadcrumbs mixed with grated cheese. Bake in a moderate oven (180C, 350F, Mark 4) for about 15 minutes.

Sour or fresh cream can be substituted for yogurt.

 *Salads*

General Instructions

For the earliest mention of salads we must go back to the days of ancient Greece where we find references to raw vegetables dressed with a mixture of oil and vinegar, or simply with curd, as well as other more complicated dressings. For example, they made a dressing of garlic and black olives pounded in a mortar and then mixed with grapes, honey and olive oil. The rich used *garum* or *liquamen* which was made from the salted down entrails of fish from which the liquid was strained and stored in jars. Its fabrication seems to go back to the Greeks of the fourth century BC. A less expensive dressing was one of leeks, garlic, honey and cheese, all pounded to a sauce.

Among the popular saladings used was lettuce, prized as a food from the earliest of time. It was grown in ancient Egypt and more than likely grew wild all over temperate Europe before being cultivated in gardens. It was offered to Min, the god of fertility, no doubt because it was thought that the milky liquid in the lettuce was an aphrodisiac. Lettuce also grew in the royal gardens of Babylon. Among the Greeks, Hippocratus, Aristotle and Theophrastus all mention it, while Pliny tells us that the Greeks called the 'white lettuce' poppy lettuce because of its soporific white juice. It was this lettuce which was known later in Italy and called *lactuca* – in modern Italian *lattuga*. Pliny found them cooling and very pleasant to eat in the summer, being good for the stomach and the appetite. Apicius, while using it mainly in salad recipes, also gives a recipe for a purée of lettuce and onion. Other ingredients also found their way into these ancient salads: endives or chicory, hollyhocks and gladioli bulbs, orchids and asphodel lilies. Purslane and chervil also were regular saladings and naturally Pliny had something to say about the latter, remarking that the Syrians used it both as a cooked and raw vegetable. The Romans ate watercress – which has its origins in Babylon – with a vinegar dressing, also it was considered as a cure for mental complaints. A really good salad in these ancient days could include savory, mint, rue, coriander, parsley, chives, spring onions, lettuce, colewort, catmint and the green flea-bane. And there is nothing to prevent us producing a similar salad today if we feel like it. Celery was considered a medicinal plant and Pliny talked of wild and cultivated varieties. Apicius used it mainly as a flavouring. Finally, the cucumber, which was cultivated in Asia and grown in India for at least 3,000 years. Cucumbers grew in Egypt on the shores of the Birket el Qarun, a lake in the province of Faiyum, near where the pyramids were being built. The Romans ate them raw or cooked, peeled and unpeeled and Apicius cooked them with honey, celery seed, brains, garum and oil. The Emperor Tiberius was so fond of cucumbers that, in order that he could eat them everyday, they were grown in movable frames, a method described by Pliny who certainly knew them as a vegetable.

How to Prepare Salads

Salads should be well coated with a dressing or mayonnaise without being soggy or drowned in either. In any dressing a good oil is an essential. Most people prefer a light olive oil, such as Ligurian oil, although a great many French cooks prefer walnut oil, which is excellent. Good quality mild vinegar is equally as important as the oil although many people prefer to use lemon juice instead.

Taste in salads varies. In France and Italy green salads are preferred, that is, made from lettuce, endive, early dandelion leaves, chicory or escarole, and served after the main course to cleanse the palate.

In Britain wooden salad bowls are preferred for green salads. Some connoisseurs say that a salad with an olive oil dressing should be served only in an olive wood bowl, but perhaps they are faddists. However, I am equally as much a faddist with my wooden salad bowls which I have collected in many parts of the world, as far apart as Kashmir, Jamaica and Madras, and which have been with me for more years then I can remember and have never been other than fondly wiped with a soft cloth or absorbent paper since we came together. However, for some of the mixed large salads, earthenware, rustic style bowls are excellent and rather nicer than wooden bowls.

Green Salad

For this choose lettuce or endive, escarole, etc. Wash well, pull apart with the fingers and dry gently. There are several drying baskets on the market these days; I have recently been converted to a 'spin-dryer' which dries green veg- etables quickly and without bruising. When the leaves are ready, make the dressing. The usual proportion of oil and vinegar (or lemon juice) is three parts oil to one part vinegar; if using a strong vinegar, then make it four parts oil. Put the vinegar, salt and pepper into the salad bowl and stir until the salt is dissolved. Add the oil and continue stirring until this is blended into the remaining ingredients. To this can be added crushed garlic, or the bowl modestly rubbed with garlic. The French rub crisp French bread with garlic, cut into tiny dice and sprinkle it over the finished salad. In the south of France they use crusts of bread sprinkled with dressing and well rubbed with cut garlic and add this to the salad. Or they put a small piece of garlic-rubbed bread at the bottom of the bowl (called *chapon à l'ail*). This gives an aroma sufficient for most people and the bread is regarded by the French as a *bonne-bouche*.

I usually mix my dressing directly in the bowl as this prevents wastage, add the salad, lifting and turning it with a wooden fork and spoon until all is coated with the dressing. In the world of salad makers there are not many, but very many, arguments, seldom a discussion, on which is the correct method of adding the dressing to the salads. Some,

for example, prefer to put the saladings into the bowl, add
the vinegar and toss it round and about before adding the
oil and other seasonings. Some people add dry mustard to
the dressings, others sugar. It is all a matter of preference or
taste.

Basic dressing

$\frac{1}{2}$–1 teaspoon salt   1 tablespoon wine vinegar
$\frac{1}{4}$ teaspoon freshly ground pepper   3 tablespoons olive or walnut oil

Mix the salt with the pepper. Combine with the vinegar in
a bowl and stir until the salt is dissolved. Add the oil and
stir well.

Cream dressing

4 tablespoons single cream   salt and pepper
1 tablespoon wine vinegar or
   lemon juice

Combine these ingredients gently, stir and use as a basic
dressing. A pleasant French dressing which makes a change
from the usual oil and vinegar.

Spring Salad

4 servings

1 head lettuce   1 green pepper
spring onions   green olives, pitted or stuffed
radishes   (optional)
2–3 tomatoes   diced piquant cheese (optional)
1 small cucumber   basic dressing (above)

Pull the lettuce leaves apart, wash well and dry thoroughly.
Drop the leaves into a large, chilled salad bowl. Peel and
thinly slice some spring onions – this recipe has no exact
quantities – and add to the salad. Thinly slice the radishes,
cut the tomatoes into quarters and add to the salad. Wash
and thinly slice the cucumber without peeling (unless you

have strong feelings about peeling cucumbers) and drop the slices in the bowl. Cut the pepper into thin strips, discarding the pith, core and seeds. If using olives, add these at this point. Finally add the cheese and dressing at the moment of serving. Toss lightly but firmly and serve.

Garlic lovers should add a little garlic.

Summer Salad

Put some crisp lettuce leaves at the bottom of a salad bowl, add wedges of peach, both white and yellow, also slices of apple and pear and finally tomatoes. Lightly tossed, the salad is sprinkled with castor sugar and with a white wine (instead of vinegar) and olive oil dressing.

Winter Salad - Celery, Apple and Walnut Salad

4 servings

1 *good head celery*   salad dressing (*p.* 248)
2 *firm green apples*   *coarsely chopped parsley*
1 *cup walnut kernels,*
  approximate

Trim and wash the celery and cut into rings. Wipe, core and cut the apples first into rings then halve the rings, do not peel. Combine the celery and apples. Break but do not crush the walnuts. Mix into the celery, add dressing, making sure the salad is well moistened, in particular the apples or they will turn brown. Toss lightly before serving, and sprinkle with parsley.

If required, the salad can be left, covered, for about 30 minutes or so before using but turn it from time to time otherwise all the dressing will remain at the bottom of the bowl.

Mixed Country Salad

This salad should be served in a really large wooden bowl, and I mean really large, and the salad should consist of almost everything which grows in the garden. All the

vegetables which need it can be cooked in the morning and
allowed to get cold. Choose peas, young carrots, French
beans or young runners, if you have them, a few artichoke
hearts or chopped mushrooms, some fresh, crisp lettuce
leaves, a few nasturtium flowers and leaves, borage with its
blue flowers (its leaves are rather prickly, so take care) and
the whole gently mixed with a home-made mayonnaise.

Such a salad deserves much attention. For those who feel
that tomatoes must be served as well, offer these separately
in a simple dressing.

French Bean Salad

cooked fresh beans (p. 150)   *basic dressing (p. 248)*

For this recipe left-over beans can be used. The beans are
simply cooled, the dressing added and served cold.

Red Cabbage Salad

4–6 servings

1 *small red cabbage*   *basic dressing (p. 248)*
coarse salt

Trim off the coarser leaves of the cabbage, shred the rest.
Put into a deep bowl and sprinkle liberally with salt: it will
turn a hideous purple colour but this disappears in time.
Leave for 4 hours. When ready to serve, wash well, dry and
mix with a generous quantity of dressing.

Cucumber Salad

1 *cucumber*   *sour cream or basic dressing*
salt   *(p. 248)*

Peel and thinly slice the cucumber, you can use a mandolin
for the slicing. Sprinkle with salt as directed (qv). Wash in
water and gently pat dry. Arrange on a salad dish and dress,
either with sour cream or yogurt, or the basic dressing.
Sprinkle with finely chopped herbs and freshly grated
pepper.

Tomato Salad

An Italian green tomato salad. The tomatoes are simply cut
into wedges, given a dressing, sprinkled with sugar and
usually with chopped herbs; in Liguria chopped basil is a
favourite herb to match with tomatoes. Firm ripe tomatoes
may be prepared in the same way.

Potato Salad

For this salad there are no set quantities of ingredients. But
it is a salad which varies considerably from the usual British
potato salad. It is not dressed with mayonnaise; also, it is
not chilled.

Preferably choose waxy potatoes and cook in their
jackets. When tender, cool just enough to be able to peel,
cut into fairly thick slices and halve the slices. Drop these
into a salad bowl – for this salad I use a fairly deep rustic
earthenware bowl – sprinkle with salt and pepper and cover
with a basic dressing. Gently toss or turn the potatoes until
they are coated with the dressing and sprinkle with chopped
herbs – chives or parsley are obvious choices – or rings of
spring onions; some cooks add crumbled hard-boiled egg
yolks, others diced cooked beetroots, but this I think spoils
the colour of the salad.

Serve at once. If the salad must be kept until later, do not
chill.

Cauliflower Salad

4–6 servings

1 kg (2¼ lb) cauliflower
280 ml (½ pt) mayonnaise
1 large carrot, shredded
1 generous teaspoon continental
  mustard

1 tablespoon single cream or top
  of milk
salt and pepper
mild paprika pepper

Prepare, break into sprigs and cook the cauliflower as
directed (p. 174) until just tender. It must remain firm and
crisp. Drain in a colander and run cold water over it. Pat

dry in a cloth. Arrange in a large salad bowl. While the cauliflower is cooking, mix the mayonnaise with the carrot and mustard and dilute with cream. Spoon the mayonnaise over the top of the cauliflower and lightly sprinkle with salt, pepper and paprika. Leave for 10 minutes to let the mayonnaise set, then serve.

A good main dish salad.

🎋 Herbs

All herbs must be fresh and used with discretion. They are used to stimulate or subtly enhance flavour, never permitted to drown it. Crushing or mincing fresh herbs will bring out their flavour. They can be added to a dish either at the beginning of cooking or at the finish; cooks disagree on this point. I usually add herbs at the beginning unless they are to be used as a garnish.

BASIL

There are some 50 varieties of this herb, all differing in height, colour and flavour. The most usual in Europe is sweet basil which has large leaves and a flavour which can be described as between a clove and liquorice, or maybe peppery. A fairly strong herb, it must be used with prudence.

Uses. In tomato and pea soups; with shellfish and white fish; with roast pork, veal, mutton or lamb; also with grills and beef stews. It goes well with tomatoes in all forms and the Italians make an excellent green herb sauce of which basil is the basis.

BAY LEAF

The leaf of a species of laurel with a strong, pungent, rather bitter flavour. Some cooks prefer to pick bay leaves a few days before using to allow some of their bitterness to evaporate. The bay grows extensively in the Mediterranean region, also in Britain. One leaf generally is sufficient to flavour a dish. It must be removed before serving.

Uses. Its uses are manifold: in soups, stocks – whether

meat or fish, in mutton broth, also in marinades. It can be used in most fish dishes, also with stewed tomatoes. It is added to milk puddings, such as rice and sweet custards. Beetroot, onion and potato soups improve with its flavour and it is an important ingredient of the *bouquet garni*.

BOUQUET GARNI

The French name for a bunch of mixed herbs, but it is international. It used to be called a faggot of herbs in old English cookbooks. It consists of three herbs tied together: 1–2 sprigs of parsley, a sprig of thyme and 1 bay leaf. The thyme and bay leaf are wrapped inside the parsley and the whole tied with thread. For some dishes an extra herb may be suggested, such as fennel or marjoram but this is usually specified in the recipe. The herbs should be removed before serving.

CHIVES

A member of the onion family with a flavour similar to the onion but more subtle.

Uses. It should be used where a light onion flavour is preferred. It can be finely chopped and used as a soup garnish; to flavour cheese and egg dishes, in particular omelettes, scrambled eggs and baked eggs. It matches with tomatoes, indeed most salads, with fish, and with cottage cheese.

DILL

A member of the parsley family and an important herb in which both the leaves and seeds are used. The leaves are pale and feathery, a little like fennel, but the plant is smaller. The flavour tends towards parsley, while the seeds resemble caraway.

Uses. It is a herb which requires real discretion in its use. A flavouring to bean, tomato, beetroot and other vegetable soups. It marries well with cabbage and turnips and, of course, is important in fish sauces and fish dishes in general.

FENNEL

Here, I am talking of the herb fennel which has been used in British cooking since the days of the Normans. It has a faintly aniseed or liquorice flavour. The feathery leaves and its stalks, which are hollow, can all be used in cooking.

Uses. This pretty herb goes well with all fish dishes and soups, with pork and wild boar and venison, is useful in marinades for hare or rabbit, and can be used in most soups and often in salads. Try it with cucumber sometime.

GARLIC

If ever a flavouring made a star come-back in British cooking it is the garlic; it never lost its popularity in Europe and other far-flung sensible places. Many have been the insults hurled at this bulb and at those who ate garlic. But today? Everyone is growing it, the British gardener is as good at plaiting garlic as his Continental counterpart, and everyone is busily explaining how they always liked this potent herb. Well, there are several varieties of this member of the lily or onion family and, although it is said to have had its origins in the region of Central Asia, today it is grown in warm climes all over the world. My old friend Pliny had much to say on the subject of the garlic, including the fact that the Israeli slaves working on the pyramids subsisted on a diet mainly of garlic and onions. It was said at one time that mariners would 'almost as lief go to sea without a compass as without a plentiful supply of garlic'.

The most usual type of garlic is probably the white skinned, but there are also mauve and pink skinned garlics. The size of the bulbs also varies from really almost shrivelled to very large. Therefore, it is often difficult to say with exactitude how many cloves one should use. However, if only a mild flavour of garlic is required, cut a clove into half and rub it around the bowl or pan in which it is to be used. If to be used in a stew or soup, peel and drop into the pan but remove it before serving.

Uses. Almost endless; wherever mutton or lamb is to be cooked; in stews and soups, stocks and broths. With sauces and egg dishes, with casseroles, baked or boiled. With steaks and poultry, game of course, it is second nature here, with mayonnaise, in salads, in short, with everything, except the sweet.

HORSERADISH

A free-growing plant in Britain recently neglected as far too many housewives buy bottled horseradish; understandably, of course, as horseradish brings one to tears like the onion. But it grows wild in woods and can even be a nuisance in the garden and is often hurled out by the irate gardener as a pernicious weed. But it has a lively and pungent flavour and some declare it to be an appetite stimulator.

Uses. Use with freshwater, smoked or oily fish, with boiled chicken, with grilled meats and roast beef in particular. It can be mixed with apple sauce and served with roast pork, also with hare and other game meat, and oddly with hard-boiled eggs.

MARJORAM

A herb native to the Mediterranean but now grown throughout the world. Its flavour is spicy, sweet and scented, akin to thyme which it often substitutes. It is often used in a *bouquet garni* and is useful in that it dries easily. Pot marjoram, as its name implies, is grown indoors but its flavour is not as good as the outdoor type. It is used in the same manner.

Uses. It can flavour omelettes, sauces and stews; goes well with carrots, courgettes, tomatoes and spinach; with onions and in mixed green salads. It can be used in fish dishes; rubbed inside poultry; with game such as venison and hare, also with beef, pork, mutton and lamb; in stuffings, with mushroom sauce and in cheese dishes.

MINT

There are so many varieties in Britain of this widely used herb, one could write a book on the subject. It has been recognised as a herb since earliest times and the Romans brought it with them on their conquest of the British Isles.

Uses. For the British mint means mint sauce and to use with peas and new potatoes. Also with carrots, cucumber, mushrooms and tomatoes. Apple mint can be used with apples and in fruit cups, as well as in some frozen and iced sweets. Peppermint is much used in herbal teas. But all mint is pungent and should be used with caution.

PARSLEY

This herb is so well-known that few people realise there are over 30 varieties of it. The type used mainly in Britain is the dark green curly leafed parsley, whereas on the Continent it is the plain-leafed parsley which is preferred. The latter is less pungent than the curly but the curly leafed does make a finer garnish, also it can be fried.

Uses. Parsley matches well with most herbs despite its pungency and is used in soups, stocks, broths, stuffings, to make parsley sauce, with egg and fish dishes; in fact, it seems there is hardly a savoury dish in which a sprig or so of parsley is not welcome.

Fried Parsley. Have ready a pan with very hot deep oil. Pick over the parsley, it must be absolutely dry, and drop it into the boiling oil leaving it for a couple of seconds only. Take out and drain. It should have retained its colour and still be crisp. Use as an edible garnish.

ROSEMARY

For remembrance, sang the poets, a sweet scented evergreen shrub and one of our best-loved herbs, pungent, refreshing and old-fashioned.

Uses. It is used extensively in Italian cooking. It dries

well, retaining much of its pungency. Used to flavour stews
and soups, especially chicken soup; it can be stuffed into the
cavity of a chicken before roasting, no other stuffing is then
needed. It goes with mutton, pork and veal, with potatoes
and in herbal teas.

SAGE

This is truly a powerful herb, at times overpowering. There
are several varieties, some of which are used only as decoration. It has been used in Britain since the sixteenth century.

Uses. Well, to the British, it means sage and onion
stuffing but it also flavours some sausages. Can be used in
creamed soups and in some countries it is an essential
ingredient with eels. Goose and duck are frequently allied
with sage and one of Italy's most famous dishes of veal is
cooked with sage.

TARRAGON

One of the great herbs, pungent with something of the
flavour of aniseed. It was one of the little 'dragon' herbs
which enjoyed the reputation of curing victims suffering
from dragon bites. The Italian name is *dragoncello*.

Uses. It is an essential herb in a number of famous sauces,
part of the *fines herbes* for omelettes, it graces a number of
soups, butters, vinegars, salads, stews and casserole dishes.
Despite its pungency, it can be used fairly freely.

THYME

'I know a bank whereon the wild thyme blows', sang the
bard but it is yet another herb we owe to the Romans who
valued it as an antidote to melancholy. It is an important
member of the herb family and there are several varieties,
all with different flavours.

Uses. Try it with fish and meat dishes, chicken and other
poultry. It is used in famous French dishes such as *boeuf à la*

bourguignonne, and is a natural with rabbit and game meats. Fresh sole takes to it kindly, so do sauces, herbal butters and egg dishes. It is best used with moderation, except with game.

❧ Vegetable Soups

Cabbage Soup

4–6 servings

2⅓ l (4 pt) meat or vegetable
   stock
2 each carrots and onions, finely
   chopped
2–3 ribs celery, finely chopped
salt and pepper to taste

450 g (1 lb) shredded white
   cabbage
1 level tablespoon flour
140 ml (¼ pt) sour cream or
   yogurt
dill or parsley, finely chopped

Bring the stock to the boil in a large saucepan, add the carrots, onions and celery and cook for 15 minutes over a moderate heat. Add salt and pepper. Add the cabbage and continue cooking until this is tender. Take a little stock from the pan and mix it with the flour to make a thin paste. Stir this into the cream. Pour this mixture slowly into the soup, stirring all the while until it reaches boiling point. At once reduce the heat and simmer for 3 minutes. Sprinkle with dill and serve.

For an even more filling soup, peeled, chopped tomatoes and potatoes can be added.

Cream of Cauliflower Soup

4–6 servings

2 small or 1 large cauliflower
30 g (1 oz) ground rice
   (optional)
280 ml (½ pt) milk

1¾ l (3 pt) white stock
280 ml (½ pt) cream
salt and pepper to taste

Prepare the cauliflower as directed and cook whole in salt water until tender. Drain and rub through a vegetable mill or purée in a liquidiser. Retain the liquid. Mix the rice with enough milk to make a thin paste. Put the stock, the remainder of the milk and 560 ml (1 pt) of the cauliflower stock into a saucepan. Bring to the boil, stir in the rice paste and, when blended, lower the heat and cook gently for 15 minutes. Add the puréed cauliflower, the cream and seasoning. Bring to a gentle boil.

Serve with a sprinkling of chopped chervil or with fried sippets of bread, plain or lightly garlic flavoured.

Dutch Cream of Carrot Soup

4 servings

340 g (12 oz) carrots
45 g (1½ oz) butter or margarine
1 medium-sized onion, finely chopped
2–3 stalks celery, diced
420 ml (¾ pt) stock
420 ml (¾ pt) water

salt, pepper and nutmeg
4 tablespoons flour
3 tablespoons single cream or top of milk
1–2 tablespoons finely chopped parsley

Wash, scrape and cut the carrots into thin rounds. Heat the butter in a large pan, add the carrots, onion and celery, stir well and cook over a low heat for 15 minutes. Add the stock and water, mix well and continue slowly cooking for 45 minutes. Take the soup from the heat, rub through a coarse sieve and return to the pan and the stove. Add salt, pepper and nutmeg to taste. Mix the flour and cream (or milk) together. Stir the mixture into the soup, stirring constantly and cook gently for 10 to 15 minutes, stirring most of the time, until the flour and cream has been amalgamated into the soup. Serve the soup hot, each plate sprinkled with parsley and, if liked, with sippets of fried bread.

Cream of Celery Soup

4 servings

450 g (1 *lb*) *celery*
1 *medium sized onion, chopped*
1 *teaspoon sugar*
30 g (1 *oz*) *butter or margarine*
30 g (1 *oz*) *flour*

560 *ml* (1 *pt*) *milk*
salt and pepper to taste
½ *cup single cream*
chopped parsley

In this recipe you can use only the outer celery stalks or
celery which is no longer young enough to be used for
salads, etc. Wash the stalks well and cut into short lengths.
Cook in water to cover, together with the onions and sugar,
until very tender. Rub through a vegetable mill or purée in
a liquidiser. Heat the butter in a large pan, add the flour
and stir to a roux. Take from the heat and gradually add the
milk, stirring all the while. Return to the stove and, still
stirring, bring slowly to the boil and cook for 5 minutes. Stir
in the purée, add salt, pepper and cream and serve hot,
sprinkled with parsley.

Pumpkin Soup

6 servings

1 *kg* (2¼ *lb*) *ripe pumpkin*
salt and pepper
30 g (1 *oz*) *butter*

1⅛ *l* (2 *pt*) *milk*
6 *thin slices toast*

For this recipe baked slices of stale French bread are better
than toast but either will do.

Peel and thickly slice the pumpkin, discarding any seeds
and fibres. Put into a saucepan with 560 ml (1 pt) of water,
add salt and pepper and cook over a moderate heat until
the pumpkin is soft. Drain well and discard the water. Rub
the pumpkin through a sieve back into the pan. Add the
butter, stir well then add enough milk to make a soup of
medium thickness: a little more milk than suggested may

be needed. Bring to a gentle boil. Put a slice of toast into each soup plate, add the soup and serve at once.

A little sugar is often added to the pumpkin when cooking, also a sprinkling of freshly grated nutmeg.

Onion Soup

4–6 servings

450 g (1 lb) onions	1¾ l (3 pt) clear stock
60 g (2 oz) butter	salt and pepper to taste
60 g (2 oz) flour	6 slices toast

Peel and coarsely chop the onions. Heat the butter, add the onions and slowly cook until soft and a golden colour. Add the flour, stir this into the onions and continue cooking until the flour changes colour. Add stock, salt and pepper, stir well and bring to the boil. Cook over a good heat for 15 minutes. Place a slice of bread in each soup bowl, add the soup, preferably without straining, and serve at once.

Instead of stock, water may be used but 2⅓ l (4 pt) will be required as the onions will need longer cooking for a good flavour and the liquid will, of course, reduce. The toast may be generously sprinkled with grated cheese before being put into the bowls, which can be put into a hot oven or under a grill to brown the toast and cheese, which will rise to the top of the bowl. Instead of toast, stale bread may be used.

Potato Soup

6 servings

1¾ kg (3 lb) potatoes	1¾ l (3 pt) hot milk and water
60 g (2 oz) butter or margarine	mixed
1–2 onions, minced	salt and pepper
	chopped parsley

Scrub the potatoes and cook without peeling in boiling salted water until soft. Drain, cool, peel and mash. Heat the butter, add the onion and cook until it is lightly browned. Add the mashed potatoes, stir well then gradually add the milk and water mixture. Stir until the soup is smooth, add salt, pepper and parsley and cook for 15 minutes.

Fried bread sippets may be served with the soup if it is served hot; if iced, it requires no addition.

Cream of Leek and Onion Soup

8 servings

310 g (11 oz) *leeks*
30 g (1 oz) *butter or margarine*
310 g (11 oz) *onions, peeled and chopped*
310 g (11 oz) *potatoes, peeled and diced*

1 l (1¾ pt) *chicken or vegetable stock*
salt, pepper, mace and nutmeg to taste
280 ml (½ pt) *milk, scalded*
2 *egg yolks, well beaten*
140 ml (¼ pt) *single cream*

Prepare the leeks as directed and cut into small pieces. Heat the butter in a large fireproof casserole, add the leeks and onions, cover the pan and cook on top of the stove until soft and a golden colour; add the potatoes, mix well to ensure they are covered with the butter then add the stock, salt, pepper, mace and nutmeg. Cover the pan and cook gently for about 30 minutes, stirring from time to time. Rub the soup through a vegetable mill or whisk in a liquidiser. Return this to the pan, add the milk, stir it well into the soup and bring carefully to the boil, stirring continuously to avoid curdling. Take the pan from the heat and add the egg yolks, beaten into the cream. Correct for seasoning.

The soup can be garnished with croûtons.

Cream of Spinach Soup

6 servings

1 *kg* (2¼ *lb*) *spinach*	2⅓ *l* (4 *pt*) *hot water*
45 *g* (1½ *oz*) *butter or margarine*	*salt and pepper*
60 *g* (2 *oz*) *flour*	*fried bread sippets*

Prepare the spinach as directed and coarsely chop. Heat the butter, add the flour and stir to a thick roux. Gradually add the water, stirring all the time. Bring to the boil and cook for 5 minutes. Add the spinach, salt and pepper, lower the heat and cook gently for 1 hour. Serve with fried bread sippets or garnished with fresh or sour cream or yogurt.

Cream of Tomato Soup

6 servings

450 *g* (1 *lb*) *ripe tomatoes*	*salt and pepper*
225 *g* (8 *oz*) *potatoes*	*fried bread sippets*
1¾ *l* (3 *pt*) *clear stock*	*finely chopped green herbs*

Chop the tomatoes, peel and chop the potatoes. Cook in stock until the potatoes are soft, adding salt and pepper. Rub through a sieve back into the pan, bring quickly to the boil, pour into soup bowls and garnish with finely chopped herbs. Serve with sippets of fried bread.

Instead of sippets, a good tablespoon of sour cream or yogurt makes a welcome garnish.

Cream of Turnip Soup

6 servings

450 *g* (1 *lb*) *turnips*	*salt and pepper*
450 *g* (1 *lb*) *potatoes*	140 *ml* (¼ *pt*) *single cream*
110 *g* (4 *oz*) *stale bread*	*finely chopped parsley to taste*
2⅓ *l* (4 *pt*) *water*	

F.F.G.—12

Wash and peel the turnips and potatoes. Cut into halves. Dice the bread. Put into a saucepan, add the water, salt and pepper and cook gently until the turnips are very soft. Rub through a vegetable mill back into the pan. Reheat and immediately before serving take the pan from the heat and stir in the cream and parsley.

Serve hot with bread sippets.

Lettuce Soup

4 servings

2 *large lettuces*
30 g (1 oz) *butter or margarine*

1¾ l (3 pt) *vegetable or chicken stock*
30 g (1 oz) *uncooked rice*

Wash the lettuce and shred finely. Heat the butter in a saucepan, add the lettuce and cook until it is soft, then add the stock, stir well, bring to the boil, add the rice and continue cooking until the rice is soft, about 15 minutes. Serve hot without rubbing through a sieve.

To this may be added finely chopped sorrel, watercress or green herbs. Serve with sippets of fried bread.

Mimosa Soup

4 servings

handful cooked green beans
2 *hard-boiled egg yolks*

1¾ l (3 pt) *clear stock*

Thinly slice the beans into strips. Crumble the egg yolks. Bring the stock to the boil and add the beans. Pour into soup bowls, add a little of the egg yolk to each bowl to create the effect of mimosa.

Gardener's Soup

6 servings

2 *carrots*   1–2 *potatoes*
2 *turnips*   *cabbage or lettuce leaves*
1 *leek or large onion*   60 g (2 oz) butter or margarine
1–2 *ribs celery*   2⅓ l (4 pt) water
spring onions   *salt and pepper*

Prepare all the vegetables as directed and finely chop. Heat
the butter in a large saucepan, add the vegetables, cover the
pan and cook slowly for 15 minutes. Add the water, salt and
pepper, bring gently to the boil, lower the heat and cook
over a moderate heat until all the vegetables are soft. Rub
through a sieve. Return to the pan, bring once more to the
boil and serve at once, preferably with fried sippets of bread.

Iced Parsley Soup

4–6 servings

225 g (½ lb) curly leafed   2 egg yolks
  parsley   280 ml (½ pt) single cream
1¾ l (3 pt) clear stock,   *salt and cayenne pepper*
  preferably chicken

Wash the parsley, chop finely both stems and leaves. Pour
the stock into a saucepan, add the parsley and bring to the
boil. Lower the heat and cook gently for 25 minutes. Whisk
in the liquidiser and strain through a fine sieve. Return the
soup to the pan and simmer. Beat the egg yolks, whisk in the
cream then stir gently into the soup, stirring all the while.
Let the soup thicken but do not let it boil, otherwise it will
curdle. Add salt and pepper, cool then chill. Serve in soup
bowls with small sprigs of parsley and a whisper of slightly
whipped cream.

This soup is rich, creamy in colour and extremely good,
also rather unusual. Failing a liquidiser, rub the soup
through a sieve or a vegetable mill.

Iced Cucumber Soup

6 servings

2–3 *large cucumbers*
1 *tablespoon lemon juice or*
 vinegar
30 g (1 oz) *butter or margarine*
30 g (1 oz) *flour*
1 l (1¾ pt) *hot stock,*
 preferably chicken

140 ml (¼ pt) *milk*
few thin slices onion
½ *cup single or double cream*
salt and white pepper to taste
finely chopped chives or tarragon

Peel the cucumbers and remove the seeds. Drop into boiling acidulated water for 5 minutes. Drain well and cut into small lengths. Heat the butter, add the cucumbers and cook for 10 minutes. Sprinkle in the flour and continue cooking, stirring all the while, then gradually add the stock, still stirring. Scald the milk together with the onion, strain and stir into the soup. Cook gently for 10 minutes. Rub the soup through a vegetable mill, stir well, add the cream, salt and pepper, cool and chill in the refrigerator.

Serve sprinkled with chopped herbs or, if preferred, with peeled shrimps or baby prawns. Instead of fresh cream, sour cream or yogurt may be used but neither should be added until the soup is chilled, otherwise it will probably curdle.

❧ Fruits

You may swear yourself black, Berry;
But you have made a mull, Berry.
I paid your bill, Berry,
As the young lady in the bar, Berry,
And your father, the elder Berry, know.
I don't care a straw, Berry,
For a goose, Berry, like you Berry;
But I'll let folks know, Berry,
That you've made yourself a regular ass, Berry,
And what'll Berry senior say.

Charles Stuart Calverley
(Victorian parodist)

❧ Strawberry

One of the most popular fruits throughout the world and, curiously, not a fruit cultivated either by the Greeks or Romans, so we have no comments from Pliny. However, the Romans had their glorious wild strawberries, still one of the delights of the hot Roman summer. Of the wild strawberry, Dr William Butler, a sixteenth century writer, wrote: 'Doubtless God could have made a better berry, but doubtless God never did.' A saying also attributed by Izaak Walton to one Dr Boteler. Linnaeus, the great botanist, claimed to have cured himself of gout by eating strawberries, and it is said the leaves of the strawberry plant make a tea which helps those suffering from dysentery.

The name strawberry has nothing to do with the straw used for mulching but probably comes from the old word strew because of the numerous runners strewed or strayed from the plant. In John Lydgate's poem on the cries of London (1430), vendors cried 'straeberry ripe', then the spelling of strew or stray.

Our present day garden strawberries are descended from two main American types, the Virginian and the Chilian, which were brought to Europe by a Frenchman. The French developed the latter while the British preferred the Virginian. The influence of the two strains can be seen in the different characteristics of the two varieties.

Probably the most usual way to serve strawberries is whole, sprinkled with sugar and cream poured over them, although some people prefer to sprinkle salt, claiming this draws out their flavour better. But there is no doubt in my mind the nicest way to eat strawberries is hand-picked and eaten on the spot still warm from the sun—and not washed. Which brings me to the question, whether to wash strawberries or not? I contend that when garden fresh the answer is no, but if you feel strongly about 'that peck of dirt' you can rinse them in a light white wine. Drowning strawberries in water ruins the exquisite bouquet which clings to the fruit. Strawberries bought in the markets and shops? This is another matter and regretfully I have to say better they should be washed.

Strawberries in Champagne
Sprinkle hulled whole strawberries with castor sugar, leave until the sugar has seeped into them and chill well. Serve in stemmed glasses in champagne (or white wine).

Strawberries Romanoff

1 kg (2¼ lb) strawberries   ½ cup each orange juice and
castor sugar to taste   curaçao
                           double cream

Hull the strawberries, put into a dish and sprinkle with
sugar. Add the orange juice and curaçao and leave in the
refrigerator for about 2 hours. To serve, turn the berries
carefully out into a glass dish. Whip the cream until stiff
with a little sugar and flavour either with curaçao or a
similar liqueur. Pour the cream over the strawberries before
serving.

Strawberry Sauce

450 g (1 lb) strawberries   kirsch
½ cup each sugar and water

Hull the strawberries and rub through a sieve. Combine the
sugar and water, dissolve slowly over a low heat then bring
to the boil and boil for 3 minutes. Mix the syrup with the
strawberries, flavour to taste with kirsch and serve over ice-
cream, pies, puddings, etc.

Compôte of Strawberries No 1

110 g (4 oz) sugar   1 kg (2¼ lb) strawberries
280 ml (½ pt) water

Make a sugar syrup. Hull the strawberries and put into a
sieve over a bowl. Pour the boiling syrup over the strawberries. Return the syrup to the pan and bring again to the
boil and repeat the process. Do this once more and the
strawberries will be just cooked, retaining their shape and
colour. Leave in the syrup until cool then chill.

Compôte of Strawberries No 2

1 kg (2¼ lb) strawberries   280 ml (½ pt) water
110 g (4 oz) sugar   2–3 tablespoons Grand Marnier

Hull the strawberries and put them into a shallow pan. Dissolve the sugar in the water over a low heat, bring to the boil and boil for 4 minutes. Flavour with Grand Marnier. Pour this mixture while still boiling carefully over the strawberries. Leave to cool then bring the strawberries quickly to the boil, take at once from the heat and leave to cool. Chill before serving.

The strawberries are hardly cooked and if handled with care will not mush or break up.

Strawberries in Whipped Cream
Hull and halve as many strawberries as required. Mix into whipped cream sweetened with icing sugar and flavoured with a little vanilla. Chill in the refrigerator for 2 hours.

Strawberries Paris Style
Mix whole, hulled strawberries with whipped cream and add enough sweetened purée of wild strawberries to add colour and a wild strawberry flavour.

Strawberry Custard

450 g (1 *lb*) *strawberries*
4 *egg yolks*
2 *tablespoons sugar*
280 ml (½ *pt*) *milk, scalded*

1 *tablespoon brandy*
280 ml (½ *pt*) *double cream*
4 *egg whites*

Hull, slice and chill the strawberries. Chill a serving dish. Beat the egg yolks until thick, add the sugar and scalded milk and cook, stirring all the time, over a low heat until the custard coats the spoon. Take from the heat, add the brandy, beat well and cool thoroughly. Whip the cream until stiff. Stiffly beat the egg whites and fold these into the cream. Now fold in the cooled custard and the chilled strawberries, turn into the serving dish and serve at once.

Strawberries Cardinal

450 g (1 *lb*) *strawberries*
140 g (5 *oz*) *raspberries*
1 *tablespoon lemon juice*

110 g (4 *oz*) *icing sugar*
60 g (2 *oz*) *blanched chopped almonds*

Hull the strawberries, turn into a glass salad bowl and put into a cool place. Hull the raspberries and rub them through a sieve. Mix with the lemon juice and icing sugar and leave in the refrigerator for 3 hours. When ready to serve, pour the iced raspberry sauce over the strawberries and garnish with the almonds.

If fresh raspberries are not available, frozen may be used instead.

❧ Raspberry

It is said we owe the discovery of raspberries to the Greek gods who went berrying on Mount Ida and returned with *Rubus ideaeus*. Since then we lesser beings have been eating raspberries sadly without giving credit to those pioneering gods.

Raspberries grow wild in profusion all over the temperate zones of Europe, Asia and the United States but it is only some four centuries ago that people began to cultivate them. Mindful of the tantalizing flavour of fresh raspberries, it is a little astonishing that they have not matched the strawberry in popularity. They allay thirst and are cooling in all feverish conditions, say the old wise men.

Can any dessert be nicer than crushed chilled raspberries served with sugar and chilled fresh cream – and a glass or two of chilled Sauternes, Muscadet or Champagne?

Raspberries with Claret or Red Wine

Spread as many hulled raspberries as required on a large
platter and sprinkle with sugar. Stir gently to disperse the
sugar and leave for some hours in a cool place. Serve in their
juice accompanied by claret or similar red wine.

Raspberries in a Raspberry Sauce

450 g (1 *lb*) *raspberries,*   60 g (2 *oz*) *sifted icing sugar*
   hulled

Take one-third of the raspberries and rub through a sieve.
Gradually beat the icing sugar into the purée. Arrange the
whole raspberries in a dish, add the sauce and chill before
serving. Excellent served with cream cheese.

Raspberry Ice-Cream

450 g (1 *lb*) *raspberries*   280 ml ($\frac{1}{2}$ *pt*) *double cream*
110 g (4 *oz*) *castor sugar*

Set the refrigerator to freezing. Hull the berries, put a few
aside to use as a garnish and rub the rest through a sieve.
Mix the sieved raspberries with the sugar and cream. Turn
the mixture into an ice tray and set to freeze for 35 to 40
minutes. When the cream begins to freeze at the edges, take
from the freezer, turn the mixture into a chilled bowl and
whisk thoroughly. Stir in the remaining raspberries, return
the mixture to the ice tray and continue to freeze.

Strawberries and blackberries may be prepared in the
same way.

🍃 Blackberry

How many of us must remember, as did Sacheverell Sitwell, the days that began with a quest for blackberries on the hills? Good as the flavour of the garden blackberry is, to my mind there is nothing to beat the flavour of what the Scots call 'the blessed bramble' with which, they say, Christ switched his donkey into Jerusalem and chased the money-lenders out of the temple. And Walt Whitman wrote: '. . . and the running blackberry would adorn the parlours of heaven'; a nice thought, to have brambles crowding round one's heavenly door.

Blackberries deteriorate quicker than most berries after being picked and should be eaten or cooked the day they are gathered. When ripe they are a shiny black, but they are not ripe simply because they are black, they must be soft as well and easily detached from the stem. Ripe, sweet and juicy they merit all the praise lavished upon them. Ripe blackberries are excellent eaten raw – what better than sun-warmed straight from the cane – and served with sugar and cream? They are often combined with apples but as their seeds are hard many people prefer to use them in dishes which require to be sieved.

Newberries, which are hybrid blackberries, are used in the same manner as blackberries.

Blackberry and Apple Cheese

1 kg (2¼ lb) ripe blackberries   sugar
1 kg (2¼ lb) cooking apples

Wash, pick and hull the blackberries. Wipe the apples, cut into small pieces and put together with the blackberries in a pan with just enough water to cover the bottom of the pan. Cook over a gentle heat until soft. Rub through a sieve and measure the pulp. Return to the pan. To 560 ml (1 pt) of fruit add 450 g (1 lb) of sugar, mix until the sugar is dissolved and boil until the mixture sets when a little is dropped on to a cold saucer. It must be very firm. Pour into small straight-sided pots and cover. The cheese may be eaten as a jam, or turned out, sliced and served with cream, or soft white cheese.

Blackberry Cordial

'Express the juice from a quart of fresh ripe fruit, adding half-a-pound of white sugar and half-an-ounce of both nutmeg and cloves. Boil altogether for a short time; strain, and add a little brandy when cold. Cork well.'

Victorian recipe

Bilberry, Blaeberry, Blueberry, or if you prefer Whinberry, Hurtleberry or Hurts, Whortleberry and Huckleberry

There are doubtless many more equally delightful names given to this pleasant little, truly blue berry which, when ripe, is sweet fleshed, tender skinned and with just enough tartness to give distinction to its flavour.

Over-ripe bilberries usually have a lifeless dull appearance and are soft and watery. So are berries which have been picked and held too long before using. As they are most perishable, it is advisable to use them as soon as possible after picking. They can be kept, unwashed, in a bowl, covered, in the refrigerator for a while.

Baked Bilberries

1 kg (2¼ lb) bilberries	110 g (4 oz) sugar
¼ cup water	pinch freshly grated nutmeg
1 teaspoon lemon juice	3–4 slices buttered white bread

Rinse the berries, pick over and drain. Put into a pan with the water, lemon juice, sugar and nutmeg. Heat gently to boiling point and take from the stove. Turn into a shallow baking dish. Cut the bread into halves or quarters and place buttered side up over the berries. Bake for about 10 minutes in a hot oven (220C, 425F, Mark 7), or until the bread is brown. Serve with cream.

Stewed Bilberries
Use the above recipe to the point of bringing the bilberries to the boil, lower the heat and simmer until soft but not mushed. A matter of a few minutes.

Bilberry Fritters
Make a fritter batter and add enough cleaned bilberries to make it thick. Have ready some hot, shallow fat, drop in a spoonful and fry until a golden brown. Drain and coat with castor sugar. Repeat with the rest.

Bilberry Pancakes or Griddle Cakes

cleaned and rinsed bilberries   *batter*

Add bilberries to the batter and fry or bake on the griddle in the usual manner.

❧ Loganberry

This large, luscious berry was brought to Britain as recently as 1907 by Frederick P. Norbury. It is named after Judge Logan who discovered what was apparently a cross between an American blackberry and a raspberry. It resembles the raspberry in character but is larger, more robust, darker coloured and more prolific. They seem a little out of favour today but when I was a child loganberries grew in every village garden. They were used in all the usual ways of berries, made into pies, tarts, jams, ice-cream, bottled and preserved. They are like all berries, highly perishable, and should be used as soon as possible after being picked and if stored for a short time must be left in a cool dry place. The

dark purple ones are the ripest and make a perfect dessert
or breakfast fruit. They are at their best hand-picked and
still warm from the sun.

🪻 *Mulberry*

The Romans, we are told, were partial to mulberries and
Pliny chatted about them in his writings. So did Pepys and
Evelyn. The mulberry tree was first introduced into Britain
in 1648 at Syon House near London. This was a white
mulberry, meant to feed silkworms. The black mulberry,
which is sweet, aromatic and juicy is meant for eating and,
indeed, should be eaten as soon as picked. Black mulberry
trees were planted in St James's Park by James I in 1609
with the intention of founding a silkworm industry, but he
planted the wrong trees and the project foundered. However, the area became a fashionable resort about which both
Pepys and his fellow diarist wrote.

As mulberries perish rapidly, they should be used
immediately after being picked (this is why they seldom if
ever appear in the markets). They can be mixed with any
acid fruits in pies, puddings and compôtes and they add a
special pleasure to apples and rhubarb. Their juice can be
made into water ices, ice-creams or drinks, alone or mixed
with other juices. Also they can be made into jams, jellies,
pies and tarts.

Mulberry Compôte
Carefully pick over the mulberries and drop them into a
shallow dish. Sprinkle with powdered sugar and mix with a
syrup made of equal parts of Chartreuse and orange juice and
a dash of ginger syrup.

❧ *Gooseberry*

These early ripening and useful berries were only introduced into Britain in the sixteenth century. They took readily to our climate and probably do as well in our changing weather as they do anywhere in the world. They ripen with luck by Whitsuntide and at one time it was traditional to serve a Whitsun gooseberry pie as the festive dish. Most varieties of gooseberry can be cooked; the green ones are the best for making gooseberry fool. The large, hairy, purplish-coloured gooseberries are sweet and make an excellent fruit for dessert. They are best served in their natural state, requiring neither sugar nor cream to assist or bring out their flavour.

Gooseberries, like their relatives in the berry and currant class, are perishable. If wishing to store them, spread without washing on a shallow tray, cover with foil or waxed paper and put in the refrigerator. Wash just before using.

Gooseberry Compôte

1 *kg* (2¼ *lb*) *gooseberries*
225 *g* (8 *oz*) *sugar*
280 *ml* (½ *pt*) *water*

1 *tablespoon apricot jam*
sherry glass kirsch

Top and tail the gooseberries and blanch for 2 minutes in boiling water. Drain. Combine the sugar and water, dissolve over a low heat then boil until the syrup is quite thick. Add the jam and kirsch, stir well then add the gooseberries and cook very gently until they are tender. Drain, turn into a dish, pour the syrup over the top. Cool and chill before serving.

Gooseberry Sauce

450 g (1 *lb*) *gooseberries*   *sugar to taste*
140 *ml* (¼ *pt*) *spinach juice or*   15 g (½ *oz*) *butter*
  milk   *nutmeg to taste*

Top and tail the gooseberries and put into a saucepan with
just enough water to prevent burning. Cook slowly until soft,
drain well and rub through a sieve. Return the purée to the
pan, add the liquid (preferably spinach as this gives the
sauce a good colour), sugar, butter and nutmeg. Simmer
and stir until the sauce is hot. Serve hot with mackerel,
boiled chicken and other poultry, or pork and game.

Gooseberry Fool

1 *kg* (2¼ *lb*) *ripe green*   140 *ml* (¼ *pt*) *water*
  gooseberries   560 *ml* (1 *pt*) *double cream*
170 g (6 *oz*) *sugar*

A fool is an old English dish of puréed fruits, usually gooseberries or rhubarb. The name may have originated from
the French *foule*, meaning pulped. Originally the fruit for
this dish was not actually sieved but simply crushed until
well pulped. Although the two above-mentioned fruits
usually are associated with a fool, any fruit which can be
stewed and puréed can be prepared in the same manner.
The fruit, when puréed, should be mixed with thick cream,
but a really thick custard sauce can be used instead although
the flavour is neither as good nor as clear; the custard gives
the fruit a slightly blurred flavour.

Top, tail and wash the gooseberries. Put the sugar with
the water into a saucepan and cook gently until the sugar
has dissolved. Add the gooseberries and cook until they are
soft. Mash or rub through a sieve, test for sweetness – a little
more sugar may be required. Leave until cold. Whip the
cream until stiff, fold in the purée, pour into stemmed glasses
and serve with Savoy biscuits or sponge fingers.

Strawberries, blackberries, raspberries, etc, can be used in the same way, but strawberries and raspberries require only to be pulped without cooking.

🐾 Cranberry

Originally called the craneberry because the fruit hung from the multiple little stems, or cranes, each berry by itself, also from the appearance of its small flower with its long central stamen resembling the long bill of the crane. Although cranberries do grow in northern Europe, in Russia for example, and can be grown in Britain, it is generally considered an American fruit for which the Pilgrim Fathers were eternally grateful when they landed in New England and were faced with adjusting their manner of eating. Those early cranberries were small but today the fruit is large and juicy. The credit for first culti-vating this useful little berry goes to one Henry Hall of Massachusetts who rooted a number of wild plants in 1816 thus starting the cranberry industry in his state.

Cranberries do not mean only sauce to the Americans, although cranberry sauce does always figure at any American turkey dinner. There are cranberry soups and cakes, relishes and biscuits, sherbets and salads, and natur-ally cranberry puddings. To store for a while, sort out the berries without washing and put into a large glass jar, cover tightly and put into the refrigerator. The two recipes below are from the States. Use a British standard measuring cup.

Old-Fashioned Cranberry Sauce

2 *cups water*
2 *cups sugar*

grated rind 1 *orange*
4 *cups cranberries*

Cook together the water, sugar and rind. Sort out and wash the cranberries and cook them in this syrup until they stop popping, about 5 minutes. Do not stir. Cool and serve cold.

Cranberry Jelly

4 *cups cranberries, cleaned*
2 *cups water*

2 *cups sugar*

Cook the cranberries in water until the berries burst. Rub through a sieve, pushing through as much of the pulp as possible. Return to the pan, add the sugar and continue cooking slowly until the sugar is dissolved, then boil rapidly until a few drops, tested on a cold saucer, jell. Turn into a rinsed mould or moulds, cool, chill and turn out to serve with turkey or other cold meats.

🎀 *Currants — Red, White and Black*

Red- and whitecurrants are closely related, in fact, the white are what you might call albino red, for they are seedlings from the red which lack the red pigment. Blackcurrants are entirely different, being more closely related to the gooseberry. The red- and whitecurrants have a characteristic but not unpleasing odour, while the black give off a heavy aroma from the stems and leaves. Whitecurrants alone, or mixed with red, make a perfect dessert fruit, but they can both be made into jams, jellies and preserves. Blackcurrants usually are made into cordials, jellies and jams, but they also make good puddings. All currants require washing before using. To store, spread the currants on a shallow tray without washing. Cover with paper and put into the refrigerator. Wash just before using.

Summer Pudding

One of England's superb puddings which can only be made to perfection during one month of summer, that brief period in mid-summer when raspberries and redcurrants are ripe together. It is a pudding easily digested and the Victorians called it 'Hydropathic Pudding'.

450 g (1 lb) each redcurrants   *sugar to taste*
  and raspberries   *8 thin slices white bread*

Wash and stem the fruit and cook in a minute quantity of water until just soft. Sweeten. Line a medium-sized pudding basin with two-thirds of the bread, wedging the slices so closely together they slightly overlap. Fill the basin with the fruit and cover the top with the remaining bread. Cover with a plate with a weight on top and leave overnight. Carefully turn out to serve, with single cream.

    Summer puddings can be made with other similar berries but this particular combination is classic.

Blackcurrant Jam

560 ml (1 pt) water   *1 kg (2¼ lb) blackcurrants*
1¼ kg (3 lb) sugar

Mix the sugar with the water in a large pan, bring to the boil and continue boiling until the syrup clears. Wash and stem the blackcurrants, add to the pan and cook rapidly for 20 minutes, test for setting by dropping a little of the jam on a cold plate. Pour into hot, sterilized jars and seal.

Iced Redcurrant Mousse

450 g (1 lb) redcurrants   *pinch salt*
170 g (6 oz) sugar   *280 ml (½ pt) double cream*
vanilla to taste

Stem the redcurrants, wash and crush them with a fork. Rub through a sieve and mix the purée with the sugar, vanilla and salt. Whip the cream until it is very stiff and holds to a point. Fold this into the purée, turn into an ice-cube tray and freeze until it is firm. Serve in chilled glasses.

Blackcurrants can be used in the same way.

❧ *Rhubarb*

Although cooked as a fruit, rhubarb is a vegetable. It was introduced into Britain from the Volga region of Russia and is a native of Siberia. It remained as a curiosity for two centuries and its use as a food is recent. In 1810 a market gardener tried to sell a consignment to the London market but found no buyers.

Rhubarb, never eaten uncooked, should be cooked in as little liquid as possible: some cooks prefer to use no water at all, cooking it with red jam very slowly until its own natural juice oozes out. All the top leafy parts should be removed and the ends of the stalks trimmed. Wash it well and cut into chunks or lengths according to the recipe or taste and pull off any stringy bits. Do not peel for this takes the red off the stalk. If not cooked correctly rhubarb can break down into a stringy mass, so it must be allowed to cook gently either on top of the stove, or in the oven, with a minimum of water and sugar for just as long as it takes for the stalks to soften, a matter of minutes.

Compôte of Rhubarb

1 *kg* (2¼ *lb*) *rhubarb*   *thin strip lemon rind*
250 *g* (9 *oz*) *sugar*

Prepare the rhubarb as directed. Cut into short lengths. Mix the sugar with half a cup of water, put into a pan and cook

gently until the sugar dissolves, add the lemon rind, bring
to the boil and cook for 5 minutes. Add the rhubarb, bring
gently to the boil and continue cooking gently until the
rhubarb is tender. Ground ginger or allspice can be added
with the lemon rind.

Rhubarb Fool

rhubarb recipe as above   *140 ml ($\frac{1}{4}$ pt) double cream*

Cook the rhubarb as above. Take from the stove, cool and
crush or rub through a sieve, or whisk in a blender. Chill.
When ready to serve, lightly whip the cream and fold it into
the rhubarb purée. Spoon into glass bowls and serve cold, if
liked, topped with a spoonful of whipped cream.

❧ Fruit Salads

When mixing fruits for a salad, care should be taken in
providing colours and flavours. Not all fruits are successful
in salads. Apples tend to become brown quickly, so do pears
and bananas. This can to some extent be overcome by
sprinkling such fruits with lemon juice as soon as they are
peeled and cut. Dark fruits, such as damsons, plums and
blackcurrants, are also best left out of salads simply on
account of their colour. Probably the best mixture is
obtained by the contrast of citrus fruits, usually somewhat
sour, with the sweet fleshiness of peaches, apricots, nectarines
and truly ripe dessert pears. Colour can be added by the
addition of a few bottled red cherries, and flavour for the
adult taste is improved with a dash of a sweet liqueur. However, the real secret of making a fruit salad is to prepare it
some time before it is required and keep it chilled.

Fresh Strawberry Salad

Hull the strawberries, put into a glass bowl, sprinkle with
sugar and lemon juice and leave until required. Do not
chill until the sugar has dissolved. This dressing brings out
the flavour of the strawberries.

Mixed Fruit Salad or Mid-Summer Salad

1–1¼ kg (2¼–3 lb) fruit   1 glass port or marsala
sugar

The fruit should be mixed: strawberries, red- and whitecurrants, a few black as well if you like, raspberries, etc.
Pick over the fruit, discard any which are not firm and
whole, hull the strawberries and other berries, gently pull
off the currants from their stems. Arrange the fruit attrac-
tively in a shallow glass bowl and sprinkle generously with
sugar. Leave for several hours in a cool but not cold place
to allow the sugar to seep gently through the fruit which in
turn provide their own juices. Immediately before serving
add the port, shake the bowl gently to distribute it, and
serve with a large crock or jug of cream.

Fruit Salad in a Syrup

225 g (8 oz) sugar   1–2 thin strips lemon rind
560 ml (1 pt) water   1 kg (2¼ lb) mixed fruit

Combine the sugar and water and put with the rind into a
small saucepan. Cook slowly until the sugar has dissolved,
bring to the boil and let it boil for 5 minutes. Strain into a
jug and leave until cool. Prepare the fruit, slicing or
quartering according to the fruit chosen, and arrange in a
glass bowl. Pour the cooled syrup over the top and chill.

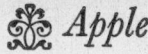 # Apple

> To eat an apple going to bed,
> Will make the doctor beg his bread.
>
> *An old adage*

Of all our fruits the apple is the national favourite in Britain. As Edward Bunyard, fruit gourmet, put it in his *The Anatomy of Dessert*: 'No fruit is more to our English taste than the Apple . . . for us the Apple is King.' Certainly the apple is one of the oldest fruits known to mankind, as excavations on ancient sites have proved, although doubts have been cast on Eve's apple, some authorities being of the opinion it was a quince, or an apricot. Be that as it may, the apple which the Scandinavians call 'the food of the gods' was introduced into Britain by the Romans and has remained with us ever since.

Apples fall into two categories: cooking and eating. Here I am concerned with cooking apples. All apples turn brown quickly when pared and cut. Soaking in cold water prevents this but it does not improve the flavour. When cooking apples, therefore, try to prepare all the other ingredients first leaving the cutting of the apples until just before using them. Apples should always be well cooked as under-cooked apples also discolour.

Stewed Apples

110 g (4 oz) sugar
280 ml (½ pt) water

1 kg (2¼ lb) crisp cooking
   apples
1 thin strip lemon rind

Dissolve the sugar in the water over a low heat in a largish pan. Boil rapidly for 2 minutes. Thinly pare and core the apples and cut into halves or quarters. Add to the sugar syrup with the lemon rind and cook gently until they are soft but still retain their shape.

Apples Stewed with Raisins

110 g (4 oz) raisins   1 kg (2¼ lb) apples

Drop the raisins into a large pan with enough boiling water in which to cook the apples. Leave the raisins in the water until they swell. Pare, core and quarter the apples. Add to the raisins and cook gently until soft but still retain their shape. Unless the apples are very tart, sugar should not be needed.

Baked Apples

1 *large firm apple per person*   *cloves, cinnamon and butter*
brown sugar

Wipe and core the apples and either prick all over with a fork or cut a thin line through the skin round the middle. Put the apples into a baking dish just large enough to hold them, adding enough water to cover the bottom of the pan. Bake in a moderate oven (180C, 350F, Mark 4) until the apples are almost soft. Take from the oven and push 1 table-spoonful of sugar into each cavity, add a clove, a little ground cinnamon and a knob of butter. Return the apples to the oven and continue baking until they are quite soft but still with a good shape. Baking time from beginning to end is between 30 to 45 minutes. Can be served hot or cold, as they are, or with cream, or a custard sauce.

Many cooks fill the apples with dried mixed fruits plus sugar and butter. If fruit is used, then the apples should be stuffed with it before being baked. In Italy they push a stick of bitter chocolate into the apples after they have been baking for a while.

Apple and Egg Cream

This is a Victorian recipe. Cook one large tart apple sweetened to taste until very soft. Rub through a sieve and leave until cold. Beat one egg white until stiff, mix into the apple and serve chilled with cream.

Baked Apple Snow

6 *large cooking apples*
2–3 *tablespoons sugar or to taste*

6 *egg whites*
butter

Bake the apples whole in a hot oven (220C, 425F, Mark 7) until soft, about 30 minutes. Cool and rub through a sieve. Add the sugar, put the mixture into a pan and cook gently on top of the stove until it thickens. In the meantime whisk the egg whites until stiff and fold into the purée while it is still hot. Rub a soufflé dish with butter. Pile the purée into the dish, smooth down lightly with a palette knife and bake in a moderate oven (180C, 350F, Mark 4) until the top is a golden brown. Serve immediately.

Apple Sauce

450 g (1 *lb*) *cooking apples*
1 *tablespoon lemon juice*
1 *small strip lemon rind*

1 *bruised clove*
1 *dessertspoon sugar* (*optional*)
15 g (½ *oz*) *butter*

Wipe the apples, coarsely chop without paring and put into a pan with the lemon juice, rind, clove and ¼ cup of water. Cover the pan tightly and cook the apples slowly to a pulp, about 20 minutes. Rub through a sieve, add the sugar and butter, beat well and serve the sauce hot. By cooking with the peel and the core all the flavour of the apple is retained.

Use with pork—roast, boiled, grilled or fried.

Apple Purée
Make as for Apple Sauce, increasing the quantity of apples and sugar. Serve in stemmed glasses, iced.

❧ Pear

The pear belongs to the same order of plants as the apple and, next to this, is one of the most extensively cultivated fruits in temperate climes. The British have long been pear amateurs as, indeed, were and still are the French who produce some wonderful species. It is hard to describe the pear's flavour. Edward Bunyard did so by saying that some pears seemed to have the flavour of a full bodied wine, others a hint of spice, or honey, or even a trace of almond or rose-water. The texture of pears is somewhat easier to define, there are those with a flesh so melting the French call them *fondant*, others with a positively crisp even gritty texture.

Like apples, pears have an ancient history and it is not surprising to read that Pliny enumerated several varieties. A rather prosaic Victorian wrote: 'when pears are pared they have a constipating tendency, whereas if eaten with their skins on they become a laxative.'

Poached Pears

450 g (1 *lb*) *cooking pears*   560 *ml* (1 *pt*) *water*
225 g (8 *oz*) *sugar*   *juice and rind* 1 *lemon*

Peel the pears. If they are large, cut in half, cut away the stems and cores: if small, leave them whole but pare and scoop out the cores. Rub the pears with cut lemon. Dissolve the sugar in the water in a pan and bring gently to the boil and boil for 3 minutes. Add the lemon juice and then the pears, a few at a time, making sure all are immersed in the syrup. Cook until they are tender and translucent. They can be served with or without their syrup, with cream, a custard sauce, ice-cream, or with a chocolate sauce.

Stewed Pears
Cook as for apples.

Pears Cooked in Red Wine
'If you would have a fine dish of pears, let these be cooked as a compôte, namely, pare them thinly, remove cores and slice them into elegant sections; lay in a pan with a few lumps of sugar and pour over sufficient claret to cover. Cook gently until the pears are thoroughly tender. A red and rich compôte.'

> An Edwardian recipe

Can be served hot or cold with a fruit sauce or with cream.

Pears Baked with Honey

4 *large dessert pears*   4 *tablespoons lemon juice*
butter   *ground cinnamon to taste*
170 *g* (6 *oz*) *honey*

Peel the pears, cut into halves and core. Arrange in a buttered oven dish, cut side uppermost. Combine the honey and juice and pour this mixture over the pears. Sprinkle with cinnamon and dot with slivers of butter. Bake in a moderate oven (180C, 350F, Mark 4) until tender, 20 to 30 minutes. Serve hot with cream, or a custard sauce.

❧ *Cherry*

'Loveliest of trees . . .' wrote Housman, and in spring 'Is hung with bloom along the bough. . .'.

Cherries were known to the Greeks and Romans and legend has it that cherries were first brought to Britain by the Romans whose legionnaires munched them on their long marches throwing out the stones which seeded along the roads thus giving Britain its precious heritage of cherry tree-lined roads. Later the cherry became a royal favourite and in Tudor times there were many references to the courtly cherry, while poets covered pages in praise of the fruit. Queen Elizabeth I was very fond of them, and Queen Victoria ordered a cherry tart for her Coronation Banquet and, we are told, had a second helping topped with ice-cream. But cherries were not only the food for royals, the so-called common folk liked them too, and we read of cherry fairs, of the singing and dancing of the professional pickers, and games of cherry bobbing.

Cherries are diverse in character and their sweetness or tartness can be incorporated into dishes both sweet and savoury. It is no wonder that recipes for their cooking run into three figures, varying from the cottage recipe to those of *haute cuisine*. It would indeed be a sad day for the world if the thousand-year-and-more cultivation and enjoyment of this delightful fruit were allowed to fade into oblivion.

Cherry Compôte

450 g (1 *lb*) *cherries, pitted*
140 ml (¼ *pt*) *claret*
1–2 *tablespoons sugar*
½ *teaspoon ground cinnamon*

2–3 *cloves*
3 *tablespoons redcurrant jelly*
double cream to taste
brandy to taste

Simmer the cherries in the claret with the sugar, cinnamon and cloves until they are tender but still hold their shape. Take the cherries out with a perforated spoon. Stir the jelly into the syrup and continue cooking until jelly dissolves. Separately chill the cherries and the sauce. To serve, stir the sauce into the cherries. Whip the cream until stiff, lightly sweeten and flavour with brandy and serve separately.

Pitting cherries is by no means difficult today as there are several varieties of cherry pitting gadgets on the market.

Cherries in Brandy

1¼ *kg (3 lb) sweet ripe cherries*   225 *g (8 oz) sugar*
brandy

Wipe the cherries with a soft cloth, cut off the stems to
2 cm (½ in) and pack the cherries into jars. Cover with
brandy, seal and store for 6 weeks. Dissolve the sugar in
3 tablespoons of water and cook over a low heat, stirring all
the time to make a syrup. Drain off the brandy from the
cherries and stir this into the syrup. Strain through muslin,
pour the syrup back into the jars, seal and store for a further
2 weeks.

🌸 *Apricot*

The apricot is a native of northern China but was extensively cultivated in Armenia for centuries and today is
cultivated in most countries with a temperate climate. It is
one of nature's most ambrosial of fruits as Shakespeare knew
when he made Titania, queen of the fairies, attempt, under
a spell, to win the affection of the uncouth mortal Bottom
by offering him some 'apricocks'. For long apricots have
been considered food for the gods, and has it not been said
that Eve was tempted by an apricot, neither apple nor
quince? As a fruit the apricot is considered by many people
irresistible and, taken sun-warm from the tree, superior to
the peach.

Apricots do not contain as much sugar as apples and
many other fruits and in their ripe state are often allowed in
moderation to diabetics. For me, apricots are best served
alone and uncooked but they do lend themselves to cooking,
drying, preserving and bottling. A considerable portion of
the world's apricot crop is taken for drying and canning.

Apricot Compôte

110 g (4 oz) sugar   450 g (1 lb) fresh apricots
140 ml (¼ pt) water   small piece vanilla bean

Dissolve the sugar in the water over a low heat then boil for 3 minutes. Add the vanilla and pitted apricots, either whole or halved and cook gently until they are soft. Turn into a shallow dish, cool and chill and serve with cream, or a custard sauce, or simply as they are.

In France they call halved and pitted apricots *oreillons d'abricots*, or little apricot ears.

Apricot Purée
Cook the apricots as for Apricot Compôte until very soft, drain and rub through a sieve. This can be used as a sauce or combined with whipped cream and served as a fool.

Apricot Fritters

poached apricot halves   oil
kirsch   icing sugar
fritter batter

Drain the apricots and pat them gently dry on kitchen paper. Put into a shallow dish and sprinkle with kirsch. Put aside for about 30 minutes. When ready to make the fritters, dip each half into the batter and fry in deep, hot oil or fat until brown. Drain on paper, arrange on a flat platter and sprinkle with icing sugar. Serve with apricot purée flavoured with kirsch. Or the fritters can be put under a hot grill for a few minutes to glaze.

Apricot Omelette Flambée
Make a plain omelette and put a little apricot purée in the centre when it is half cooked. Roll up in the usual manner and sprinkle the top with icing sugar. Pour over it warmed kirsch, rum or brandy and ignite. Serve at once while still flaming.

🎚 Peach

For most people peaches are regarded as the most luscious of all fruits. I remember my own first peach, hothouse grown in Britain which, to me then a child, appeared horribly hairy. I did not like peaches I decided then and there, and it has taken me a long time to realise my mistake. What I did not know then, as Edward Bunyard claims, 'the eating of peaches is an art which has its techniques as well as its traditions'. And he pursues the subject at length, describing how a royal gardener of one of the French kings, before eating his peach, admired it from all sides and exclaimed: 'What richness of colour: how admirably downy'. Odd, for it was this very downiness that had repelled me.

Like most fruits, peaches have their long and fascinating history and, for those interested, that of the peach is rewarding. Peaches, like apricots, originated in China, so it is generally thought, in particular the white fleshed peach which also grows profusely in northern India. Modern varieties of peaches, it is said, do not vary much from those planted by the Romans and the Chinese long, long ago. Apart from being a delectable fruit to eat raw, warm from the tree, they are a useful fruit for canning, bottling and freezing.

Nectarine

This is a variety of peach, smooth skinned, rosy hued and generally smaller than the average peach. They are so much of the same family that pits sown from one tree may grow to be the other, i.e. plant a peach pit and you may well get a nectarine. The flesh is melting and fragrant and it is important to gather nectarines when ripe, for unripe nectarines are astringent. They can of course be cooked in any of the ways of peaches but in Britain hothouse grown and somewhat rare it would seem better to serve them raw as a dessert fruit with a glass of chilled Sauternes or another white wine of one's choice.

Baked Peaches Stuffed with Macaroons

6 *large ripe peaches*   *peach brandy*
8–10 *macaroons*   140 *ml* ($\frac{1}{4}$ *pt*) *dry white wine*

Pour boiling water over the peaches and carefully slip off their skins. Cut each into half and take out the pits. Arrange the peaches in a large, shallow baking dish. Crumble the macaroons and soak them in peach brandy. Fill these into the cavities and pour white wine over the top. Bake in a moderate oven (180C, 350F, Mark 4) until the peaches are soft, about 25 minutes.

Baked Peaches with Pork

6 *large ripe peaches*   *sugar*
butter   *lemon juice*

Pour boiling water over the peaches, slip off their skins and cut each into half, removing the pits. Brush the cut sides with softened butter, put a knob of butter into each cavity and sprinkle lightly with sugar. Put the peaches under a grill and let them cook until glazed. Sprinkle lightly with lemon juice and serve with roast pork or ham.

Poached Peaches

225 *g* (8 *oz*) *sugar*   2–3 *tablespoons rum*
280 *ml* ($\frac{1}{2}$ *pt*) *water*   *whipped cream*
6 *large ripe peaches*

Combine the sugar and water and cook over a moderate heat for 5 minutes. Pour boiling water over the peaches, slip off their skins, halve and pit and carefully drop into the syrup and cook gently until tender. Take out with a perforated spoon and arrange in a shallow serving bowl. Cook the syrup until it is thick and pour this over the peaches. Add the rum, stir gently, cool and chill. Serve with whipped cream which can be flavoured with sugar and peach brandy.

Instead of whipped cream, raspberry cream flavoured with kirsch can be poured over the peaches.

Peaches with Sauternes

6 *large peeled, halved and pitted*   2–3 *tablespoons icing or castor*
   peaches   *sugar*
1 *cup each Sauternes and water*

Put the peaches into a shallow wide pan. Combine the remaining ingredients and pour over the peaches. Cover and cook gently until the peaches are tender but still retain their shape. Arrange in a serving bowl, pour the syrup over them, cool and thoroughly chill.

❧ *Plum, Damson and Greengage*

The many varieties of plum are products of the cultivation of the wild plum. Certain varieties of plums and greengages are good eaten raw, and some can be eaten cooked, either as compôtes or in pies and puddings. According to one source, plums are good for people with nervous disorders and experiments in a boy's institution carried out at the turn of the century found that eating plenty of plums reduced the boy's irritability in a marked manner. Maybe we should all eat more plums in these hectic days.

Greengages are a variety of plum, the sweetest and best eating of all the plums and said to be named after a member of the Gage family who introduced them into Britain at the end of the eighteenth century.

Damsons have a distinctive and fine flavour and although they can be eaten raw, usually they are cooked in the same manner as plums and greengages. Incidentally, damsons are used to make a damson brandy. A small dark, purple plum, the *Zwetchen*, is used to make Slivowitz, a potent Slav drink. Prune plums are a particular variety of plum suitable for drying.

Plums can be stored for several weeks if their skins are not broken but, like all fruits, they are better eaten soon after picking, as their flavour deteriorates.

Poached Plums or Greengages

1 *kg* (2¼ *lb*) *plums*   *pinch salt*
sugar to taste   *water*

Wash the plums and put them into a pan together with sugar, salt and enough water to prevent burning. Cook gently until the fruit is tender, about 10 minutes.

Ground cinnamon, orange or lemon juice, cherry brandy, or red wine can be added for additional flavour; however, a white wine for greengages.

✿ *Quince*

Yet another fruit with an ancient history, some authorities say not only was it a quince which lured Eve but quinces were also the Golden Apples of the Hesperides that the swift-footed Atalanta stopped in her tracks to retrieve, thus losing her race against a suitor and so compelled to marry him. In ancient days too it was claimed that if quinces were present at a wedding feast they assured love and happiness, obviously a good reason to reinstate the neglected quince. The quince came to Britain from Austria only in the six-teenth century but it was well-known in France for centuries. The French produced, and still do, the delicately flavoured *cotignac* to which Joan of Arc was so partial.

Eaten raw the quince is astringent, but cooked it has an

excellent flavour. In the more recent past quinces were the great standbys for home doctors, bringing relief from coughs and colds, sore throats and bad digestions. Perfumes are made from their blossoms. There are many varieties of this interesting fruit, the most usual being a pale gold colour, pear or apple shaped. When cooked they blend well with other fruits, especially apples. Quinces should be stored in a cool, dark place. Remember that quinces require long, slow cooking to bring out their colour and flavour.

Baked Quinces

6–8 *quinces*
sugar to taste

tiny pinch salt
280 *ml* (½ *pt*) *water*

Pare, core and slice the quinces. Arrange in a shallow baking dish, sprinkle with sugar and salt, add the water, cover and cook in a slow oven (150C, 300F, Mark 2) for about 2 hours, or until tender and a good red colour. Uncover, sprinkle lightly with some more sugar and continue cooking until the syrup is thickened. Serve hot or cold.

Quince Compôte

¾ *l* (1¼ *pt*) *water*
juice and rind small lemon
pinch salt

4–6 *quinces*
340 *ml* (12 *oz*) *sugar*

Put the water, lemon rind, juice and salt into a pan. Pare, core and halve the quinces then thinly slice and drop at once into the water. Cook over a low heat until tender but not broken. Drain off the fruit, stir the sugar into the hot liquid and bring to the boil. Boil for 2 minutes, return the fruit to the pan, lower the heat and cook gently for a further 30 minutes. By this time the fruit will be a good red colour. Cool, chill and serve with cream.

Quince Butter

quinces   *sugar*
water

Wash, cut the fruit into small pieces, cut off the blossom end
but leave the cores, seeds and peel. Put into a pan with
water, using equal quantities of water to fruit. Bring to the
boil, lower the heat and cook gently until very soft. Rub
through a sieve. Measure the quantity of pulp and add half
as much sugar to the pulp. Bring this to the boil and continue to cook gently, up to an hour, stirring constantly,
until the mixture cools down. If the flame is too high, the
mixture will splutter most unpleasantly. When the butter is
thick, test on a plate. It is ready when no rim of liquid
separates round the edge of the butter.

✿ Crabapple

Not a fruit for eating raw for it is too sour, colourful though
it is. It is a fruit of ancient lineage and the Japanese and
Chinese have been cultivating it for centuries both for
culinary and decorative purposes. However, it can be made
into jellies, pickles or jams.

Crabapple Pickles

1¼ *kg* (3 *lb*) *crabapples*   225 *g* (8 *oz*) *sugar*
1–2 *small pieces cinnamon*   560 *ml* (1 *pt*) *vinegar*
1 *teaspoon whole cloves*

If possible, choose crabapples of uniform size and of good
colour. Pare and core, cut into quarters and cook them over
steam until very soft. Tie the spices in a small piece of
muslin or bag. Put them into a pan with sugar and vinegar,

add the fruit and bring all to a gentle boil. Cook at a gentle boil for about 20 minutes. Pour into sterilised jars and seal tightly.

Crabapple Jelly

1¼ kg (3 lb) crabapples   cloves, root ginger or lemon rind
1 l (1¾ pt) water   sugar

Wash the fruit, cut into quarters without paring or coring and put into a pan with the water. Cook until the fruit is soft and mushy, adding if required a little more water. Add spices or flavouring while the crabapples are cooking. Strain through a jelly cloth, do not squeeze the bag or the jelly will cloud, measure the juice and return to the pan. Bring to the boil and add 450 g (1 lb) of sugar to each 560 ml (1 pt) of juice. Stir while the sugar is dissolving, then boil briskly for 10 minutes or so until a set is obtained. Pour into jars and cover.

❊ *Fruit Soups*

It is curious that the British have forgotten many of their interesting dishes and generally are surprised at being offered fruit soups, yet, in one of the earliest references to soups in Britain they were described as being 'a kind of sweet, pleasant broth made with fruit or vegetables and spices.' Fruit soups usually are eaten cold at the beginning of a meal and can be garnished with croûtons or cream or raw fruit. The late Sir Compton Mackenzie once remarked on fruit soups being served 'after the meal' which he found to be the correct place for them. If serving a fruit soup with a pronounced flavour, it should be followed by a highly seasoned dish that can hold its own against the soup.

Apple Soup

1 *kg* (2¼ *lb*) *cooking apples*   560 *ml* (1 *pt*) *dry white wine or*
small piece cinnamon   *cider*
juice and rind 1 *lemon*   *sugar to taste*
30 *g* (1 *oz*) *butter*   *croûtons*
1 *tablespoon flour*

Wipe the apples and coarsely chop. Put into a pan with the
cinnamon, lemon juice and rind and 2 to 3 cups of water.
Cook until the apples are very soft and rub through a sieve.
Heat the butter, blend in the flour, gradually add the wine,
stirring all the time, and 1 cup of water. Add sugar, remembering this is a soup and should not be too sweet, stir in
the apple purée and let it all come to the boil. Serve iced
with croûtons, or whipped cream, or small meringues as
a garnish.

Cherry Soup

A country recipe from France.

30 *g* (1 *oz*) *butter or margarine*   *sugar to taste*
30 *g* (1 *oz*) *flour*   3–4 *tablespoons kirsch or cherry*
1¾ *l* (3 *pt*) *water*   *brandy*
1 *kg* (2¼ *lb*) *pitted cherries*   *triangles buttered fried bread*

Heat the butter, add the flour and stir to a light roux.
Gradually add the water and, when completely blended,
add the cherries and sugar. Bring to the boil, lower the heat
and cook until the cherries are very soft. Add the kirsch, stir
well and bring the soup to a bubbling boil. Put triangles of
bread into individual soup bowls and add the soup while it
is still bubbling hot. Some French cooks serve cherry soup
with 'ladies fingers' or 'cat's tongues' or small wine biscuits.

Blackberry Soup
A lovely soup to make from September blackberryings. The recipe comes from Austria but a similar soup is made in Germany and Poland.

1 *kg* (2¼ *lb*) *blackberries*
2–3 *thin slices lemon*
1⅛ *l* (2 *pt*) *water*
60 *g* (2 *oz*) *sugar*

2 *cloves*
1 *small piece cinnamon*
iced whipped cream

Wash and pick over the fruit, put aside a few to use as a garnish, and put the rest into a pan with the lemon, water, sugar, cloves and cinnamon. Bring slowly to the boil and cook gently until the berries are very soft. Rub the soup through a sieve, cool and chill. Serve generously garnished with whipped cream, or, just before serving, stir whipped cream into the soup and serve garnished only with a dash of cream and the reserved blackberries.

Mixed Fruit Soup
This soup has no particular recipe. It is simply a mixture of strawberries, raspberries, currants and any other fruit available. All are cooked together in water until very soft, rubbed through a sieve, sweetened and left to cool and chill. Served in soup bowls with cracked ice as a garnish.

FREEZING
by Brenda Sanctuary

❧ Introduction

The pleasure of growing your own vegetables and fruit is being able to pick produce and eat it within minutes, but of course, there is a limit to the family's tolerance of the same vegetable day after day when in season and this is when the freezer comes into its own. Having a freezer means there is no wastage of produce because 'pick and freeze' should be the motto of all garden and freezer owners. Freezing means having your vegetables and fruit in and out of season and certainly saving money.

Freezers

There are basically two types of freezer, upright or chest, both have their virtues, although I prefer the upright model.

Upright freezers take up less floor space than the chest freezer, consequently they are often easier to house but are slightly more expensive to run. The chest freezer though cheaper to run has the disadvantage that it is more difficult to rotate produce because of the difficulty one often has in packing this type of freezer.

Upright freezers need de-frosting more often than the chest model, though it is not necessary to de-frost freezers more than twice a year. It is very important to de-frost your freezer as quickly as possible, putting all your food into large paper freezer bags, which can be bought from any food freezer shop; these should then be covered with newspaper or a large blanket. After de-frosting, wipe the freezer thoroughly, then dry and turn on the 'fast freeze' switch and restock. Check what you have in your freezer as you re-stock it.

Keep the freezer as full as possible because a half-full

freezer uses more electricity than a full one. Always instal the freezer in a room that is not too warm and where the air can circulate round the freezer easily. A freezer in a small enclosed space uses more electricity, forms more ice and therefore will need more de-frosting.

When buying a freezer it is wise to have a good look around and to find one that is big enough for the family. So often first-time freezer buyers tend to buy a freezer that is too small and, in no time at all, a larger freezer has to be bought. It is a good idea to visit your local freezer food shop and ask their advice because they often have new freezers that are 'shop soiled' but are excellent value for money.

Blanching

Blanching is most important as this stops the action of the enzymes which would destroy the Vitamin C, texture, flavour and colour of the vegetable or fruit.

For blanching you need a large saucepan and a blanching basket or a large sieve. A chip basket is not suitable as the wires are spaced too far apart and the smaller vegetables or fruit will fall into the saucepan. For each pound of vegetables or fruit you will need two gallons of boiling water, this can be used up to six or seven times for the same vegetable or fruit. Put a pound of prepared vegetables or fruit into the blanching basket. When the water is boiling rapidly, plunge the vegetables or fruit into the boiling water and then bring back to the boil as quickly as possible and start timing the 'blanching time'. Do not over-blanch as this over-cooks the vegetable or fruit and they become mushy. When the blanching time is reached, take the basket from the saucepan, turn the vegetables or fruit into a colander and plunge them into a large bowl of very cold water, preferably iced, and keep cold water running into the bowl until the vegetables or fruit are really cold. Take care not to let the cold running water fall directly on to the vegetables or fruit. When the vegetables or fruit are cold, drain well and pat dry on kitchen paper and follow freezing instructions.

Freezing

About two hours before freezing vegetables or fruit, set the freezer to 'fast freeze' so that the temperature is really low and the food gets frozen quickly. The quicker food is frozen the smaller the ice crystals that form round the food and these will preserve the food, whereas slow freezing causes large ice crystals to form and these damage the food cells and cause loss of food value. *Remember to turn the 'fast freeze' switch off after freezing.*

Normal Freezing

After the vegetables or fruit have been blanched, cooled and dried, pack them into polythene or waxed boxes, or polythene bags. Never fill polythene bags more than three-quarters full and leave 1 to 3 cm ($\frac{1}{2}$ to 1 in) headspace above the vegetables and fruit in boxes to allow for any expansion during freezing.

It is important to exclude any air before freezing. To remove the air from boxes, after putting on the lid, lift one corner of the lid to allow any air to escape, then snap down and seal with freezer tape. To remove the air from polythene bags, twist the top of the bag as near the contents as possible, push a drinking straw into the bag and carefully suck out any air, so that the bag clings to the vegetable or fruit; fix securely with freezer wire ties.

Open Freezing

'Open freezing' means that the vegetables or fruit are frozen on freezer trays or baking sheets. The advantage of 'open freezing' against ordinary freezing is that you have 'free-flow' vegetables or fruit and these are easier to use and also defrost.

To 'open freeze', put the blanched, cooled and dried vegetables or fruit onto a freezer tray or baking sheet, lightly cover with cling film wrap, greaseproof paper or foil and put into the freezer. When the vegetables or fruit are hard, pack into polythene or waxed boxes or polythene bags.

Dry Sugar Freezing

Put the prepared fruit in layers with sugar, allowing 110 g
(4 oz) castor sugar to each 450 g (1 lb) of fruit.

Syrup Freezing

Put the prepared fruit into rigid containers and cover with
cold sugar syrup, leaving 2½ cm (1 in) headspace. Cover with
crumpled foil or greaseproof paper to hold the fruit under
the syrup. Cover tightly, seal and freeze. Allow 280 ml (½ pt)
of sugar syrup to each 450 g (1 lb) of fruit.

Light Sugar Syrup

Make a syrup using 450 g (1 lb) castor sugar to 1⅛ l (2 pt) of
water.

Heavy Sugar Syrup

Make a syrup using 900 g (2 lb) castor sugar to 1⅛ l (2 pt) of
water.

Purée

If fruit is over-ripe but sound, freeze it as a purée. Rub the
fruit through a nylon sieve or purée in an electric liquidiser.
Add sugar to taste either before freezing or later, before
cooking, marking container accordingly. Put purée into
rigid containers leaving 2½ cm (1 in) headspace. Freeze.

Fruit can be cooked first, then made into a purée, cooled
and put into containers, again leaving 2½ cm (1 in) headspace. Freeze.

Ascorbic Acid

To prevent certain fruits such as apples, pears, peaches and
apricots becoming discoloured lemon juice can be added to
the cold sugar syrup: 1½ tablespoons to 560 ml (1 pt) of
syrup. As lemon juice is acid it is better to use Ascorbic
acid – Vitamin C – as this does not flavour the fruit.
Dissolve ¼ teaspoonful of Ascorbic acid crystals in each
560 ml (1 pt) of syrup. If you have difficulty in finding
Ascorbic acid crystals, use Vitamin C tablets instead, dis-

solving the tablets in a little water before adding to the syrup. When using Vitamin C tablets follow the manufacturer's instructions about the number of tablets to each 560 ml (1 pt) of water.

Packaging and Labelling

It is most important to pack and label your produce carefully. There are different types of packages made specifically for deep-freezing that are available. Plastic boxes, waxed cartons or polythene bags are all suitable for vegetables and fruit.

Plastic boxes and waxed cartons can be used many times, as long as they are well washed and dried after use. As a saving the large plastic boxes containing ice-cream make excellent containers, also useful are yogurt and cream cartons and margarine tubs for freezing small amounts of purée or individual portions. When freezing vegetables or fruit that are liable to stain waxed cartons, it is a good idea to line the carton or tub with a polythene bag.

Polythene bags can be bought in different sizes and thicknesses, though it is advisable to use a thicker weight, about 200 gauge, as torn polythene bags can cause freezer burn and this causes loss of colour, flavour, texture and quality in the vegetables or fruit. It is also possible to use polythene bags again if they are well washed, turned inside out and then dried.

When sealing plastic boxes or waxed containers always use a strong freezer tape because ordinary adhesive tape will peel off or crack in the freezer. There are two methods of sealing polythene bags after all the air has been extracted. If you want to re-use the bag, twist a paper covered wire tie-fastener round the top of the bag. There are also sealing machines on the market that fasten very effectively but the disadvantage of this method is that the polythene bag cannot be used again because it is difficult to remove the seal without tearing the bag.

Make sure all produce is labelled correctly with the name of the produce, weight and date. Tie labels onto bags and stick special freezer labels onto boxes or tubs and always use a felt pen, freezer pen or gardening pencil. It is also helpful to label vegetables with one colour label and fruit with another colour label.

Always over-wrap all foods that have a strong smell to avoid cross-flavouring.

Have a freezer log book and write down all details when you freeze vegetables and fruit so you know exactly what you have in your freezer and can use produce in rotation. Do not forget to cross out the various items of frozen food that have been removed from the freezer. In order that it is quick and easy to select the produce you require I would advise you to pack your fruit and vegetables on different shelves or, if using a chest freezer, in different baskets. It is worth remembering to pack your produce in convenient sizes for your own family needs.

Vegetable	To prepare	Blanching time	To freeze	To use	Freezer life
Artichoke Globe	Remove outer coarse leaves. Trim stems and tops. Wash thoroughly in cold water.	7 minutes	Open freeze. Pack into boxes.	Thaw overnight in a 'fridge or 4 hours at room temperature.	1 year
Artichoke Jerusalem	Scrub and clean. Cut up or slice. Leave in cold water.	1–2 minutes	Open freeze. Pack into boxes.	Thaw for 4 hours at room temperature.	3 months
Asparagus	Cut off the woody base of the asparagus. Wash in cold water and scrape the stems. Divide into thick and thin stems.	Thick stems: 4 minutes. Thin stems: 2 minutes.	Open freeze. Pack into boxes.	Tie in bundles and thaw overnight in a 'fridge or 4 hours at room temperature.	1 year

Vegetable	To prepare	Blanching time	To freeze	To use	Freezer life
Aubergine	Wash and slice into 1 cm (½ in) slices. Leave the aubergine slices in salted water for half an hour. Rinse thoroughly and drain.	4 minutes	Open freeze. Pack into polythene bags or boxes.	Cook frozen or thaw overnight in a 'fridge or 4 hours at room temperature.	1 year
Beans Broad	Shell the beans.	2 minutes	Open freeze. Pack into polythene bags.	Cook frozen.	1 year
Beans French	Wash and trim the ends. Leave the beans whole.	2 minutes	Open freeze. Pack into polythene bags.	Cook frozen.	1 year
Beans Runner	Wash and trim the ends. Leave small beans whole or slice if very long.	2 minutes	Open freeze. Pack into polythene bags.	Cook frozen.	1 year

Vegetable	To prepare	Blanching time	To freeze	To use	Freezer life
Beetroot	Wash and remove part of the stem, leaving about 7 cm (3 in) to prevent the beetroot from 'bleeding'. Cook the beetroot until tender, about 30 minutes for small beetroot, 1 hour for larger beetroot. Cool and remove the skins. Leave the small beetroot whole, slice the large beetroot.		Open freeze. Pack into polythene bags or boxes.	Thaw overnight in a 'fridge or 4 hours at room temperature.	9 months
Broccoli	Cut off large leaves and cut stems into 15 cm (6 in) sprigs.	3 minutes	Open freeze. Pack into boxes.	Cook frozen.	1 year
Brussels Sprouts	Use small Brussels sprouts, remove any damaged leaves and trim the stalks.	3 minutes	Open freeze. Pack into polythene bags.	Cook frozen.	1 year

Vegetable	To prepare	Blanching time	To freeze	To use	Freezer life
Cabbage Green Red	Wash thoroughly and shred the cabbage.	1½ minutes	Pack into polythene bags, seal and freeze.	Cook frozen.	1 year
Carrot	When small: remove tops, wash and scrape carrots and leave whole. When big: remove tops, wash, peel and cut into slices or dice.	Whole: 3 minutes. Sliced and diced: 2 minutes.	Open freeze. Pack into polythene bags.	Cook frozen.	1 year
Cauliflower	Strip off outer leaves, wash the cauliflower and break into flowerettes. Leave in salted water until ready to blanch.	3 minutes	Open freeze. Pack into boxes.	Cook frozen.	6 months
Celery	Wash well and remove any outer tough fibres. Cut into 5 cm (2 in) pieces.	3 minutes	Pack into polythene bags, seal and freeze.	Thaw before cooking.	1 year

Vegetable	To prepare	Blanching time	To freeze	To use	Freezer life
Chicory	Choose compact heads, trim stalks and remove any outer leaves. Leave in salted water until blanching.	2 minutes	Pack into boxes. Seal and freeze.	Cook frozen.	1 year
Courgette	Pick young courgettes, wipe and cut into 1 cm (½ in) slices. Leave in salted water, drain and blanch.	1 minute	Open freeze. Pack into boxes.	Thaw partially.	1 year
Cucumber	Not suitable for freezing but can be frozen as a made-up dish such as soup or mousse.				
Kale	Choose young leaves, remove from stalks and wash well.	3 minutes	Pack into polythene bags, seal and freeze.	Cook frozen.	1 year

Vegetable	To prepare	Blanching time	To freeze	To use	Freezer life
Kohlrabi	Use small roots about 5–7 cm (2–3 in) across. Trim off root ends and tops, peel, leaving small roots whole but dicing the larger roots.	Whole roots: 3 minutes. Diced roots: 2 minutes.	Open freeze. Pack into polythene bags.	Cook frozen.	1 year
Leek	Trim off tops and roots and remove outer leaves. Wash leeks thoroughly in cold water. Cut larger leeks into 2½ cm (1 in) slices.	Whole: 4 minutes. Sliced: 2 minutes.	Pack into boxes, seal and freeze.	Cook frozen.	6 months
Lettuce	Not suitable for freezing but can be frozen when made up as a soup.				
Marrow	Young marrows can be peeled and cut into 2 cm (¾ in) slices.	3 minutes	Open freeze. Pack into boxes.	Cook frozen.	9 months

Vegetable	To prepare	Blanching time	To freeze	To use	Freezer life
Onion	Large onions can be peeled and sliced or chopped. Small pickling onions peeled and left whole.	Sliced or chopped: 2 minutes. Small onions: 3 minutes.	Pack into polythene bags or boxes, seal and freeze. When frozen overwrap the bag or box with foil and seal to prevent any odours affecting other food in the freezer.	Cook frozen.	6 months
Parsnip	Use young parsnips. Wash and cut off the tops and trim the roots of the parsnips. Peel and cut into quarters lengthwise or dice.	2 minutes	Open freeze. Pack the dice into polythene bags and the quarters into boxes.	Cook frozen dice in boiling water for 10 minutes or thaw quarters for 3 hours before roasting.	1 year

Vegetable	To prepare	Blanching time	To freeze	To use	Freezer life
Peas	Shell young peas.	1 minute	Open freeze. Pack into polythene bags.	Cook frozen.	1 year
Peppers	Wipe the peppers and remove the stalks. Cut in half and remove the seeds and membrane. Leave as halves for stuffing or cut into slices lengthwise.	Halves: 3 minutes. Slices: 2 minutes.	Open freeze. Pack halves into boxes and pack slices into polythene bags.	Cook frozen.	1 year
Potatoes	Freeze small new potatoes. Wash and scrape the potatoes and keep in cold water until blanched. Older potatoes can be frozen as made-up dishes such as potato croquettes, chips or duchesse potatoes.	3 minutes	Pack into polythene bags, seal and freeze.	Cook frozen.	1 year

Vegetable	To prepare	Blanching time	To freeze	To use	Freezer life
Pumpkin	Not suitable for freezing but can be frozen as a ready-made thick purée for soup or pumpkin pie.				1 year
Radish	Not suitable for freezing.				
Spinach	It takes time to freeze spinach when fresh and it is easier to freeze spinach when cooked. Strip the leaves from the stalks and wash thoroughly in cold salted water. Drain and put into a large saucepan and cook until tender. Drain and press out excess water, cool and chop finely.		Pack into polythene bags, seal and freeze.	Cook frozen with a little butter.	1 year
Swede	Not suitable for freezing.				

Vegetable	To prepare	Blanching time	To freeze	To use	Freezer life
Tomato	Tomatoes are not suitable for freezing for eating with salad, as they collapse when thawed but they are excellent for cooking. To freeze whole, wipe tomatoes and plunge into boiling water, drain and remove the skins. To freeze as tomato purée, cut into quarters, simmer with salt, pepper, herbs and a little water for 10 minutes. Rub through a nylon sieve.		Whole: Open freeze and pack into polythene bags or boxes. Purée: Put the purée into rigid containers and freeze.	Thaw whole tomatoes and purée overnight.	1 year
Turnip	Peel and trim the turnips. Leave small turnips whole and cut large turnips into small dice.	Whole: 4 minutes. Diced: 2 minutes.	Open freeze. Pack into polythene bags or boxes.	Cook frozen.	1 year

Herbs

Herbs freeze well but as they become limp when thawed it is not possible to use them for garnishing. Use frozen herbs as fresh but when a recipe mentions a certain quantity of dried herbs, use double the amount of frozen herbs. Herbs have a freezer life of six months.

The following herbs are suitable for freezing:

Basil
Chives
Dill
Fennel
Marjoram
Mint
Parsley
Rosemary
Sage
Tarragon
Thyme

Horseradish and garlic are not suitable for freezing but Creamed Horseradish Sauce can be frozen for two months and Garlic Butter is also useful to have in the freezer. Both Horseradish Sauce and Garlic Butter should be packed in small rigid containers and then over-wrapped securely to avoid cross flavouring.

There are three methods of freezing herbs:

1. Wash and dry the herbs, chop finely. Pack thickly into ice-cube trays, adding a little water and freeze solid. Turn out the cubes and pack into polythene bags and tie securely. Use the cubes, while still frozen, in casseroles and sauces.

2. Wash and dry the herbs, chop finely and pack in small containers, very small polythene bags or made-up foil envelopes. Seal securely with freezer tape and freeze.

3. Wash and dry the herbs and divide into sprigs. Open freeze and then pack into polythene bags. When using the herbs, you can crumble them up while still frozen to save time chopping.

Fruit	To prepare	To freeze	To use	Freezer life
Apple	Peel, core and slice. Put into cold water, drain. Blanch for 1–2 minutes. Cool.	1. Open freeze. Pack into polythene bags.	Thaw 3 hours at room temperature.	1 year
	Peel, core and quarter. Cook in sugar syrup until soft. Sieve.	2. Pack into boxes. Cover with light sugar syrup. Freeze.		6 months
		3. Put into small containers leaving headspace. Freeze.		6 months
Apricots	Wipe over, cut in half, remove stones. Blanch for 1–2 minutes. Cool.	1. Pack with dry sugar in boxes. Freeze.	Thaw 4 hours at room temperature.	1 year
		2. Pack in boxes, cover with light sugar syrup. Freeze.		

Fruit	To prepare	To freeze	To use	Freezer life
Berries Bilberry Blackberry Loganberry Mulberry Raspberry Strawberry	Pick over fruit, rinse and dry.	1. Open freeze. Pack into polythene bags. 2. Pack into boxes, cover with light sugar syrup. Freeze. 3. Pack with dry sugar, seal and freeze.	Thaw 2 hours at room temperature.	1 year
Cherry	Remove stalks and stones.	1. Open freeze. Pack into polythene bags. 2. Pack into boxes, cover with heavy sugar syrup. Freeze. 3. Pack with dry sugar, seal and freeze.	Thaw 4 hours at room temperature.	1 year
Crabapple	Not suitable for freezing.			
Cranberries	Stem, rinse and dry.	Open freeze. Pack into polythene bags.	Thaw 3 hours at room temperature.	1 year

Fruit	To prepare	To freeze	To use	Freezer life
Currants Black Red White	Strip from stalks, rinse and dry.	1. Open freeze. Pack into polythene bags. 2. Pack with dry sugar, seal and freeze.	Thaw 2 hours at room temperature.	1 year
Damsons Greengages	Wash, halve and stone. Poach with sugar and water. Cool.	Pack in boxes. Freeze.	Thaw 4 hours at room temperature.	1 year
Gooseberry	Top and tail, rinse and dry.	1. Open freeze. Pack into polythene bags. 2. Pack into boxes, cover with heavy sugar syrup. Freeze.	Cook frozen.	1 year
Nectarines	Dissolve 225 g (8 oz) castor	Freeze.	Thaw 3 hours at room temperature	1 year

Fruit	To prepare	To freeze	To use	Freezer life
Peaches	sugar in 560 ml (1 pt) water, bring to the boil and add 1 tablespoonful lemon juice. Pour syrup into rigid containers. Peel nectarines or peaches, halve, stone and slice. Drop into syrup.			
Pear	Peel, halve and core. Lightly poach in light sugar syrup. Cool.	Pack fruit into boxes, cover with syrup. Freeze.	Thaw 3 hours at room temperature.	1 year
Plums	As apricots.	1. Dry sugar pack. 2. Syrup pack.		3 months 1 year
Quince	Peel, core and slice. Simmer in heavy sugar syrup. Cool.	Pack into boxes, cover with syrup. Freeze.	Thaw 3 hours at room temperature.	1 year
Rhubarb	Pick young, trim, rinse and cut into 2½–5 cm (1–2 in) lengths. Blanch for 1 minute. Cool.	1. Pack into bags, freeze. 2. Pack into boxes, cover with heavy sugar syrup. Freeze.	Thaw 3 hours at room temperature.	1 year

🎕 Index

Other non-fiction available from Magnum Books